Tropic Cooking

Tropic Cooking

The New Cuisine from Florida
and the Islands of the Caribbean

Joyce LaFray Young

Published by Ten Speed Press
900 Modoc, Berkeley, California 94707

Printed in Canada

ISBN: 0–89815–234–8

Book design: Seventeenth Street Studios, Oakland
Typesetting: Another Point, Inc., Oakland

4   5   —   02   01   00   99   98   97

This book is dedicated to the fond memory of my father, John Joseph Cornyn, Sr., who would have enjoyed these recipes, along with his Dagwood sandwiches; and to my big brother, John Joseph Cornyn, Jr., who had the greatest faith in me through the toughest of times.

Contents

Acknowledgments

To my husband, Richard for tasting all of these recipes.

To my good friend, B. J. Burns, who was here through the good times and the bad.

To Susan Lichtman, whose expertise, dedication, and enthusiasm for this project has been a joy.

To Jackie Wan, who "pulled it all together" and whose knowledge of international cuisine has made this project one of the most enjoyable ever.

To Sandra Moore, who toiled many hours typing the manuscript and keeping everything in order.

To Dolores Juler and Jane Smiley, whose enthusiasm gave me encouragement.

To the hundreds of great Florida and Caribbean chefs and cooks who contributed their knowledge and excellent recipes.

To my sister, Lea Cornyn, who kept me company for many trips to Florida and Caribbean restaurants.

To Chef Rennie Smith of New York City, who has been a delight and a true inspiration for this book.

To Bern Laxer of Bern's Steak House in Tampa, Florida, for his confidence.

To Marina Polvay and Culinary Communications for sharing their culinary know-how.

To my daughters, Julie and Christy, to Sandy and Rosalee Berger and to the Cedars Medical Center Development staff for tasting the recipes.

To Moses Brissett, my tailor, who introduced me to one of the best Caribbean cooks, Elfreda Clarke.

To Elfreda Clarke, who taught me the techniques of good Jamaican cooking while still wondering why the recipes couldn't read "just a little of this and a little of that."

To Miryam Ionita, my neighbor, for her wonderful tips on preparing tropical fruits and vegetables.

To Chris Rollins, Director of the Preston B. Bird and Mary Heinlein Fruit and Spice Park in Homestead, Florida, for his interesting and informative classes on tropical fruits and vegetables.

To Barbara Seldin, food editor and Miami talk show hostess, for her great "Dining-In" Miami recipes.

To Hal Stayman, Chief Operating Officer of La Chaine des Rotisseurs, U.S.A., for his restaurant recommendations.

To Marilyn Rose of the Florida Department of Natural Resources, a fine cook and an expert in preparing fish and shellfish, for her contributions.

To Enid Donaldson, food consultant to the Jamaican Tourist Board, for her culinary expertise.

To Anne Marie Marecheau of the Grenada Tourist Board and Arnold Tours for their hospitality.

To Karen Weiner Escalara Associates, Inc. of New York, who helped contribute much of the information about the Caribbean and much of their time recommending "what to taste" and "where to stay." A special thanks to Karen Weiner, Marilyn Marx, Bob Burrichter, and Frances Borden.

To Janell Smith and J. R. Brooks and Son, Inc. of Homestead, Florida, for their expertise on tropical fruits and vegetables and their many suggestions for this book.

To Mitchell Mangos for their expert advice.

To Janet Maizner of Maizner & Franklin, Ft. Lauderdale, for her information on visiting the Caribbean.

To Joe Petrocik and Myron Clement of the Clement-Petrocik Company of New York.

To the Cooperative Extension Service, University of Florida, Institute of Food and Agricultural Sciences.

To the Florida Tomato Exchange.

To the Florida Department of Agriculture and Consumer Services.

To the Gulf and South Atlantic Fisheries Development Foundation, Inc.

To Glenda Obrecht and the Florida Department of Citrus for their contributions.

To Peter and Ricki Fischer who put me up at their beautiful Florida Keys home while I was writing much of this book.

To the tourism associations of Florida, Barbados and Antigua, the British Virgin Islands, Cayman Islands, French West Indies, Grenada, Haiti, Jamaica, Puerto Rico, Trinidad and Tobago, and the U.S. Virgin Islands.

To my good friends, Bernie Moyle and Ed de Cayia, who made me believe that it isn't how you start, but how you finish.

Special thanks to Roberto Perez, manager of the Goodway Supermarket, and to Edwin Santos, who helped me choose the freshest fish for testing these recipes; to "Mama" (Insley Wardally), and her children and grandchildren, who were a pleasure to visit with in Grenada; to Island House owners Art and Sue Rochlin, and associates David Woodward and Corinna Duczek, for their artful inspiration; and to Louis Rosemont for use of his painting, "The Marketplace."

Introduction

There is no richer sensory experience than a visit to the tropics. Just close your eyes and let your imagination take you to a place where balmy breezes gently caress swaying palms; where juicy fruits, vegetables, and green vegetation grow in lush abundance; where clear blue waters lap the soft white sandy beaches. Add the sound of reggae music and the scent of tropical flowers and you'll have it all. Or almost all. There's one more element to the picture, something most visitors to the area overlook, and that's the wonderful tastes, the gustatory delights of the local cuisine.

My interest in tropical cuisine began years ago on a pleasure jaunt to the beautiful Caribbean island of Jamaica in the West Indies. Feeling much like Christopher Columbus must have, I discovered taste sensations that I had never before experienced. The native cuisine had a perfect blending of herbs and spices, and a myriad of fresh ingredients contributed flavors that were very distinctly "island." There was coconut milk and ginger beer to quench your thirst, and fish cakes and curried chicken baked in heavenly pastry to appease the appetite. Markets were ablaze with color and activity, farm women gently hawking their exotic root vegetables and huge quantities of fresh spices.

Ever since I was six years old, cooking has been my favorite pastime—and eventually, food became something of a passion for me. As a student in Italy, I had plenty of time for dining, and gastronomy became as much of an attraction as the sightseeing. I traveled to Athens to sample the moussaka, to Istanbul for the blended teas, to Granada to savor the fruity sangria, to Hungary for the paprikash, to Paris for the sauces, and to Brussels to feast on mussels and waterzooi. I married the owner of a Japanese restaurant and quickly became addicted to sushi and sashimi.

Now here was a new and exciting cuisine, as intriguing as the islands themselves. And my passion took a new direction as I began to explore a whole new world of tastes and aromas. I sampled food at local restaurants, sought out experts, professional and amateur, collected recipes, and experimented in my own kitchen. And I continued to travel to learn more about this "tropic cooking."

But before I go on with an explanation of the cuisine itself, let me define the geographical area with which I'm concerned. Technically, the tropics lie in the region along the equator bounded on the north by the Tropic of Cancer, and on the south by the Tropic of Capricorn. The tropics boast warm-to-hot temperatures all year round, averaging between 70° and 85° most of the year. The sub-tropics are in the zone 300–700 miles on either side of the tropics. Weather in the sub-tropics consists of warm and sunny days, with nights averaging between 45° and 50°. On rare occasions, temperatures will dip to produce frost. Central America, Malaysia, the Philippines, India, Hawaii, and much of South America and Africa are tropical or sub-tropical. But my focus is on just two small areas that lie within this region—Florida and the Caribbean islands, which are situated to the south and east of Florida.

While that might seem like an unlikely prospect for good eating, a closer look reveals quite the opposite, for tropical cooking represents an exciting intermingling of African, Spanish, French, British, Indian, Dutch, and North American customs and techniques (mainly Southern cooking). A grand blend of spices and seasonings and sometimes exotic island produce makes this a delightfully different cuisine. Add to this a touch of the "New American Cuisine," and you are in for some real adventures in food.

The earliest settlers of the Caribbean region were the gentle Arawak Indians. They were agricultural people and cultivated sweet potatoes, cassava root, garlic, tobacco and corn, and harvested papaya and guava. From them came the use of allspice (pimento) and hot chili peppers. They are thought to have been the first to grind flour for bread from the cassava root. Long before Ponce de León's arrival, the Seminole Indians discovered Florida. Their methods of preparing the native fruits and vegetables are also part of the heritage. The Indians cooked meat, fish, and fowl on wood gratings over a hot fire. They called it *barbacoa*—the original barbecue. They are also known to have used a form of clay cookery.

In 1492, on his first voyage to the New World, Christopher Columbus sailed into the Bahamas, and the rest, as they say, is history. The French, Spanish, Portuguese, English, Dutch, Danish and other European nations began settling throughout the beautiful region, sometimes fighting over land rights (the island of St. Croix, in the U.S. Virgin Islands, has actually flown seven flags!). By the early 1700s, every Caribbean island was a European colony. Even today, most of the islands remain under the flag of a foreign country (Dutch, French, British, or U.S.A.).

There are four basic groups that are heavily influenced by their colonial heritage: the Hispanic group, which includes Cuba, Puerto Rico, and the Dominican Republic; the French group, which includes Haiti, Guadeloupe, Martinique, and St. Bartholomew; the British group, which includes Jamaica, Barbados, and Grenada; and the Dutch, which includes Aruba and Curaçao. Reminders of colonial ties are evident to this day, as reflected in the architecture, language, customs, and—food. It was only natural that the early European settlers would bring along their favorite food—rich pastries, meat dishes, sauces, and methods of seasonings. Jamaicans have inherited the British love of beef, while Guadeloupe residents welcome visitors to their *haute cuisine Française* as well as their spicy *cuisine Creole*. In Puerto Rico, the food is definitely Spanish.

Of all the European styles of cooking that have contributed to the Caribbean melting pot, the Spanish and French influences have been most significant and long-lasting. But neither has had the unifying impact of the "African factor." During the colonial period, hundreds of thousands of slaves were imported from the gold coast of Africa to work on the colonial sugar plantations in the West Indies. They brought with them the peas, beans, peanuts, okra, and ackee fruits of their homelands, along with time-tested methods of preparation. This influence remains strong throughout much of the Caribbean because the slaves, who were the cooks for the upper classes, shared their gastronomical traditions among themselves and passed them on to the new generations.

When slavery was abolished, plantation owners imported field hands from China and India. This has added a bit more to the culinary collage. Curry for instance, is a favorite spice in island cooking.

While certain of the islands can be said to have their own styles of cooking (Jamaica, Haiti, or Martinique, for instance) there has always been a good deal of contact between islands. This has resulted, over the years, in a good deal of similarity in cooking styles among the islands.

Until recently, Florida had been considered a culinary wasteland—a land of backyard barbecues and greasy fish-fries. But this description is far from accurate. If anything, there is now an even greater mix of cooking types here than there is on the islands. To begin with, the Florida "crackers," those who were born and raised in the Sunshine State, have their own culinary traditions—cooking methods that have stood the test of time and recipes that have been passed down from generation to generation. Another factor has been the migration into Florida of people from neighboring states. From them we get the down-home Southern school of cooking. Since the beginning of the 1890s, trade and emigration have brought the Caribbean closer to Florida. Immigrants from Cuba, Haiti, Puerto Rico, Barbados, Trinidad, Jamaica, and other islands have arrived in large numbers, and their cooking styles have also been assimilated into our culture. The latest thing to hit the state has been the New American Cuisine, with its emphasis on fresh produce, light sauces, fearless combinations, and fine presentations. Out of this, a style of cooking that is unique to Florida—the New Florida Cuisine, if you will—is beginning to take shape and make itself known. Basically, it is the New American Cuisine applied to foods indigenous to Florida, with a touch of island seasoning.

Because of this grand mix of cooking influences, it is difficult to put labels on the cooking of Florida and the Caribbean islands. There is a common ground to it all, though, and that has to do with the raw materials. Since the growing season in the tropics and sub-tropics runs the year round and the climate favors many warm-weather crops, there is always an abundance of fresh fruit, herbs, and vegetables, ordinary and extraordinary. Citrus fruits (of course!), tomatoes, corn, peppers, eggplants, mangoes, papaya, avocados, passion fruit, squash, guava . . . the list is endless and essentially knows no season. Then there's a seemingly infinite variety of fresh seafood—grouper, snapper, mullet, flying fish, lobsters, crab, shrimp, conch—more than 500 species of fish inhabit the island and coastal waters. Because of this, there is a heavy emphasis on seafood in tropic cooking. Tropic cooks also tend to use spices and peppery seasonings generously. Many spices actually come from the Caribbean—cinnamon, nutmeg, cocoa, allspice, tamarind—others, whatever their origin, have been adopted, like so much else in tropic cooking.

I invite you now to explore with me the delights of tropical cuisine. Assembled in the pages of this book are the secrets of many generations and of many cultures. I've included a sampling of the most delicious recipes that I have collected over the years from native islanders, Florida "crackers," restaurateurs both old and new, and also many which I have created myself. Modern shipping methods make almost all tropical fruits and vegetables available in any part of the country, most times of the year. Seek out the specialty food shops in your locale for some of the more unusual spices and seasonings. If all else fails, you can probably use a substitute for some impossible-to-find items (see Tropical Substitutions). There are two other sections you can turn to for help: the Can Do section, which will give you tips on handling mangoes, coconuts, pineapples, etc. and the Tropical Glossary.

I hope you will enjoy your adventure with tropic cooking as much as I have.

Beverages

Sugar Syrup

Keep this handy for your Caribbean drinks.

½ cup sugar
½ cup water

Mix sugar and water in a saucepan. Bring to a rapid boil. Simmer for a minute or two. Cool and measure correct amount for each drink.

Serves: 1

Tranquility

This tropical refresher is served at the New Kingston Hotel in Kingston, Jamaica.

½ ounce fresh lime or lemon juice
1 ounce Jamaican rum
1 ounce pineapple juice
1 ounce fresh orange juice
1 ounce Cointreau
Dash of grenadine syrup
Fruit for garnish

Put all ingredients, except fruit, in a bar shaker with crushed ice. Shake well. Strain. Serve in a large brandy snifter with straw. Garnish with fresh pineapple wedge, orange slice, and cherry.

Serves: 1

Calico Jack

Negril Beach Village in Jamaica is a place where people enjoy doing whatever strikes them at any particular moment. Why not sit back, kick up your feet, and enjoy this tasty specialty, one of the village favorites.

½ ounce overproof rum
½ ounce Appleton Special rum or other rum
2 ounces pineapple juice
½ ounce fresh lime juice
Dash of Triple Sec
Pineapple stick and lime slice for garnish

In a bar shaker, blend the first 5 ingredients well. Pour over ice cubes or serve "up" garnished with a pineapple stick and a lime slice.

Serves: 1

Sunset Glow

As you sit on a cozy veranda watching the sun set on tropical island waters, this libation should put you in a most seductive mood which in turn will add a nice glow to your cheeks. (This is not guaranteed, but probably will happen.)

1 ounce overproof rum
1 ounce Appleton Special rum or other rum
1 ounce Rumona rum liqueur or other rum liqueur
⅓ cup fresh orange juice
1 ounce strawberry syrup
Strawberry for garnish

Combine all ingredients except the strawberry in the container of a blender. Blend well. Serve over a large piece of cracked ice. Garnish with a large strawberry sliced (lengthwise) almost in half, but not quite, and slid onto the rim of the glass.

Serves: 1

Jack Frost

Montego Bay, Jamaica is best seen on a small motorbike or moped, which makes for easy access to the top of the island where the view is truly breathtaking. After a hard day's biking, Appleton rum on the rocks with a slice of lime or this chilled favorite really hits the spot. It's served at the elite Royal Caribbean Hotel in Montego.

1½ ounces Jamaican rum, light or gold
½ ounce Rumona rum liqueur
⅓ cup pineapple juice
2 tablespoons confectioners' sugar or powdered sugar
¼ cup evaporated milk
Pinch of allspice

Put the first 5 ingredients into the container of a blender along with a small amount of cracked ice. Blend until the drink is smooth and frothy. Pour into a tall chilled glass and sprinkle allspice on top.

Serves: 1

Miami Magic

Miami is truly an exciting city, a business center, and a mecca for sports, entertainment, and sightseeing. It's no wonder it is often called the capital of the Caribbean. After a glimpse of its dazzling skyline at night, here's a touch to make it all seem "magic."

2 ounces overproof dark rum
½ teaspoon Triple Sec
½ ounce mango nectar
Slice of lime
Green maraschino cherry for garnish
Freshly grated nutmeg for garnish

In a bar shaker filled with ice cubes, combine the first 4 ingredients. Strain into a medium-sized champagne glass. Garnish with a cherry and freshly grated nutmeg.

Serves: 1

"Jump Up" Sour

Now listen good! A great "Jump Up" fete of dancing, laughing, and feasting also calls for some nice island rum!

2 ounces white rum
1 ounce mango nectar
½ ounce Triple Sec
1 ounce pineapple juice
Orange slice lightly sprinkled with fresh ginger for garnish

Mix liquid ingredients together with ice in a bar shaker. Shake and pour into an old-fashioned glass. Garnish with a slice of orange that has been sprinkled with lightly grated fresh ginger.

Serves: 1

Tropical Kiss

Walking along the white sand beaches of Grenada with that special person in your life—all you need is a sip of this delicious drink to get you headed in the right romantic direction. Kisses and moonlight seem to go hand-in-hand with this concoction.

1½ ounces light rum
½ ounce guava nectar
½ ounce pineapple juice
½ ounce grenadine syrup
1 ounce cream of coconut*
Twist of lime peel for garnish

Put all ingredients, except lime peel, into the container of a blender along with crushed ice. Blend for 15 seconds. Pour into a chilled champagne glass. Garnish with a twist of lime peel.

Serves: 1

*See Tropical Glossary.

Miami Beach Rumbana

In the tropics guanabana, or soursop*, as it is commonly called, can grow to six pounds. It is a dark green fruit that is covered with soft spurs and contains a spongy pulp. When I first tasted the fruit I was in Grenada, West Indies and was impressed with its tangy flavor. It was very different from anything else I've tasted! The Cubans love guanabana-flavored ice cream. It's also nice in cocktails—a real island taste.

¾ ounce white rum
1 ounce guanabana nectar**
¾ ounce Crème de Banana
Twist of lime peel and maraschino cherry for garnish

Stir liquid ingredients together over ice in an old-fashioned glass. Serve with a twist of lime and a maraschino cherry. Substitute pear nectar if guanabana is not available.

Serves: 1

* See Tropical Glossary.
** I particularly like the Goya brand of guanabana nectar.

Big Bamboo

Be sure to accompany this drink with music from a low-key steel drum band and "lotsa lovin." Like the song goes, "Well, I ask my lady what should I do to make she happy, to make love true." She said, "The only thing I want from you is a little piece of the big bamboo."

2 ounces light rum
½ ounce fresh lime juice
½ ounce grenadine syrup
½ ounce Triple Sec
1 ounce fresh orange juice
Mint sprigs for garnish

Combine all ingredients except garnish in a bar shaker filled with ice. Strain into a glass filled with lots of cracked ice. Garnish with mint springs.

Serves: 1

Guava Treasure

The guava is a member of the myrtle family, as are its aromatic cousins—the clove, allspice, and the bay-rum tree. Its perfume-like flavor and even consistency make for a fruit that you would swear was made in heaven!

Although this popular fruit has been associated with the Hispanic culture, it grows heartily around the globe. Guavas in the United States come largely from Florida, although they're occasionally imported.

My husband, Richard, created this delight on one of his experimental nights at our very "tropically-stocked" bar.

1½ ounces vodka or white rum
½ ounce guava nectar*
½ ounce fresh orange juice
½ ounce grenadine syrup
½ ounce Triple Sec
Twist of orange peel for garnish
Mint sprig for garnish

Put all ingredients (except garnishes) in a bar shaker with cracked ice. Shake well. Pour into a chilled old-fashioned glass. Add ice to fill glass to the top. Garnish with a twist of orange peel and a mint sprig.

Serves: 1

*I use the Goya brand—it is consistently good. The nectar is a blend of guava fruit pulp, sugar, and ascorbic acid.

Calabash Rum Punch

Saturday is market day in St. George's, Grenada, and it's fascinating to watch vendors peddling all types of fresh fruits, vegetables, spices, and handicrafts. After a day of shopping there, I was delighted upon my return to be handed an ice cold glass of this refreshing punch which is made daily by maitre d' Jeff Donne at the Calabash Resort.

1 ounce fresh lime or lemon juice
1 ounce Sugar Syrup (see page 5)
1 ounce water
2 ounces dark rum (Mount Gay, preferably)
Angostura bitters to taste
Freshly grated nutmeg for garnish

Crack ice by placing cubes in palm of hand and hitting with a soup spoon. Fill glass with ice and pour in ingredients. Stir. Serve with freshly grated nutmeg on top.

Serves: 1

Guan-Tana-Bana Shake (Soursop*)

Rum may be the oldest of all distilled spirits. The Arabs helped perfect the art of distillation as early as the Middle Ages. Its combination with many fruits has been legend over the years. It's delightful combined with guanabana juice, also commonly known as soursop juice.

Soursop, a member of the genis *Annona*, has a white flesh that contains black seeds and is rarely cooked. "Cousin" fruits in the same family as the soursop that you may have tried are the sugar apple, atemoya, and cherimoya.

1 ounce light rum
2 ounces whipping cream
1 ounce mango nectar
1 ounce guanabana nectar (soursop*)
1 ounce guava nectar
¼ medium-sized banana, sliced
Maraschino cherry and lime slice for garnish

Put all the ingredients (except garnishes) in the container of a blender with about ¾ cup crushed ice. Blend for about 20 seconds. Pour into a tall glass. Garnish with a cherry and a slice of lime.

Serves: 1

*See Tropical Glossary.

Cuba Libre

Once in a while, an old standby drink tastes better than ever. Variations on rum types make this a different drink every time. A toast to the beautiful people with such a fine Hispanic heritage.

1½ ounces light rum
3 ounces cola
Juice of ½ fresh lime
Lemon wedge for garnish

Pour rum over ice cubes or crushed ice in a highball glass. Add cola. Garnish with a lemon wedge.

Serves: 1

Negril Stinger

One of the most beautiful beaches in the world is in Negril, Jamaica. After one of these tantalizing creations, it will look even prettier. I use an extra smooth premium rum if Appleton is not in the liquor closet.

2 ounces Appleton Special rum or other rum
1 ounce Tia Maria*
Lime slice for garnish

Mix the liquid ingredients and pour over lots of ice. Garnish with a lime slice if desired.

Serves: 1

*Tia Maria is a Jamaican liqueur derived from an original coffee liqueur recipe that has been closely guarded for generations.

Guava Sunrise

The perfect way to start a day in the tropics is with a Guava Sunrise. Try it instead of a Bloody Mary.

2–3 dashes grenadine syrup
1½ ounces rum
Guava nectar
2 maraschino cherries for garnish

Put grenadine in an old-fashioned glass filled with ice cubes. Add rum. Fill with guava nectar. Stir lightly and garnish with 2 cherries.

Serves: 1

Hurricane Classic

This drink was created in Miami in honor of the Hurricanes, University of Miami's national championship football team. Try making it with a smooth liqueur like O'Darby Irish cream.

3 ounces O'Darby Irish cream liqueur
1 ounce light rum
3 ounces fresh orange juice

Place all ingredients in the container of a blender along with ¾ cup crushed ice. Mix well. Serve in an hour-glass shaped glass.

Serves: 1

Jeff's Special

Lazy days and magical nights at the Calabash Resort at L'Anse aux Epines in Grenada demand a tasting of this creation by maitre d' Jeff Donne. It's refreshing because it's not too sweet.

1 ounce Malibu (may substitute a coconut liqueur)
1 ounce Cointreau or De La Grenade*
2 ounces white or dark rum
2 ounces pineapple juice
Fresh slice of pineapple and maraschino cherry for garnish

In a bar shaker, combine all the liquid ingredients. Shake well and serve over cracked ice. Garnish with a pineapple slice and a cherry.

Serves: 1

*This liqueur has a delightful rum base with orange spice and is a product of Grenada, West Indies.

Tropical Dreams

Here's a drink that offers you an exhilarating way to end a memorable day in the tropics.

¾ ounce light rum
¾ ounce apricot brandy
½ ounce peach nectar
¾ ounce Triple Sec
½ ounce fresh lemon juice

Combine ingredients with ice in a bar shaker. Shake well. Strain into a chilled cocktail glass.

Serves: 1

Island Jazz

This recipe was created by my friend and husband, Richard, who as a teenager back in the 50s, had one of those dance bands. (You remember those guys with the pink and gray jackets and slick crew cut hairdos.) The crew cut and pastel jacket are gone now, but he still loves music, including the music of the islands. I've noticed he increases the rum measure as the music becomes more exciting.

2 ounces light rum
1½ ounces apricot brandy
½ ounce pineapple juice
½ ounce fresh lime juice
1 teaspoon powdered sugar
Pineapple slice, lime slice, and mint leaf for garnish

Combine rum, brandy, pineapple juice, lime juice and powdered sugar with ice in a bar shaker. Shake and strain into a 14-ounce glass. Add ice to fill glass. Garnish with a large slice of fresh pineapple, a slice of lime, and a mint leaf.

Serves: 1

Blue Grenada Seas

Here's a drink that's cool, colorful, and incredibly refreshing, just like a visit to beautiful Grenada, West Indies.

½ ounce blue Curaçao liqueur
½ ounce apricot brandy
1 ounce light rum
½ ounce lemon juice
1 ounce cream of coconut*
Maraschino cherries and an orange slice for garnish

Put the first 5 ingredients in a bar shaker filled with ice. Shake well and strain into a chilled deep-saucer champagne glass. Garnish with maraschino cherries separated by a ½-inch slice of orange.

Serves: 1

*See Tropical Glossary.

Cuban Kick

You'll want to get out your dancin' shoes and do the Bossa Nova after a few sips of this drink, which packs a sneaky kind of wallop!

1 ounce light rum
1 ounce Liquore Galliano
¾ ounce apricot brandy
1 ounce fresh lemon juice
1½ ounces pineapple juice
1½ ounces fresh orange juice
Banana slice for garnish

Combine liquid ingredients with ice cubes in a cocktail shaker. Shake well and serve in a 12-ounce glass filled with ice cubes. Slice a 1-inch section of banana. Remove the peel. Split almost in half with a sharp knife and attach to the rim of the glass.

Serves: 1

Mango Orange Blossom Breeze

One afternoon as my husband Richard and I sat out on the patio enjoying the Florida sunshine and cool breezes, he invented this wonderfully refreshing drink. He said the smell of orange blossoms from a nearby tree gave him the idea.

¼ cup mango, peeled and sliced
½ ounce orange Curaçao liqueur
1½ ounces rum

Put all the ingredients in the container of a blender along with some crushed ice. Blend well and pour into a chilled cocktail glass.

Serves: 1

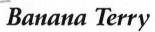

Banana Terry

Dinner at 9:00... Reggae music from a nearby boat party... Banana Terry... Never mind the mosquitos... This is heaven.

1 ripe banana
3 ounces fresh coconut milk*
1½ ounces condensed milk
1 ounce Crème de Banana

*See Tropical Glossary.

3 ounces white rum
Banana slice, maraschino cherry, and fresh pineapple ring for garnish

Blend first 5 ingredients in a bar shaker filled with cracked ice. Pour into a 12-ounce cocktail goblet.
Garnish with a banana slice, a cherry, and a pineapple ring.

Serves: 1

Tim-Tim Time

"Tim-tim" are the Creole words used by narrators to introduce stories from long ago. There is an intriguing antique shop in Pointe-à-Pitre, Guadeloupe, French West Indies owned by storytellers Simone and Andre Schwartz-Bart. This would be a nice drink to sip while listening to their many tales of pirates and sunken treasure ships.

1 ounce Ronrico rum
½ ounce Triple sec
½ ounce fresh lemon juice
Dash of Sugar Syrup (see page 5)
Strawberry for garnish

Put all the liquid ingredients in a bar shaker filled with ice. Shake and strain into a chilled old-fashioned glass. Garnish with a fresh strawberry.

Serves: 1

Rumrunner

Originally, light rum came from Cuba. Later, Puerto Rico took over the production of light rums and now benefits quite nicely because of their increasing popularity. Variations on rum drinks are limitless as you are probably beginning to find out. Here's an interesting combination.

1 ounce blackberry brandy
1 ounce fresh lime juice
2 ounces white rum
½ ounce grenadine syrup
1 ounce water
Lime slice for garnish

Combine all ingredients, except garnish, in a bar shaker filled with ice. Shake well. Serve in a tall glass. Garnish with a slice of lime.

Serves: 1

Yellowbird

Try this mild but somewhat potent tropical drink from the Tryall Golf and Beach Club in Hanover, Jamaica. I became addicted to Yellowbirds on my first honeymoon.

1¼ ounce light rum
¼ ounce apricot brandy
¼ ounce Liquore Galliano
¼ ounce fresh lime juice
2 ounces fresh orange juice
Slice of orange and maraschino cherry for garnish

In a bar shaker, blend liquid ingredients by shaking well. Pour over ice into a 10-ounce highball glass. Garnish with a slice of orange and a cherry.

Serves: 1

U. S. Bomber

Ever since the United States intervention in Grenada, West Indies, in 1983, the beautiful "Isle of Spice" has become, once again, a mecca for those looking for the ultimate in peaceful and serene settings. Those who have been there will never forget the gentleness of its people, the tropical lushness of its terrain, and the excellence in its cuisine.

It's a kick to sip this drink specially created at Delicious Landing Restaurant in St. George's.

1 ounce honey
1 ounce Crème de Banana
1 ounce Liquore Galliano
2½ ounces overproof white rum
1½ ounces fresh lime juice
Orange slice and maraschino cherry for garnish
1 teaspoon grenadine syrup

Combine honey, Crème de Banana, Galliano, rum, and lime juice in a bar shaker. Stir well. Fill a 12-ounce cocktail goblet with cracked ice. Pour in mixture.

Ice should smoke as the bomb cools its way through.

Garnish with an orange slice and cherry. Pour grenadine syrup on rim of the glass to complete the illusion of a bomb explosion.

Serves: 1

Perfect Piña Colada

I lived in Cleveland, Ohio, for seven years. During that time I would often daydream, imagining myself back in the tropics, sitting on a sunny beach, sipping something cool. When it came time to return to Florida, my first thought was, "I can't wait to have a *real* piña colada!"

2 ounces pineapple juice
2 ounces rum
2 ounces cream of coconut*
½ ounce fresh lime juice
1 tablespoon coconut shavings
Maraschino cherry and orange slice for garnish

Combine all ingredients except garnish in the container of a blender. Blend on high for 60 seconds or more. Pour into a chilled glass. Sprinkle coconut shavings over top and garnish with a cherry and an orange slice.

Serves: 1

*See Tropical Glossary.

Beach Club Piña Colada

Drinking warm weather coolers at the Tryall Golf and Beach Club in Hanover, Jamaica is a sport in which many visitors indulge. You'll like this easy piña colada which is one of their specialties.

2 ounces cream of coconut*
¼ ounce apricot brandy
¼ ounce light rum
2 ounces pineapple juice
¼ ounce Sugar Syrup (see page 5)
Dash of cinnamon
Dash of pure vanilla extract
Fresh pineapple stick, grated coconut, and maraschino cherry for garnish

In a blender or container of a food processor, blend all ingredients (except garnishes) with crushed ice. Serve in a 10-ounce highball glass or hurricane-shaped glass.
Garnish with fresh pineapple stick, grated coconut, and cherry.

Serves: 1

*See Tropical Glossary.

Come Monday Colada

This tasty little variation of the piña colada will make you feel as though you've just landed on a Caribbean island. Maybe it's the fresh coconut shavings that lend that special tropical flavor.

Shredded coconut will store for several days if kept in a tightly-covered container. There's no need to sweeten the shavings. Coladas are nice frozen, too, according to my assistant, Sandra, who has a sweet tooth.

1½ ounces rum
1 ounce cream of coconut*
4 ounces pineapple juice
Fresh pineapple stick, coconut shavings, and a maraschino cherry
    for garnish

Combine rum, cream of coconut and pineapple juice in the container of a blender. Pour over ice cubes in a tall frosted glass. Garnish with a pineapple stick, coconut shavings and a cherry.

Serves: 1

*See Tropical Glossary.

Banana Colada

Here's another island variation of the popular piña colada.

Add some tropical music, close your eyes and spend a few minutes reliving your favorite tropical vacation.

1½ ounces rum
½ ounce Anisette liqueur
½ ounce Crème de Banana
½ ounce blackberry liqueur
¾ ounce grenadine syrup
1 ounce cream of coconut*
½ banana, sliced
Maraschino cherry and banana slice for garnish

Place rum, Anisette, Crème de Banana, black raspberry liqueur, grenadine syrup, cream of coconut, banana slices, and ¾ cup crushed ice in the container of a blender. Blend for 15–20 seconds. Pour into a tall glass and garnish with a cherry and a banana slice.

Serves: 1

*See Tropical Glossary.

Caribbean Mai Tai

The blend of fruit juices brings this drink a unique tropical taste. The coconut is what really gives it character.

2 ounces overproof white rum
½ ounce fresh lime juice
½ ounce almond syrup
1 teaspoon sugar
2 ounces fresh orange juice
2 ounces apricot juice
2 ounces pineapple juice
¾ ounce coconut milk*
Dash of grenadine syrup
Mint sprigs for garnish
Maraschino cherry and lime slice for garnish

Place all ingredients (except garnishes) in the container of a blender or bar shaker. Process or shake. Strain into a tall glass filled with ice. Garnish with a cherry and a lime slice.

Serves: 1

*See Tropical Glossary.

Limey Rum Mai Tai

Summer thirsts seek tropical quenchers like the mai tai. You'll love the sweet refreshing taste of lime juice in this one.

1½ ounces light rum
½ ounce fresh lime juice
½ ounce almond syrup
1 teaspoon sugar
2 ounces fresh orange juice
Dash of grenadine
Lime slice and maraschino cherry for garnish

In a bar shaker, combine all ingredients (except garnishes). Shake well. Strain over ice in a tall glass. Garnish with a lime slice and a maraschino cherry.

Serves: 1

Mai Tai Mama

Grenadine syrup always adds excitement to drinks with its bright rose color and its fruity taste. Mamas everywhere like this mix.

1½ ounces rum
½ ounce fresh lime juice
½ ounce almond syrup
1 teaspoon sugar
2 ounces fresh orange juice
Lime slice for garnish

Put the first 6 ingredients in the container of a blender. Blend. Strain over ice in a highball glass. Garnish with a slice of lime.

Serves: 1

Crazy Mai Tai

The term "rum-running" refers to the Prohibition-era activity of smuggling rum into this country from Cuba and other Caribbean islands—a most interesting history, full of enjoyable anecdotes and stories. Make yourself one of these drinks, and curl up with a good book about this era. It's a good way to spend a lazy Sunday afternoon!

½ teaspoon powdered sugar
2 ounces dark rum
1 ounce Triple Sec
½ ounce grenadine syrup
½ ounce fresh lime juice
Maraschino cherry and pineapple wedge for garnish

Put the first 5 ingredients in a bar shaker filled with ice. Shake well and strain into a large old-fashioned glass that is half filled with crushed ice. Garnish with a maraschino cherry and a pineapple wedge.

Serves: 1

Rum Daiquiri

The history of rum is an interesting one, from the famed Caribbean pirate's cry of "Yo-ho-ho and a bottle of rum" to the strong sound of the Temperance Union radicals' "Away, away with rum by gum!" Would one ever believe that George Washington's 1758 election to the Virginia House of Burgesses was supposedly related to the distribution of 75 gallons of rum to voters? Perhaps so, after indulging in some interesting rum concoction like this simple but delicious Rum Daiquiri.

1 teaspoon sugar
½ ounce fresh lime juice
2 ounces extra-smooth premium light rum
Orange slice and maraschino cherry for garnish

Mix the sugar with the fresh lime juice. Pour into a bar shaker. Add the rum. Shake with cracked ice until very cold. Strain into a cocktail glass that is filled with lots of ice. Add an orange slice and a maraschino cherry for garnish.

Serves: 1

Banana Daiquiri

Banana is one of the few fruits that can be picked full size but green and stored for ripening without loss of flavor. If you need to ripen yours, hang in a cool shady place and they will gradually ripen. Here's an easy-to-make banana cooler for a lazy summer's day.

2 ounces of dark rum
½ ounce fresh lime juice
½ ripe banana, thinly sliced
1 teaspoon sugar
Slice of banana for garnish

Place all ingredients in the container of a blender. Blend for about 30 seconds. Stir mixture. Add a couple of cubes of ice and then blend for another 30 seconds.
Garnish with a freshly peeled slice of banana.

Serves: 1

Caribbean Sparkler

Depending on the "proof" rum one uses, this drink can be relatively harmless or deceptively potent!

Chilled white sparkling wine
½ ounce white rum
¼ ounce Crème de Banana
1-inch slice of banana with peel for garnish

Fill a chilled champagne flute almost to the brim with the sparkling wine. Add the rum and Crème de Banana and stir. Slice banana vertically into a 1-inch slice, split almost in half with a sharp knife and slide on side of the glass.

Serves: 1

Frozen Mango Daiquiri

The mango is often called the apple of the South, but the mango might well be of more importance to people of the tropics than the apple is to their counterparts in more temperate areas because the mango is so versatile. Ripe mangoes are good in salads, sauces, desserts, breads, and beverages, such as this refreshing Frozen Mango Daiquiri.

¾ cup ripe mango, peeled and diced
⅓ cup fresh lime juice
3 tablespoons sugar
⅓ cup rum

Place ingredients in the container of a food processor or blender along with 4 cups of crushed ice. Blend until smooth. Serve in chilled glasses.

Serves: 2

Dark and Stormy

Bill Gottlieb, owner of the remarkably inexpensive Caribe Restaurant at Perry Street and Greenwich in New York City told me that he often prepares this drink at his retreat in Montserret, French West Indies. It is also very popular at his trendy restaurant where bandana-clad waitresses pulse to the foot-stomping tunes of Bob Marley and other friends.

At the Caribe they prepare this drink with commercially bottled ginger beer, but it's also good with the homemade version (see page 34).

By the way, this is great when you're down with a cold.

3 ounces Mount Gay dark rum
3 ounces ginger beer, bottled or fresh
Fresh lime slice

Pour rum and ginger beer over freshly cracked ice. Squeeze the lime juice over all. Drop in squeezed lime slices.

Serves: 1

Island "On-The-Rocks" Coffee

This drink is a little different from your average morning "pick-me-up." The rum imparts a delectable smoothness to the coffee.

1 ounce rum
Black coffee, double strength
Sugar to taste
Whipped cream
Maraschino cherry for garnish

Pour the rum into a glass filled with ice cubes. Fill with coffee. Sweeten with sugar to taste. Top with whipped cream and a maraschino cherry.

Serves: 1

Orange Surprise

The "surprise" will be the lift your spirit will get from this healthful invention from Klaus's Cuisine Restaurant in Holly Hill, Florida. It's a "hoot."

1 scoop orange sherbet
4 ounces fresh orange juice
1 ounce Cointreau
Splash dark rum
Finely minced orange peel and orange slice for garnish

Put the first 4 ingredients in the container of a blender. Blend until foamy. Pour into a tall glass. Garnish with finely minced orange peel and ½ slice of orange.

Serves: 1

Martiniqua

On the island of Martinique, the natives have their own version of the Margarita—one that reflects the cultural blendings of the African, European and Hindu people that have settled there over the centuries. If you sit back, close your eyes, and take a sip, you can almost picture yourself there, too.

Lemon wedge
Sugar
Shredded coconut
1½ ounces dark rum
½ ounce Cointreau
½ ounce fresh lemon juice
1 egg white
Dash of blue Curaçao liqueur

Rub the rim of a chilled champagne glass with a lemon wedge. While still damp, insert the rim in a saucer of sugar and then in a saucer of coconut.

Combine rum, Cointreau, lemon juice, egg white and crushed ice in a blender for 20 seconds. Pour into the prepared glass. Add a dash of blue Curaçao to the center of the drink.

Serves: 1

Peter Island Special

"Presentation" has a lot to do with the experience one has while dining out. You'll love this drink from Peter Island Hotel and Yacht Harbour in the British Virgin Islands. It resembles the beautiful blue ocean water surrounding the islands.

¼ ounce fresh lime juice
1 teaspoon sugar
1½ ounces blue Curaçao liqueur
1 ounce fresh orange juice
Angostura bitters
Orange slice and maraschino cherry for garnish

Blend first 4 ingredients in the container of a blender or food processor. Serve over ice in a 10-ounce highball glass with a dash of bitters on top. Garnish with a fresh orange slice and a maraschino cherry.

Serves: 1

Tropical Seas

Here's an incredibly smooth drink to conclude a brunch, lunch, or dinner in the tropics!

½ ounce blue Curaçao liqueur
½ ounce Triple Sec
½ ounce Cointreau
2 ounces cream of coconut*
Ice

Mix all ingredients in a bar shaker filled with ice. Shake well. Strain into a chilled cocktail glass.

Serves: 1

*See Tropical Glossary.

Curaçao Baby

Here's a drink that's a perfect blend of old France and the tropics suitable for topping off a late dinner.

1 ounce Armagnac
½ ounce orange Curaçao liqueur
Dash bitters
Twist of lime peel for garnish

Combine Armagnac, Curaçao, and bitters over crushed ice in an old-fashioned glass. Garnish with a twist of lime peel.

Serves: 1

Armagnac Champagne Royale

Here's a tribute to the French West Indies whose French cuisine alone is worth a trip to the islands!

1 ounce Armagnac
1 ounce orange Curaçao
6 ounces brut champagne, well chilled
Orange slice for garnish

Measure Armagnac and orange Curaçao into a champagne flute that has been chilled. Top off with well-chilled champagne. Garnish with a slice of fresh orange.

Serves: 1

Martinique Cooler

A touch of Cassis added to a rather dry wine makes for a fashionably cool thirst quencher.

4 ounces Chablis or dry white wine
1 teaspoon Sirop De Cassis* (blackberry syrup)

Pour the Chablis into a glass that has been well chilled in the freezer. Add the Sirop and stir well.

Serves: 1

*This is a non-alcoholic blackberry syrup imported from Bordeaux by Hartley & Parker, Inc., Miami, Florida. What a great taste!

Caribbean Sunset

Island bartenders in the Caribbean are highly revered for creating such refreshing libations as this Caribbean Sunset. Keep one close at hand as you watch the sun cast its beautiful warm colors against the late afternoon sky.

1 6-ounce can frozen orange juice concentrate, undiluted
2¼ cups (3 juice cans) semi-sweet white wine
½ cup heavy cream
1 egg white
Orange peel or mint springs for garnish

Place the juice, wine, cream, and egg white in the container of a blender. Add crushed ice to within 1 inch of the top of the container. Cover and blend until very frothy.

Pour into wine glasses and garnish with twists of orange peel or mint sprigs.

Makes: 8 5-ounce servings

Sexy Margarita

Your Margarita will taste better with fresh lime juice but if you absolutely must, you may substitute the bottled variety. Enjoy this famous drink—one that's bound to be as popular among your friends as it is in the tropics.

Lime wedge and salt for glass rim
2 ounces tequila
1 ounce fresh lime juice
1 ounce Triple Sec
1 tablespoon confectioner's sugar
Lime slice for garnish

Rub rim of cocktail glass with lime wedge. While still damp, insert rim in a saucer of salt to coat.

Combine remaining ingredients with ¾ cup cracked ice in blender and whirl until slushy. Pour into the prepared glass and garnish with a lime slice.

Serves: 1

Blue Margarita

This delightful libation was created by Raymond Anderson, a waiter at The Foundling, a private women's club (sorry guys!) on Miami Beach whose membership and fraternity (sorority?) I cherish along with their fabulous gourmet meals and great bar drinks.

1 ounce tequila
½ ounce blue Curaçao liqueur
Splash of Triple Sec
Salt
Splash of fresh lemon juice
Lime slice for garnish

Put the first 5 ingredients in the container of a blender along with ¾ cup crushed ice. Blend for 3 minutes or until slushy. Serve in a chilled champagne glass that has been rimmed with salt. Garnish with a slice of lime.

Serves: 1

Island Brew

Try this brew for a refreshing way to relax after a walk along the beach on a tropical summer day. Smell the ocean breeze.

1 6-½-ounce can lager beer
4 ounces lemon-flavored Perrier
Lime slice for garnish

Fill a tall, chilled beer glass halfway with your favorite lager beer. Pour in the Perrier. Rim glass with lime and garnish with a slice of lime.

Serves: 1

Sorrel Drink

The sorrel, also known as roselle, is a tropical flower that grows throughout the Caribbean islands. It has a slightly acidic taste and is delicious when mixed with the flavorful island spices and fruits.

I first tasted this delightfully refreshing drink at a church "island" bazaar in Miami, but it was served "sans" alcohol. The food and drink were prepared by the ladies of the church who were from the islands of Jamaica, Trinidad, Martinique, and Guyana.

When I asked my Jamaican friend, Elfreda Clarke, if she had a good sorrel recipe, she showed me how to make this one which was her own special version.

¼ cup dried Jamaican sorrel* (roselle, available in most Latin American markets)
2 cinnamon sticks
1 5-inch piece fresh ginger, peeled and chopped
3 cups sugar or less (may use other sweeteners, such as honey)
2½ quarts boiling water
½ cup medium-dark overproof rum
2 teaspoons ground cinnamon

Combine the sorrel together with the cinnamon sticks, ginger pieces, and sugar in a very large crock. Pour the boiling water over all and cool. Cover and set aside at room temperature for 2 days. Strain the liquid through cheesecloth or a fine sieve and return to the crock. Stir in the rum and cinnamon. Let it stand at room temperature for 2 more days. Strain again and refrigerate until thoroughly chilled. Serve in glasses that have been chilled and filled with crushed ice.

Yield: About 6½ pints

*See Tropical Glossary.

The Winged Moped

If you're visiting the islands, you might try sightseeing by moped or small bike, as many of us do. This drink will make you feel as if your bike had wings, so be sure to imbibe only *after* sightseeing.

To add that special Caribbean flavor, find a spot near a steel drum band, preferably under the aged flora so typical of the islands. This drink is sweet, so you may opt to wait and have it as an after dinner treat.

½ ounce Triple Sec
Juice of 3 Key limes or 1 Persian lime
1 ounce apricot brandy
Lime slice for garnish

Fill bar shaker with ice and add first 3 ingredients. Shake well. Strain into a cocktail glass. Reserve 5–6 ice cubes to add to the glass. Garnish with a fresh slice of lime.

Serves: 1

Grenada Lady (Pretty in Pink)

Whenever I prepare this drink, I am reminded of the beaches of Grenada and their vivid, beautiful colors: the deep emerald and turquoise of the ocean, the bright blue sky, the soft white sand, and the "clear-as-gin" air.

1½ ounces gin
½ ounce Crème de Banana
½ ounce fresh lemon juice
1 teaspoon grenadine syrup
1 egg white
Strawberry for garnish

Mix all liquid ingredients in a bar shaker filled with ice cubes. Shake and serve over crushed ice in a chilled champagne glass. Top off with a fresh strawberry.

Serves: 1

Carambola Gin Sparkle

The carambola is a small, tart fruit, widely grown in tropical regions. Sliced crosswise, it reveals a beautiful five-pointed star shape. Other names this pretty "star fruit" goes by are: foreign peach, balimbing, Chinese gooseberry, and bilimbine. Whatever the name, the fruit is absolutely delicious and very versatile.

2 ounces gin
5 ounces sparkling water
2 slices carambola fruit

Measure gin into a tall frosted glass filled with ice. Add water. Stir. Squeeze one slice of carambola into the glass and garnish with the second.

Serves: 1

Melon Ball

This recipe is from La Teresita de Marti restaurant in Key West, known to the locals as "La-Te-Da." It's very refreshing on a hot day in the Florida Keys.

1 ounce vodka
1½ ounces melon liqueur
3 ounces fresh orange juice
Orange slice and fresh orchid for garnish

Fill the blender ⅔ full of cracked ice. Combine vodka, 1 ounce of the liqueur, and juice. Blend until smooth. Serve in a 16-ounce stemmed glass and top with a ½-ounce float of the liqueur. For an elegant touch, garnish with an orange slice and a fresh orchid.

Serves: 1

Malaga Sangria

This Spanish beverage from the Malaga Restaurant in Miami, Florida, is ideal for nearly any occasion. It goes well with poultry, seafood, and beef.

1 bottle (750 ml) Spanish red wine (Rioja)
1 cup lemon soda
4 tablespoons sugar, or more to taste
Juice of 2 seedless limes
1 cup mixed fruit cocktail, drained and slightly crushed
1 orange, seeded and sliced
Assorted fruit for garnish

Pour wine and lemon soda into a glass pitcher. Add sugar, lime juice, fruit cocktail, and orange slices. Add lots of ice and stir well. Pour into wine goblets. Garnish with fruit.

Serves: 2–4

Mango Fandango

Mangoes, low in calories, fat, and sodium, are a healthy way to add a little tropical punch in any diet. They can be used at any stage of maturity. However, it's important that the fruit be ripe when used for this cooling tropical drink.

4 ounces fresh orange juice
¼ cup fresh mango, peeled and chopped
½ fresh banana, cut up
1 ounce fresh lime juice
1 teaspoon powdered sugar
4 ice cubes
Fresh mint sprigs for garnish

Combine all ingredients in the container of a blender. Blend on high for about 60 seconds or until mango is puréed. Serve in a chilled old-fashioned glass and garnish with mint sprigs.

Serves: 1

Strawberry Whip

From the 19th Hole at the PGA National in Palm Beach Gardens, Florida, comes the Strawberry Whip. It's said that this drink can do wonders for your golf game.

½ cup fresh strawberries
½ cup fresh orange juice
½ cup strawberry yogurt
1 tablespoon honey
Fresh strawberry for garnish

Place all ingredients in the container of a blender. Blend for a few seconds. Serve in a tall, chilled glass. Garnish with fresh strawberry.

Serves: 1

Tamarind Coolers

The first time I tasted fresh tamarind was in Grenada at the Saturday morning marketplace, a festive occasion when the country folk come into St. George's to sell a variety of exotic fruits, vegetables, and mounds of wonderfully aromatic spices. The tamarind is a brown pod-like fruit about 3–4 inches long. It grows in bunches on very large trees. I cracked open the pod which revealed a very tart, juicy pulp surrounding a long, dark brown seed. It was refreshing and nice to suck on.

12 whole tamarind seeds, shelled
4 cups water
½ cup sugar, or to taste
1 teaspoon fresh lime juice

Soak the tamarind seeds in the water for 30–40 minutes. Remove seeds. Add the sugar and lime juice. Chill for about 1 hour. Serve over cracked ice in very well-chilled glasses.

Serves: 4

French West Indies Cooler

One of the most memorable things about a hot summer's day are the refreshing drinks that send icy streams down the sides of frosty drink glasses. You'll say "ahhh-hh" when you taste this.

4 ounces Chablis or other white wine
6 ounces Perrier
½ fresh lime
½ ounce maraschino cherry juice

In a tall glass, combine the Chablis and Perrier. Squeeze the lime juice into the glass, then drop in the lime shell. Stir. Add the cherry juice. Stir. Fill glass with lots of cracked ice and stir again until glass is frosty.

Serves: 1

Tuacarita

The flavor of Tuaca liqueur is unique and tantalizing. I love it, perhaps because it brings back memories of my school days in Italy, or maybe just because it tastes so refreshing on a hot tropical day.

Salt for rim
1 ounce Tuaca* liqueur
1 ounce fresh lime or lemon juice

Wet the rim of a chilled champagne glass (with a lemon or lime wedge if you have one). Insert the rim in salt. Place ingredients in a bar shaker with shaved ice. Shake well. Serve in the frosted salt-rimmed champagne glass.

Serves: 1

*A delicious Italian liqueur.

"Why Don't We Get Drunk" Sangria

As a carefree student abroad, I traveled to Granada, Spain, where I sampled this very mellow libation. As a less carefree but still fun-seeking adult, I refined it while on a visit to Jamaica. Try it for your next party!

½ gallon Burgundy wine
Juice of 4 oranges
Juice of 1 lemon and 1 lime
1 cup fresh peaches, peeled and sliced
1 cup fresh apples, peeled and sliced
¾ cup sugar
½ cup brandy (cognac or Armagnac, preferably)
A few pinches of cinnamon

Mix all ingredients except brandy and cinnamon in a large earthenware pitcher. Chill in refrigerator for 24 hours. Add brandy just before serving. Pour over ice in large goblets. Sprinkle with cinnamon.

Serves: 8–10

Fruity Island Punch

Due to the great consumption of rum in the 1700s, some historians have felt that the Boston Tea Party could easily have been the Boston Rum Party. Records of that time indicate that per person consumption of rum was several gallons per year, as compared to the current 1.5 gallons per person per year—which all figures indicate is now beginning to rise. I drink tea in great quantities. But after researching hundreds of great rum drinks recently, I might well agree that had it been a Rum Party I would have been a willing sponsor. In any event, why not have one now and feature this punch?

25 ounces overproof white rum
1 cup pineapple juice
1½ cups fresh orange juice
1½ cups fresh lime juice
½ cup sugar or sugar to taste
2 liters (67.6 ounces) ginger ale
Sliced fruit: pineapple, oranges, and limes
Maraschino cherries and mint leaves for garnish

Mix the rum, pineapple juice, orange juice, and lime juice in a punch bowl. Add sugar and adjust to your taste. Add plenty of ice. Stir well. Add the ginger ale. Decorate with the sliced fruit and maraschino cherries. Add mint leaves, if desired.

Serves: About 30

Jamaican Rum Punch

Jamaican Rum Punch is a familiar favorite at most of the hotels on the island. It's an easy recipe to remember, but be sure not to confuse the measure. Well, I guess it's okay to mix up "3" and "4" occasionally, especially on a hot summer day! Try a number of different rums.

1 part of sour (lime or lemon juice)
2 parts of sweet (Sugar Syrup—see page 5)
3 parts of strong (rum)
4 parts of weak (water and crushed ice)
Freshly grated nutmeg

Combine liquid ingredients in a bar shaker. Shake well. Pour over cracked ice in an 8-ounce glass. Garnish with freshly grated nutmeg.

Yield: Whatever amount you desire.

Jamaican Berry Rum Punch

Elfreda Clarke, a lovely lady with a reputation for great cooking, was born in St. Catherine's, Jamaica, but lived in Kingston for much of her life. For about five years now, she's been living in Miami. I was lucky enough to meet her recently and have her share some excellent recipes with me, and a few glasses of this lively sweet punch. It can be made ahead and seems to improve with age, just like lots of people I know. Here's enough for a party.

1 bottle (750 ml) overproof white rum
1 bottle (750 ml) Kelly's Strawberry Syrup* (available in West Indian markets)
1½ cups fresh lime juice, (may use part lemon juice)
2½ quarts water
20–30 whole allspice seeds (pimento)
Sugar to taste

Pour rum and strawberry syrup into a large wide-mouthed jug. Strain the lime juice through a wire strainer to remove all pulp. Add to rum mixture and stir. Add water, more or less depending on taste desired. If you desire a sweeter taste, add some sugar. Mix well.

Siphon punch into glass bottles with screw-on caps. Add 4–6 allspice seeds to each bottle; they will float on top. Cap tightly. No need to refrigerate.

Yield: About 5 (750 ml) bottles

*Kelly's Strawberry Syrup is an artificially flavored strawberry syrup. You can substitute any similar brand.

Jamaican Ginger Beer

Fresh ginger roots, or "hands" as they are sometimes called by the island-ers, are widely available in Latin and Oriental markets and are becoming more available in supermarkets. Elfreda Clarke (see Jamaican Berry Rum Punch, page 33) showed me how to prepare this wonderful drink, too. She added a little rum, just for flavoring. After tasting the finished product, she exclaimed with a big, toothy smile, "I just *love* ginger beer!"

1 pound fresh ginger, chunked, then peeled and grated by hand into a
    large glass bowl*
4 quarts water
½ cup fresh lime juice
1 teaspoon vanilla extract
1 ounce white Jamaican rum (optional)
1 pound sugar or to taste

After grating the ginger, pour ginger with juice that has accumulated into a large saucepan that contains 1 quart of boiling water. Cover and turn off the heat. Let sit until mixture is cool.

When cool, strain twice through a wire mesh strainer to remove ginger pieces. Only the ginger water should remain. Discard pieces in strainer. Add the lime juice to the ginger juice. Pour mixture into a very large glass con-tainer (5 quarts or thereabouts) with lid. Add remaining 3 quarts of water, vanilla, and rum. Mix well. Add about 1 pound sugar (more or less—depending on your taste).

"Put it down" (translation—place in the refrigerator) until chilled. Be sure to stir the mixture from the bottom before serving as it tends to settle. Serve with lots of ice. Keep chilled in the refrigerator and it will keep for months.

Yield: 4 ½ quarts

*To remove grated pieces from your grater, place in a pan of hot boiling water. Pick off pieces.

Passion Fruit Punch

Partaking of the tangy passion fruit is often said to soothe the sensual and lusty passions of "savage" taste buds. I'm always willing to cater to my sen-sual cravings, as I'm sure you will be after just a few sips.

¼ cup passion fruit juice, strained (available at most gourmet shops)
¼ cup fresh lime juice
2 cups white grape juice, chilled
3 cups pineapple juice, chilled
1 12-ounce can dry ginger ale, chilled
1 cup white rum or bourbon
Lime slices and mint leaves for garnish

Combine passion fruit juice, lime juice, grape juice, and pineapple juice. Add ginger ale and liquor. Serve over crushed ice with lime slices and mint leaves as garnishes. A wonderfully cooling treat!

Serves: 8

Spiced Rum Punch

Fruit and rum punches are often served at festive occasions and weekend parties on the islands. Here's an easy-to-prepare punch that can be made in a snap. Use the sweetest oranges you can find.

1 bottle (750 ml) spiced rum*
¾ cup pineapple juice
Juice of 6 oranges
Juice of 6 lemons
¾ cup powdered sugar
1½ quarts ginger ale
Orange and lemon slices and maraschino cherries for garnish

Combine the first 5 ingredients in a large bowl and stir well. Add ginger ale just before serving. Chill with a large block of ice. Garnish with orange and lemon slices and maraschino cherries.

Serves: 20–22

*I particularly like this punch made with Seagram's Captain Morgan brand, which also makes a good piña colada.

Tropical Punch

Rennie Smith, who is famous for his Caribbean catering in New York City, makes certain that his food and beverages look as good as they taste. He gave me this simple but delicious recipe while chatting over a cup of coffee at the Barbizon Hotel in the Big Apple. Use a silver punch bowl if you've got one.

1 quart mango nectar
1 quart papaya nectar
1 quart pineapple juice
1 quart fresh orange juice
1 6-ounce package orange Koolaid
2 quarts water
Sugar to taste
Block of ice
2 oranges, sliced
Island flowers such as hibiscus, orchids, and periwinkle

Combine mango, papaya, pineapple, and orange juices well. Stir in Kool-aid (this gives color), and water, and sugar to taste. Add the block of ice. Garnish ice with orange slices and island flowers.

Yield: 6 quarts

St. George's Rum Punch

Listening to Terry Lampert, co-owner of Delicious Landing in St. George's, Grenada, describe how to prepare this refreshing libation, I was reminded how pleasant to the ear the Grenadian accent is. Terry explained in his young and sexy British-like accent, that when making the nutmeg syrup, quartering the nutmeg enhances the flavor. Nutmeg has a hard outer casing that holds the flavor in. Blanching the nutmeg gets rid of the small amount of acid that nutmeg contains. The nutmeg syrup adds a special flavor to this rum punch.

3 cups fresh lime juice
3 cups fresh orange juice
3 cups Nutmeg Syrup (recipe follows) or 2½ cups sugar
3 cups pineapple juice
1½ bottles (750 ml) dark rum
1 cup apple juice
1 cup pineapple chunks
1 cup frozen, pitted, unsweetened cherries
6 ounces angostura bitters

Blend the lime juice, orange juice, nutmeg syrup, pineapple juice, and rum well. Add apple juice, pineapple chunks, cherries, and bitters. Stir well.

Nutmeg Syrup

12 nutmeg pods or shells
Sugar to thicken

Cut pods into quarters. Place in large pot. Blanch pods by pouring boiling water over them. Pour out the hot water and add 5 quarts cold water to cover the nutmeg. Leave to soak overnight.

Boil for 20 minutes. Leave in the liquid for 24 hours. Strain; reserve and measure liquid. Bring liquid to a boil. As it comes to a boil, add ¾ cup sugar for every 2 cups of liquid. Boil until liquid reaches consistency of maple syrup.

Yield: About 5 quarts

Tropical Eggnog (Coquito)

This refreshment, rich and very flavorful, is a welcome change from ordinary eggnog. It is served at the Hyatt Dorado Beach and the Hyatt Regency Cerromar Beach Hotels in Puerto Rico. Located on the island's balmy north shore, these hotels were once part of Rockefeller's private playground. This recipe was developed by the Cerromar's Swiss executive chef, Gerard Messerli, who was formerly Rockefeller's personal chef. By the way, Coquito is Spanish for "little coconut."

4 egg yolks
1 15-ounce can cream of coconut*
1 14-ounce can sweetened condensed milk
1 12-ounce can evaporated milk** (or more to taste)
1 bottle (750 ml) white rum
Cinnamon

In a large bowl, whisk together egg yolks, cream of coconut, sweetened condensed milk and evaporated milk. Cover and refrigerate for 2–3 hours. Just before serving, stir in rum and sprinkle with cinnamon.

Serves: 25

*See Tropical Glossary.
**May substitute half-and-half.

Peanut Butter Punch

On one of my homeward bound trips, I stopped in for a quick bite at Vee's Snack Bar in the Grenada airport. I struck up a conversation with Vera Graves, who owns the snack bar and we started talking about island drinks. She said a friend from Trinidad had given her this recipe, and she insisted that I try it.

1¾ cups evaporated milk
1¾ cups water
2 teaspoons vanilla extract
3 tablespoons peanut butter
Sugar (optional)
Freshly grated nutmeg

Combine all ingredients except the nutmeg in the container of a blender. Blend for about 10 seconds. Garnish with grated nutmeg.

Serves: 4

Evander's White Sangria

Evander Preston is a classic example of a person who does what he wants, when he wants to. He is the only jewelry store owner I know of who has a complete gourmet kitchen in his place of business...and the kitchen often takes priority. From Pass-a-Grille beach on the West Coast of Florida, this is one of the best white sangrias I've tried (and I've tried a few!).

Regular Batch

1 fifth white wine (Chablis is fine)
5 ounces Triple Sec
5 ounces French brandy

Combine and serve over ice cubes or chilled in champagne flutes.

Serves: 6–8

Vat Batch

1 fifth plus 1 gallon Chablis
1 liter Triple Sec
1 liter French brandy

Combine ingredients together in a large glass pitcher or bowl. Refrigerate. Add ice to glasses when ready to serve, if desired.

Serves: A crowd

Sparkling Cooler

To guarantee the "sparkle," chill glasses for a least 1 hour before serving so that you are certain to have a super-frosty drink.

2 ounces grapefruit juice, chilled
1½ ounces pineapple juice, chilled
2 ounces apricot nectar, chilled
2 ounces tonic water, chilled
Lime slice and maraschino cherry for garnish

Combine juices. You may refrigerate this mixture until needed. When ready to serve, add the tonic, stir well, and pour into a well-chilled glass. Garnish with a lime slice and cherry.

Serves: 1

Fresh Limeade

It's easy for me to get all the fresh limes I want because I need only step outside and pick them from one of my lime trees. As always, freshest is best, so of course, the fresher lime you use, the better your fruit drink will be.

1 cup fresh lime juice
4 cups water
Honey to taste
Fresh mint sprigs and maraschino cherries for garnish

Combine juice and water. Add sugar or honey to taste. Pour in tall, chilled glasses half-filled with ice. Stir. Garnish with fresh mint and cherries.

Serves: 4

Mauby Drink

Mauby, sometimes spelled mawby, is the bark of the carob tree. It makes a refreshing drink that is thought to be very healthful and good for digestion. I tried this at Vee's Snack Bar at the Port Saline Airport in Grenada and thought it was very good, although very sweet.

Islanders make it with a variety of spices. I enjoy it with extra cinnamon served over ice.

4 ounces mauby bark (available in Latin American and
    West Indian markets)
9 cups water
2 bay leaves
1 stick cinnamon
1 cup brown sugar

In a large saucepan, place the mauby bark, bay leaves, and cinnamon. Cover with 8 cups of water. Cook over medium heat and then bring to a boil. Reduce heat and simmer for about 10–15 minutes. Cool. Strain and refrigerate until cold.

To prepare a brown sugar syrup, combine the brown sugar and remaining water and cook over medium heat until the sugar is dissolved. Cool and refrigerate.

To make a mauby drink add about ¼ cup of the brown sugar syrup to ½ cup of the mauby juice. Mix well. Add ice to fill a tall 10- or 12-ounce glass. Pour mixture over all. Stir well.

Serves: 4

Lime Cooler

The full tropical flavor of the lime is the very essence of a summer's day. You will find that this refreshing cooler soothes not only your taste buds but your mind, as well.

For variety, use carbonated water.

3 tablespoons sugar
Juice of 3 limes
2 cups crushed ice
Maraschino cherry and lime slices for garnish

Combine sugar and lime juice in a one-cup measuring cup. Add water to mixture to make 1 cup. Pour mixture over crushed ice in the container of a blender. Cover and process until slushy. Serve in a tall, chilled glass with a straw and spoon. Garnish with a cherry and lime slice.

Serves: 1

Nutmeg Nog

A very seductive flavoring, nutmeg, used in the right places, can produce some very satisfying libations. Try this around the holidays and serve ice cold out by the pool.

12 egg yolks*
1 cup sugar or less
1 quart milk
1 bottle (750 ml) overproof white rum
1 quart heavy whipping cream
1 tablespoon freshly grated nutmeg
½ teaspoon cinnamon
Freshly grated nutmeg for garnish

Beat yolks until thick. Beat in sugar. Stir in milk and rum. Chill for about 4 hours, covered.

Whip heavy cream until stiff (peaks will form). Fold into the chilled egg mixture. Add nutmeg and cinnamon and stir in. Chill for 1 hour or so before serving. Sprinkle with freshly grated nutmeg.

Yield: 1 gallon, or about 25 5-ounce servings

*Reserve the whites for lemon meringue pies.

Tropical Frappé

This frosty drink has a fine rich flavor and aroma and can be whipped up in a jiff. Good for breakfast or as an afternoon cooler. I have one at least a few times a week at breakfast.

1 cup fresh orange juice
1 banana, peeled and cut into chunks
5 fresh strawberries, fresh or frozen, stems removed
Lime slice for garnish

Place the first 3 ingredients in the container of a blender or a food processor along with 1 cup of crushed ice. Blend for 5–10 seconds. Pour into a tall, chilled glass. Garnish with a slice of lime.

Serves: 1

Appetizers

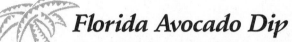

Florida Avocado Dip

Avocados grow throughout the semi-tropical sections of Florida, with most coming from the Miami area and the Gulf Coast. Florida avocados are different from the California variety, and, in my opinion, are highly underrated. Florida avocados are plump, waxy green like the color of a polished emerald outside, with a green-yellow meat inside. Sublime. Not like the pear-shaped nubs often weighing under a half pound.

Here's a zesty dip you can make with any variety of avocado. It's especially nice with heated nachos. If it will be a little while before you are ready to serve it, sprinkle the dip with a few drops of ascorbic acid. This will prevent discoloration. By the way, the California avocado will also make up nicely in this recipe.

2 ripe avocados
2 teaspoons fresh lime juice
½ teaspoon salt or salt substitute
¼ cup diced Spanish onion
1 medium tomato, peeled and finely chopped
2 cloves garlic, mashed
1 small jalapeño pepper, finely chopped*
½ teaspoon minced fresh cilantro (coriander leaves)
Sliced black olives for garnish

Cut the avocados in half. Remove the pits and carefully scoop out the flesh, being careful not to pierce the shells.

Place the flesh in a mixing bowl and mash with a fork. Add lime juice and salt. Mix well. Add the remaining ingredients, except the olive. Mix thoroughly. Scoop the mixture into the reserved avocado shells. Garnish with sliced black olives. Serve with sliced cucumbers, squash, cauliflower, or chips.

Yield: About 2 cups

*You may substitute any hot pepper.

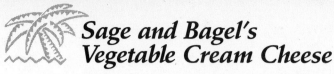

Sage and Bagel's Vegetable Cream Cheese

Shortly after moving to Miami Beach in 1986, I felt my appetite go completely out of control. I gorged myself on huge helpings of chopped chicken liver, blintzes, lox, nova, and an unending array of herbed and flavored cream cheeses. Each deli seemed to be better than the last. One of the best is the Sage Bagel and Appetizer Shop in Hallandale. Their Vegetable Cream Cheese is a cinch to make in a food processor, and the variations are endless. Thanks, Milt and Sid.

¼ cup green pepper, shredded
¼ cup peeled cucumbers, shredded
¼ cup radishes, shredded
¼ cup scallions, shredded
2½ 8-ounce packages cream cheese, softened

Mix vegetables (you may use other veggies, too) and cream cheese together very well. Chill and serve on bagel chips, bagels, crackers, or celery. The dip is not only good for you but very colorful.

Yield: 3–4 cups

Hot Artichoke Seafood Spread

Here's a "taste of Florida" from the Kissimmee-St. Cloud area. If you must, you can use frozen crab meat instead of the fresh, but as always, "fresh is best."

1 14-ounce can artichoke hearts, drained and finely chopped
2 cups mayonnaise
2 cups freshly grated Parmesan cheese
1½ cups fresh crab meat, drained and picked through
½ teaspoon Tabasco sauce
½ cup toasted almonds
Assorted crackers

Preheat oven to 350°. Liberally grease a 1½-quart glass baking dish.
Combine artichoke hearts, mayonnaise, cheese, crab meat, and Tabasco sauce. Mix well and spoon into the baking dish. Top with almonds. Bake for about 15–20 minutes or until hot. Serve on crackers.

Serves: 4–6

Boiled Peanuts

Boiled peanuts taste great right out of the pot . . . so says my Southern-bred publishing assistant Sandra Moore. In the warmest, nicest Southern accent you'll ever hear, she'll tell you how daddy just loves to take 'em to the ballgame right after mother fixes 'em. Such a nice lady! She stayed up four hours waiting for the peanuts to finish so that I could taste them. Definitely addicting.

Once boiled, store in plastic bags in the refrigerator or freezer. Keep cold!

2 pounds fresh raw peanuts in shells (available in many supermarkets)
3 tablespoons salt or to taste

Wash the peanuts well. Place them in a huge cast-iron pot or the biggest pot you have. Pour in enough water to almost fill the pot. Add salt and stir.

Cover and cook over high heat. Bring to a rolling boil. Reduce heat only enough to prevent the water from boiling over. Keep heat on at least medium-high as much as possible while keeping peanuts at a rolling boil. Add water as needed to keep the peanuts in water. When you add water, increase heat to high until peanuts are boiling again.

Boil for 3½–4 hours. After about 3½ hours, test to see if they're done: spoon out a peanut, let it cool briefly, then open the shell and bite into one. Boiled peanuts should be soft, not crunchy or hard. Test every 15 minutes until done.

Drain, rinse well, and cool slightly before serving

Yield: 2 pounds

Salmon-Caviar Canapés

Here's a quick and easy appetizer-snack that's ready in a pinch. If caviar is not on your list of "delights" garnish with a little chopped dill pickle.

1 7½-ounce can red salmon
1 tablespoon minced onion
1 12-ounce package cream cheese
1 tablespoon fresh chopped dill
Rye toast or crackers
Caviar and freshly chopped parsley for garnish

Drain the liquid from the salmon and mash the salmon with a fork. Add the remaining ingredients and mix well.

Serve on rye toast or any type of cracker. Garnish with caviar and freshly chopped parsley.

Yield: 1 dozen canapés

Hot Tuna-Mango Surprise

Mangoes can be messy little creatures to peel and seed, but they're well worth the fuss. One way to do it is to first score the skin into four sections. Then peel and slice the juicy fruits away from the seed. Use only ripe mango fruit for this recipe.

1 6½-ounce can chunk tuna
1 8-ounce package cream cheese, softened
2 tablespoons minced fresh onion
1 teaspoon Worcestershire sauce
½ teaspoon fresh lemon juice.
1 teaspoon Vegit* seasoning or seasoning salt
1 large slice fresh mango, peeled
½ cup slivered almonds
Fresh parsley sprigs for garnish
Saltine crackers

Preheat oven to 325°. Mix the first 6 ingredients together. Place the mango slice on the bottom of a small well-greased ovenproof baking dish. Cover the fruit with the tuna mixture, using a spatula. Sprinkle with almonds and bake for about 20–25 minutes or until almonds are browned.

Garnish with fresh parsley. Use a sharp knife when serving so pieces of mango can be cut up and served with the spread on the saltines.

Serves: 4–6

*Vegit is an all natural seasoning available in most supermarkets and health food stores.

Ted Peter's Smoked Fish Spread

For a large party, make up a generous batch of this Smoked Fish Spread. It's been served by the tons at Ted Peter's outdoor restaurant in St. Petersburg, Florida, since the restaurant opened in 1950. Serve with crisp saltines and enjoy in front of a super sunset. You won't be able to stop eating.

2 cups finely diced onion
1 cup finely diced celery
1½ cups sweet relish with pimentos
1¼ quarts salad dressing
3½ quarts flaked smoked fish (boned), mullet preferred (available at most seafood markets, or smoke your own)

Mix ingredients well. Chill. Best if served within 2–3 days.

Serves: A party

Best Tuna Canapés

Lucky for me, life on Maimi Beach allows for a great selection of Jewish rye breads. If you're in the area, try Joseph's Bakery on 71st Street. Joseph is a Hungarian chef, and he makes one of the best.

I am also an aficionado of great tuna salads. Enjoy this one served on your own favorite Jewish rye bread on a bed of onions, tomatoes, and lettuce. Cut each slice into fourths and serve open faced or close it if you wish!

1 6½-ounce can solid white tuna in water, drained
2 tablespoons finely minced celery
3 tablespoons mayonnaise
1 tablespoon Kraft's Horseradish Sauce
1 tablespoon sweet relish, drained
¼ teaspoon dill weed
1 dash Louisiana Hot Sauce
1 teaspoon dark brown mustard
4 slices fresh Jewish rye bread
Tomato slices, onions, and lettuce for sandwiches

Flake tuna and mix well with all ingredients. Spread on toasted rye bread.

Serves: 6

Land's End! Fish Spread

If you hang out for awhile at the Half Shell Raw Bar in Key West, Florida, you may just run into Mr. Margaritaville himself, Jimmy Buffet. You can imagine the satisfied look on his face as he indulges in a jumbo margarita and this tasty dip. Here's the recipe just as it is prepared at Land's End Village.

1 pound smoked fish (kingfish, tuna, or sailfish)
¼ onion, peeled
1 stalk celery, peeled
Mayonnaise
Tabasco sauce to taste
Fresh lime juice (Key lime juice, if available)

In the container of a food processor, grind the smoked fish, celery, and onion in a mixing bowl until well minced. Add enough mayonnaise to bind and season with Tabasco and lime juice.

Yield: 1 pound

Joe's Seviche

Joe's Stone Crab Restaurant, located on the south end of Miami Beach, is best known for its stone crabs, of course, but its seviche is one of the best. It's a nice first course to eat before devouring that wonderfully fresh specialty of the house. When you make it yourself, be sure to allow at least 4 hours for the shellfish to marinate. For those of you who have not yet enjoyed this tropical delicacy, the lime juice marinade changes the texture and literally cooks the shellfish.

1 pound bay scallops or sea scallops cut smaller
6 scallions, chopped (white part only)
1 cup fresh lime juice
½ cup fresh orange juice
6 tablespoons finely chopped onion
4 tablespoons finely chopped parsley
2 tablespoons finely chopped green pepper
½ cup olive oil
½ teaspoon oregano
1 teaspoon salt
Freshly ground pepper to taste
Crushed red pepper to taste
Tabasco sauce to taste

Marinate scallops and scallions in lime juice and orange juice. Chill at least 4 hours. Drain well. Discard marinade. Add remaining ingredients. Mix and serve on lettuce leaves.

Serves: 6

Seviche Martinez

Florida Governor Bob Martinez, a former restaurateur, gave me this recipe when he was mayor of Tampa. Perhaps his culinary expertise helped propel him into his present position as governor! He calls for sea bass, but you can use just about any firm white fish with good results. It's especially good with a Sauvignon Blanc wine.

2 pounds sea bass, washed and cut into bite-sized pieces
Juice of 18 Key limes or 6 Persian limes
1 1-pound can tomatoes, finely chopped with liquid reserved
½ cup finely chopped onion
½ cup finely chopped green pepper
½ cup finely chopped green olives
3 tablespoons finely chopped fresh parsley
¼ teaspoon basil
¼ teaspoon oregano

¼ cup pure olive oil
Dash of Tabasco sauce
Salt and pepper to taste
Hungarian paprika and parsley for garnish
Thin slices of avocado

Place fish in a glass bowl with the lime juice. Cover and refrigerate for 5 hours, periodically stirring and turning the fish. One hour prior to serving, drain the lime juice and add remaining ingredients, including the reserved tomato juice. Place in a serving dish.
Garnish with paprika, parsley and thin slices of avocado.

Serves: 4–6

Pier House Caribbean Conch Seviche

This recipe was given to me by the Pier House chef in Key West, Florida. This spicy seviche is best when made with fresh Key lime juice, of course.

If you are any kind of Floridian or have traveled to the Florida Keys, you never make the mistake of pronouncing "conch" nearly to rhyme with "launch." This beautifully pink-colored, subtly-flavored gastropod is pronounced "konk"—now don't forget, especially, when you're in Florida or the Caribbean.

1 pound raw conch
¾ cup Key lime juice (may substitute bottled or regular lime juice
   if necessary)
1 small cucumber, finely chopped
1 small red onion, finely chopped
1 fresh jalapeño pepper, finely chopped
1 sweet red bell pepper, finely chopped
2 tablespoons chopped fresh parsley
6 tablespoons vegetable oil
2¾ cups coconut milk*
Dash of Tabasco sauce
½ teaspoon oregano
1½ tablespoons sugar
½ teaspoon salt
⅛ cup shaved coconut
Dash of freshly ground black pepper
Lettuce
Bermuda onion, cucumber, fresh basil, and alfalfa sprouts for garnish

One day ahead, with a meat grinder or food processor grind the conch into small pieces, add to lime juice, and marinate for 24 hours.

*See Tropical Glossary.

Combine the cucumber, onion, peppers, and parsley. Drain off ⅔ of the lime marinade from the conch and discard the ⅔ marinade. Add the conch and lime juice to the oil, coconut milk, seasoning and vegetables. Mix thoroughly.

Serve on a healthy bed of lettuce with thinly sliced Bermuda onion, alfalfa sprouts, thinly sliced cucumber, and a sprig of fresh basil. Garnish with a fresh hibiscus flower, if you have one.

Serves: 6–8

Conch Fritters with Key Lime Mustard Sauce

Fort Lauderdale entrepreneur Anthony Gillette has mixed Florida fare of the past and present to create a "New Florida Cuisine." Most of the ingredients used at his restaurant, the Historic Bryan Homes Restaurant, are indigenous to Florida, as in this wonderful recipe. The secret to making the fritters is to thoroughly chill the batter. If you can't find Key limes for the sauce, go ahead and use regular limes—the sauce will turn out just fine. Just be sure to let it "age" a few days before you use it.

1 pound conch, blanched and finely ground*
1 medium green pepper, finely diced
1 pound onions, finely diced
2 teaspoons baking powder
½ teaspoon celery seed
1 large egg
2 teaspoons chopped parsley
½ teaspoon cayenne pepper
2 teaspoons Worcestershire sauce
1 clove garlic, mashed
¼ teaspoon black pepper
Pinch of baking soda
1 cup milk
1½ cups sifted flour

Mix all the ingredients together well, adding the flour last. Allow the dough to sit overnight in the refrigerator.

Heat the oil to about 350°. Carefully drop the fritter mix by the spoonful into the hot oil. Cook until golden brown. Remove and place on paper towels to remove grease. Serve with Key Lime Mustard Sauce.

Serves: 4–6

*Grind conch into small pieces in a meat grinder or in the container of a food processor.

Key Lime Mustard Sauce

2 cups mayonnaise
¼ cup Dijon mustard
¼ cup fresh Key lime juice or Persian lime juice
½ teaspoon freshly grated lime peel*
2 tablespoons Tabasco sauce
2 tablespoons Worcestershire sauce
Salt, freshly ground pepper, and cayenne pepper to taste

Mix all the ingredients together. Allow the sauce to sit in the refrigerator for a couple of days. The sauce may also be used right away, but the flavor gets better as it sits.

Yield: 2¼ cups

*Use a "zester" (see Cooking Terms).

Caribbean Conch Fritters

The flesh of the conch is light and flavorful; its taste, incomparable. Some have likened it to whelks, clams, or squid, but it's one of those foods that really has a taste all its own.

Conch is often difficult to find (try your local seafood grocer—he may have a supply frozen). At this time there is not a large supply of conch available, but efforts are being made to farm and cultivate larger quantities. Turks and Caicos islands in the Caribbean play host to this conch mariculture of the delicious mollusks.

Here's a great recipe by Chef Hermann Hiemeyer of the Hyatt Regency Grand Cayman, British West Indies, should you be lucky enough to come by some fresh conch.

1 pound conch
3 stalks celery, finely chopped
1 large carrot, finely chopped
1 onion, finely chopped
1 leek, finely chopped
½ cup butter
Pinch of thyme
Pinch of basil
Pinch of oregano
Pinch of salt
Pinch of freshly ground pepper
¼ teaspoon baking powder
4 eggs

¾ cup flour
Splash of milk
2 quarts vegetable oil or more

Put the conch through a meat grinder or food processor.

Sauté all the vegetables in butter for about 3 minutes. Add in the herbs. Place the mixture in large bowl together with the conch, baking powder, eggs, flour, and milk. Mix well to a thick yet runny consistency. Chill.

Heat the oil to 350° for frying. Using a large oval spoon, form 1-inch thick dumplings. Allow them to fall straight into the deep fryer. Cook for about 4–6 minutes. Serve with tartar sauce, dill mayonnaise, salsa, sour cream sauce, or your favorite hot sauce. Maybe try some Old Sour (page 289).

Serves: 6

Lorelei's Lobster Fritters

This tasty dish is served at the Lorelei Restaurant in Islamorada, in the Florida Keys. It makes as good a snack as it does an entrée. You can use the spiny lobster or any other variety, just as long as it's fresh.

8 ounces lobster meat, finely chopped
½ green pepper, finely chopped
½ onion, finely chopped
3 eggs, well beaten
½ cup bread crumbs
½ cup flour
1 teaspoon baking powder
Cumin to taste
Salt and freshly ground pepper
Vegetable oil for frying

Combine all ingredients. Roll into 2-inch balls. Place into ½-inch of hot oil. Fry until golden brown.

Serves: 2

Verona Watson's Fried Oysters

Oysters from Black Point or Thompson's Gap, Cedar Key, Florida, are definitely among the best in Florida. Here's a relatively simple recipe for oysters that improves with the freshness of the catch, wherever they come from.

1 egg
½ cup water
1 dozen oysters
White cornmeal

Pepper
Vegetable oil for deep-frying
Vinegar
Lemon juice

Make an egg wash by beating the egg and water together. Dip the oysters into the egg wash and roll in white cornmeal seasoned with pepper. Chill.

Deep-fry at 350° for 3–4 minutes. Cook a little longer for real brown crispness. Serve with vinegar and lemon juice on the side for seasoning.

Serves: 2

Sizzlin' Crab Meat Appetizer

Beyond the fun of "crabbing" (if you've ever tried catching you own) is the joy of devouring them afterwards. I've made this recipe with a number of varieties: lump crab, blue crab, Alaskan crab, and the relative newcomer, the fabulous golden crab. Use fresh crab meat for this delicately seasoned appetizer, if possible. You may substitute frozen if absolutely necessary, but be sure to drain it very well.

3 pounds crab meat
1 medium green pepper, finely diced
1 pimento, finely diced
2 teaspoons dry English mustard
½ teaspoon white pepper
2 eggs, beaten
Butter or margarine for greasing shells
1 cup mayonnaise for coating
¼ pound grated Swiss cheese
Hungarian paprika to taste
4 teaspoons freshly grated parsley
Leafy greens and lemon wedges for garnish

Preheat over to 350°. Squeeze excess water out of the crab meat. In a medium-sized bowl, combine green pepper, pimento, mustard, white pepper, and eggs. Blend well. Add crab meat to the mixture. Mix very gently.

Grease 6 large baking sea shells very well. Heap the crab meat rather loosely into the shells or coquilles. With a rubber spatula, coat each with mayonnaise. Sprinkle with the grated cheese, paprika, and parsley. Bake for 15–20 minutes. Serve nice and hot, surrounded by leafy dark greens and lettuce wedges.

Serves: 6

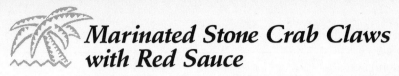

Marinated Stone Crab Claws with Red Sauce

Of the thousands of species of crabs worldwide, one is particularly popular in Florida and that is the delicious stone crab. In Florida, by law, the only part which may be removed is the claw, which when removed, rejuvenates itself. Jumbo crab claws will be twice as delectable and are most impressive at a fancy affair. The sauce with this delicious appetizer is light in color, but nice and tangy.

2½ pounds cooked fresh stone crab claws, about 18–24
1 cup tarragon vinegar
⅔ cup salad oil
⅔ cup sugar
2 teaspoons salt or salt substitute
2 cloves fresh garlic, minced
Lemons for garnish
Red Sauce (recipe follows)
Leafy salad greens
Lemons for garnish

Crack the claws. Remove the shell and moveable pincer while leaving meat attached to the remaining pincer (this may take some practice). Now, combine vinegar, salad oil, sugar, salt and garlic. Mix well until the sugar and salt dissolve. Pour the mixture over the crab claws and cover. Marinate in the refrigerator for 2–6 hours. Drain. Serve on a bed of leafy salad greens with small bowls of red sauce and a garnish of halved lemons wrapped in cheesecloth and tied with thin green ribbons.

Serves: 4–6

Red Sauce

1 cup mayonnaise
¾ cup ketchup
1 tablespoon Worcestershire sauce
1 tablespoon horseradish
½ teaspoon Louisiana hot sauce, or more

Mix all of the ingredients thoroughly and chill before serving.

Yield: About 2 cups

Caribbean Crab Ring

This is an easy make-ahead creation that guests rave about. Use fresh spices, if possible, for a truly unbeatable taste.

6 ounces fresh crab meat, or 1 6-ounce package frozen crab meat, thawed
1 teaspoon unflavored gelatin
¼ cup cold water
2 8-ounce packages cream cheese, softened
2 tablespoons sherry
¾ teaspoon Vegit seasoning (available in most health food stores)
1 2-ounce jar pimentos, sliced, drained, and chopped
¼ teaspoon cayenne pepper or to taste
½ teaspoon freshly ground pepper
¼ cup fresh parsley sprigs
Papaya and mango slices for garnish

Sprinkle water over the gelatin to soften. Stir over a pan of hot water until dissolved. Beat in cream cheese until mixture is smooth.

Stir in crab, sherry, Vegit seasoning, pimentos, cayenne pepper, freshly ground pepper, and 2 tablespoons of the parsley, chopped. Pour into a 3-cup fish-shaped mold and refrigerate for about 4 hours or until set.

To serve, set mold in hot water until slightly melted. Turn out mold on to a large plate. Serve surrounded by a variety of crackers. Garnish with fresh parsley sprigs, papaya, and mango slices.

Serves: 8–10

Hot and Crabby Dip

For ultimate flavor, use fresh crab meat purchased at your local fish market. You may also prepare this with frozen crab meat that has been properly drained of excess liquid. Use crusty bread for dipping; Cuban or French bread is great.

4 cups lump crab meat, drained and well-picked through
½ pound butter or margarine
4 small onions, chopped
1 pound sharp Cheddar cheese, diced
¾ cup ketchup
4 tablespoons Worcestershire sauce
¼ cup dry sherry
Several dashes of Tabasco sauce
Salt and freshly ground pepper to taste
Cuban or French bread for dunking

In a double boiler, melt the butter and sauté the onions for a few minutes, until translucent. Add cheese, ketchup, Worcestershire sauce, sherry, and other seasonings. Stir constantly until smooth. Add the prepared crab meat and blend well into the cheese mixture.

Serve immediately, or you may refrigerate and then reheat when ready to serve. Serve with long fondue forks and chunks of bread.

Serves: 8–10

Mussels in Wine Sauce (Moules Marinière)

After a morning shopping spree at the Galleria Mall in Fort Lauderdale, I enjoy treating myself to a huge plate of Moules Marinière just across the street at Les Trois Mousquetaires restaurant, the creation of Andre Labouri and his partners. A trip there definitely proves that one does not have to travel to Brussels for the finest in mussels and friendly service. Enjoy this appetizer with fresh French bread and a dry white wine, and top it off with a heavenly chocolate mousse. Without a doubt, it is a victory when one surrenders to fine French cuisine, especially in Florida.

4 pounds fresh mussels, well scrubbed to remove all sand
1 cup water
3 cups white wine
4 tablespoons butter
1 medium onion, chopped
4 cloves garlic, minced
2 tablespoons freshly chopped parsley
1 stalk celery, peeled and chopped
3 tablespoons flour mixed with 1 tablespoon water
1 cup fish stock*
Salt and freshly ground coarse black pepper to taste
¼ teaspoon curry powder
1½ teaspoons basil
1½ teaspoons tarragon
1½ teaspoons thyme
1½ teaspoons oregano

Steam mussels in water and 1 cup of wine for about 8 minutes or until opened. Rinse shells very well to ensure sand is gone. Remove mussels from shells. Reserve both mussels and shells.

Melt butter in a heavy sauté pan. Sauté onions, garlic, parsley, and celery until translucent. Add mussels and cook for about 2 minutes. Stir in flour mixed with water to form a roux.* Cook for about 1 minute.

*See Cooking Terms.

Add 2 cups of wine, fish stock, seasonings, and herbs. Simmer about 4 minutes.

Place mussels back into shells. Spoon sauce over all. Serve on large flat plates with a big basket of crusty bread.

Serve: 6–8

Mussels Stuffed with Hazelnuts

'Tis true that "Mussels in Brussels" are great, but they serve some interesting variations in Florida, too. Like sushi and good Scotch, mussels get better the more one becomes accustomed to them. Here's a favorite appetizer that I've prepared for years.

18 mussels, cleaned
2 tablespoons fresh lemon juice
1 tablespoon chopped shallots
1 pound sweet butter
2 tablespoons chopped hazelnuts
1 tablespoon minced garlic
3 tablespoons fresh bread crumbs
1 tablespoon fresh chopped parsley
1 tablespoon chopped chives
Leafy greens and lemon wedges for garnish

Steam the mussels in a small amount of water with 1 tablespoon of the lemon juice and the shallots until the shells open. Remove the top shells and discard any mussels that remain closed. Cool.

Mix the remaining ingredients very thoroughly—kneading with your hands works the best. Cover each mussel in its shell generously with the mixture. Place briefly under broiler to brown lightly. Serve on a bed of leafy greens with lemon wedges for garnish.

Serves: 4

Fresh Oysters with Champagne

The Fontainebleau Hilton in Miami Beach, Florida, manages to combine fine art masterpieces of the Old World with the breezy look of the tropics. I was served this outstanding dish in their Dining Galleries restaurant nearly six years ago, but the recipe will remain in my repertoire forever. This is particularly delicious when served with a very dry champagne, perhaps with that left over from its preparation. Garnish delicately with a good caviar.

12 fresh oysters
1 minced shallot
1 cup heavy cream
½ cup champagne
1 tablespoon sweet butter
Caviar for garnish

Shuck the oysters, being careful to preserve the juice. Wash the shells and save. The cooked oysters will be served in the original shells.

Place the oysters in a saucepan with preserved oyster juice and cook on medium heat for 2–3 minutes. Remove the oysters and keep warm. Add shallots, cream, and champagne to the hot oyster juice. Reduce the sauce by ⅓.* Swirl in the butter. Taste and correct seasoning if necessary. Serve the oysters in their shells with a bit of the sauce in each one. Garnish with caviar.

Serves: 2

*See Cooking Terms.

Shrimp Merlin

Merlin the magician performed some interesting feats of magic. So has Marina Polvay, consultant to the famous Forge restaurant on Miami Beach, with this heavenly shrimp appetizer.

3 pounds large shrimp, shelled and deveined
3 quarts water
1 tablespoon thyme
½ teaspoon basil
4 hard-boiled egg yolks
4 tablespoons white wine vinegar
2–3 tablespoons sugar or more to taste
1 teaspoon dry mustard
¼ teaspoon freshly ground black pepper
Easy Homemade Mayonnaise (recipe follows)
½ cup capers
2 medium onions, sliced into very thin strips
½ cup whipped cream
½ cup sour cream, whisked smooth

In a large pot, bring water to boil. Add thyme and basil. Drop in the shrimp. Bring to boil again. Reduce heat and simmer for 5 minutes or until the shrimp are pink. Drain and cool completely.

Press the 4 egg yolks through a sieve into a large bowl. Add vinegar, sugar, mustard, pepper, and mayonnaise. Blend well. Add capers and onions. Blend well. Fold in whipped cream and sour cream. Add the shrimp. Taste for seasoning. The taste should be sweet and sour. You may wish to add more pepper and a pinch of salt.

Serves: 8

Easy Homemade Mayonnaise

½ teaspoon powdered mustard
1 teaspoon water
½ teaspoon salt or to taste
⅛ teaspoon freshly ground white pepper
Dash of cayenne pepper
2 large egg yolks or 1 whole large egg
2 tablespoons lemon juice
1 cup vegetable oil

Soak the mustard in the water for 5 minutes to develop the flavor. Put it in the container of a blender. Add the next 5 ingredients and ¼ cup of the oil. Cover and turn on the motor at high speed. Then quickly turn off the motor. Set the motor at high speed again and add the remaining ¾ cup oil in a steady, gradual stream and blend until thick. Turn off the motor. Transfer mayonnaise to a jar. Cover and refrigerate until ready to use.

Yield: 1½ cups

Simply Snappy Shrimp

These tender, delicate, mouth-watering creatures are the most popular shellfish in the United States. No wonder, considering their outstanding flavor, ease of preparation, and health-giving goodness. The fresher the shrimp, herbs and cheese, the better this appetizer will taste, and the more amazed your guests will be with this easy seafood recipe.

1 pound small fresh raw shrimp, peeled and deveined
½ teaspoon freshly chopped chives
1 clove garlic, minced
¼ cup butter or margarine
1 teaspoon salt
1½ tablespoon sherry
1 tablespoon freshly grated Parmesan cheese

In a 10-inch frying pan, sauté chives and garlic in butter or margarine until tender. Add shrimp and simmer 2–3 minutes or until the largest shrimp is opaque in the center when tested by cutting in half. Add salt and sherry. Sprinkle cheese over shrimp. Serve hot.

Yield: 50–60 hors d'oeuvres

Hot Shrimps

Here is a simple-to-prepare snack or appetizer that tastes great with a jumbo Blue Margarita (see page 26). My British friends call the cocktail shrimp "shrimps," hence the name Hot Shrimps.

½ cup chopped onions
2 tablespoons olive oil
1 10-ounce can tomatoes and green chiles
1 pound medium sharp Cheddar cheese, shredded
1 4½-ounce can cocktail shrimp, drained
Dash of cayenne pepper
Crackers or nachos

Sauté the onion in the oil until soft. Add tomatoes and green chiles. When mixture steams, add the cheese. Cook on low heat until mixture is smooth. Stir in shrimp. Serve hot in chafing dish with crackers or nachos.

Serves: 4–6

Bern's Steak Tartare

On the west coast of Florida, which boasts a number of excellent dining establishments, Bern's Steak House is consistently one of the first places named when visitors ask, "What is the best restaurant in the area?"

But if you were to ask me the same question, I would probably add that it is not only one of the best restaurants in the area, but also in the United States. It has consistently been voted "Best Restaurant" in the state of Florida by *Florida Trend Magazine.* Owner Bern Laxer attributes its success to his attention to product quality and detail, as in this steak tartare recipe, for instance, which I finally convinced him to give me.

Be sure to serve this immediately after preparing. You will undoubtedly exclaim, "Ah, perfection!"

5½ ounces steak, as fresh, lean, and red as possible
4 tablespoons finely chopped shallots
2 tablespoons finely chopped green pepper
2 tablespoons red wine mixture*
1 teaspoon Spice Island brand fines herbes
¼ teaspoon salt
⅛ teaspoon freshly ground pepper
1 egg yolk
4 celery strips, peeled and thinly sliced for garnish
4 onion slices, peeled and thinly sliced for garnish
Fresh parsley for garnish

Hand chop the steak into very small pieces, removing any strains of fat or

*Mix 80% red wine with 20% cream sherry.

gristle. Chop shallots and green peppers into the steak so that the meat is chopped a second time. (Or you may put into the container of a food processor and process for 7 seconds.) Add other ingredients, except for garnish. Blend well, but do not purée.

Garnish with celery strips, onion slices, and parsley. Serve with a brown bread wedge, toasted with caraway butter.

Serves: 4–8

Baked Grapefruit with Chicken Livers

Chalet Suzanne, a cozy Florida Inn in beautiful Lake Wales, Florida, is surrounded by lush tropical orange groves. Dinner there starts with this rather unusual fruit appetizer and ends with a most satisfied customer.

2 chicken livers
Flour
Salt and freshly ground pepper
Vegetable oil
½ grapefruit
1 tablespoon butter, melted
½ tablespoon granulated sugar mixed with
½ tablespoon ground cinnamon

Dust the chicken livers with flour seasoned with salt and pepper. Grill or sauté the livers in vegetable oil and set aside. Cut out the center of the grapefruit, and cut around the sections to loosen, being careful not to pierce the skin. Fill center of the grapefruit half with melted butter and sprinkle with the sugar-cinnamon mixture. Broil until slightly browned. Garnish with the chicken livers. Serve as an appetizer.

Serves: 1

Tomatoes Stuffed with Guacamole and Chicken

The key to this dish is to use tomatoes that have been ripened on the kitchen counter, in a fruit bowl, or in a ripening bowl until they're fully red. A few days at room temperature usually brings tomatoes to perfection.

6 medium-sized tomatoes, cut into "sunbursts"*
1½ cups diced cooked chicken
1½ cups diced ripe avocado
¼ cup vegetable oil

*To make a "sunburst," turn the tomato over, stem end down and blossom end up. Cut down about ¾ of the way through to make 6–8 wedges which are still joined at the base. Fan out the wedges to resemble flowers.

2 tablespoons red wine vinegar
¾ teaspoon chili powder
½ teaspoon salt
¼ cup chopped onion
2 garlic cloves, chopped very fine
Bibb lettuce
Fresh parsley sprigs for garnish

In a medium-sized bowl, combine the chicken and avocado. In a small bowl, combine the oil, vinegar, chili powder, salt, onions, and garlic. Pour over the chicken mixture. Toss gently to coat. Chill.

Spoon about ½ cup of the mixture into each tomato. Place each tomato on a bed of Bibb lettuce and garnish with a sprig of parsley.

Serves: 6

Tropical Shrimp Bits

You'll find this appetizer to be very refreshing. It's a variation on a lovely "snack" I tried from a sidewalk food vendor while discovering Barranquilla, Colombia. Add more hot sauce if you want to "sweat," but be sure that it is very, very chilled.

1 pound tiny shrimp* or cut-up shrimp, shelled and cooked
1 cup water
¼ cup chopped onion
½ carrot, chopped
½ stalk celery, chopped
2 cloves garlic, peeled
1 bay leaf
2 tablespoons ketchup
2 teaspoons horseradish
1 teaspoon Lea & Perrins Worcestershire sauce
½ teaspoon hot sauce or to taste
Salt and freshly cracked black pepper to taste
1 tablespoon finely chopped green pepper

Add the water to a saucepan and bring to a boil. Add onion, carrot, celery, garlic, and bay leaf. Cover and reduce heat to low. Simmer for 30 minutes. Strain out vegetables and discard. Reserve vegetable juice.

In a small bowl, mix together the ketchup, horseradish, Worcestershire sauce, hot sauce, salt, pepper, and green pepper. Slowly add vegetable juice and mix well. Add the shrimp. Refrigerate until nicely chilled. Serve in small chilled glasses with demitasse spoons.

Serves: 4

*The small shrimp are often referred to as popcorn shrimp.

Salads and Salad Dressings

Orange and Avocado Salad

Everyone knows that Florida grows great oranges, but not everyone knows that Florida also grows wonderful avocados. And they're huge, many weighing in at two pounds or more. Here's a tasty salad that uses both and is very refreshing on a hot summer day.

    1 avocado, peeled, pitted, and sliced
    1 tablespoon fresh lemon juice
    1 medium orange
    ⅓ cup salad dressing
    2 tablespoons fresh orange juice
    Salt to taste
    Boston lettuce

Sprinkle the avocado with lemon juice. Peel, seed, and slice the orange. Blend the salad dressing, orange juice, and salt. Alternately arrange the avocado and orange on the lettuce. Spoon dressing over all.

Serves: 2

Avocado and Grape Salad

Here's an interesting combination from Carl Allen's Historical Cafe in Auburndale, Florida. From the outside, the cafe looks a lot more like a pioneer outpost than an eatery. On the inside, there are literally thousands of antiques on display. Tables are fashioned from old sewing machine bases and old postcards are carefully epoxied into the table tops.

The menu consists of some ordinary Florida fare like swamp cabbage and sweet potato pie, but you might also like to try the fried rattlesnake, catfish, or armadillo. Owner Carl Allen is mighty proud of his recipes and he should be.

1 pound large purple grapes, peeled and seeded
1 medium avocado, peeled and cut in 1¼-inch chunks
½ cup finely chopped pecans
1 tablespoon mayonnaise
3–4 tablespoons sour cream
Small dash sweetener, sugar or honey

Combine the grapes and avocado in a small bowl. Mix the remaining ingredients together and pour over the fruit. Toss lightly to coat all. Serve immediately.

Serves: 6

Island Pineapple Rum Chunks

Rum and fresh spices combine with fresh pineapple to create a most tantalizing salad or dessert.

1 ripe pineapple, quartered
½ teaspoon fresh cinnamon
1 teaspoon freshly grated nutmeg
¾ cup white rum
Maraschino cherries for garnish

Cut the pineapple, leaving the stem intact on each quarter (see the "Can Do" section). Remove chunks. In a bowl, combine the pineapple with the other ingredients and marinate refrigerated for about 4 hours. Return chunks to pineapple quarters. Garnish with cherries and serve very cold.

Serves: 4

Antigua Mixed Fruit Cocktail

This recipe was created by Gwen Tonge, who teaches cooking in Antigua, French West Indies. It's an elegant fruit salad that features many of the fruits indigenous to the island.

1 cup peeled and diced pineapple
1 cup peeled and diced mango
1 cup peeled and diced papaya
1 cup peeled and diced banana
1 cup orange sections
2 tablespoons fresh lemon juice
1 cup Sugar Syrup (see page 5)
Freshly grated nutmeg and mint sprigs for garnish

Mix all the fruit together gently. Pour Sugar Syrup over the fruit. Chill. To serve, scoop the fruit into chilled glasses. Garnish with nutmeg and mint sprigs.

Serves: 4

Fresh Fruit Salad

There's a cozy, rather modest little restaurant in the Homosassa Springs area on the west coast of Florida, not too far from Clearwater, where some of the most beautiful beaches in the state exist. Many of the Little Inn Restaurant's customers say the owners here serve up some of the best meals in the state—and at very moderate prices. Their dressings are great—best when served over fresh fruit.

1 cup mayonnaise
½ cup honey
¾ teaspoon Hungarian paprika
1 teaspoon celery seed
2–3 tablespoons fresh lime juice
1 drop green food coloring
1½ cups mixed fresh fruit (substitute 1 20-ounce package frozen mixed fruit, if necessary)

Combine all the ingredients except the fruit. Mix well and chill. Place the fruit on the plate and top with chilled dressing.

Serves 4

Mango Combo

There's nothing like sweet, juicy fruit to perk you up in the morning. Here's a fruit salad that I like for breakfast when blueberries are in season. It's simple and oh, so appetizing!

1 large mango, peeled and diced
½ cup fresh blueberries
½ cup fresh halved strawberries
½ cup peeled and sliced kiwifruit
1 teaspoon sugar or sugar substitute
2 Key limes, if available, or ½ Persian lime

Wash fruit well. Combine all fruit and mix gently. sprinkle sugar over fruit and squeeze lime over all. Use seedless limes or be sure to pick out seeds. Mix once again and let marinate in refrigerator for about 30 minutes. Serve in chilled glass bowls.

Serve for breakfast out on the patio or use as a light dessert.

Serves: 4

Spiced Melon Balls

Try this as a side salad or use as a dessert. It was created by Executive Chef Gerard Messerli and is served at the Hyatt Regency Cerromar Beach Resort in Dorado, Puerto Rico.

1 firm honeydew melon, formed into balls
1 firm cantaloupe, formed into balls
1 large bunch black grapes, seeded
½ cup water
½ cup sugar
2 whole vanilla beans
¼ cup Port wine
¼ cup chutney, chopped

Mix the fruit well. Chill. In a medium saucepan, heat the water, sugar, vanilla beans, wine, and chutney until the sugar melts and the mixture is smooth. Cool. Remove the vanilla beans. Add the sugar mixture to the fruit. Marinate refrigerated for about 3 hours. Serve chilled.

Serves 4–6

Carambola Salad
with Spicy Lime Dressing

A visit to southern Florida demands a trip to the Preston B. Bird and Mary Heinlein Fruit and Spice Park (That's a mouthful!). It is a living museum of fruit and spice plants from all over the world. Leisurely strolling on the 25-acre grounds, one can view 500 varieties of fruit, spices, nuts, and plants.

Director Chris Rollins regularly gives seminars on unusual fruits and vegetables. This man truly knows his p's and q's (this could stand for prickly pears and quince). I was fascinated by the varieties I had never seen or heard of before. Having lived in the sub-tropics for 12 years I was quite familiar with the carambola, which is often called star fruit, but many of those in the audience had never heard of it.

Fresh green leaf lettuce, torn into pieces
1 avocado, peeled and sliced
1 6-ounce jar marinated artichoke hearts, drained
1 sweet carambola, sliced and seeded
Spicy Lime Dressing (recipe follows)
Ripe seeded black olives for garnish

Place lettuce leaves on each of four individual salad places. Add the avocado, marinated artichoke heart pieces, and carambola. Sprinkle lightly with dressing and garnish with olives.

Spicy Lime Dressing

1 cup fresh lime juice
½ cup honey
1 small onion
1 clove garlic
1 small red pepper
4 sprigs of fresh parsley

In the container of a blender, combine the lime juice, honey, onion, garlic, and red pepper. Process until all ingredients are puréed. Add sprigs or parsley and blend for just a second. Chill until ready to use.

Serves: 4

Watermelon Salad

Here's a cooler that is guaranteed to perk up spirits on a hot day. Serve it along with Fish Escovitch and Red Peas and Rice.

4 cups watermelon, seeded and cut into cubes
½ cup freshly grated coconut
1 cup Sugar Syrup (see page 5)
¼ cup fresh lime juice
Lime slice for garnish

Chill the watermelon well before cutting. Arrange watermelon cubes in four frosted glass dessert bowls. Sprinkle coconut over all. Mix together the Sugar Syrup and lime juice. Pour this mixture over the fruit in each bowl. Garnish with a slice of lime.

Serves: 4

Tropical Fruit Bowl

Here's a very light, refreshing fruit salad that can be served as a dessert or as a perfect complement to any morning brunch. Serve with the St. George's Rum Punch (see page 36) and Strawberry Muffins (see page 118).

2 cups water
1½ cups sugar
Juice of 1 lemon
Juice of 1 Persian lime or 2 Key limes
3 tablespoons orange Curaçao liqueur or other fruit liqueur
1 cup blueberries
1 cup seedless green grapes
1 large pineapple, peeled, seeded, and cut into chunks

1 large honeydew melon, peeled, seeded, and cut into chunks
2 large Valencia oranges, peeled and sectioned (may also use navel, Hamlin, or Temple oranges)
3 kiwifruit, peeled and sliced horizontally
1 large cantaloupe, peeled and cut into chunks
Freshly whipped cream for topping
Mint leaves for garnish

Pour the water into a large saucepan. Add the sugar, lemon juice, lime juice, and liqueur. Heat over medium-low for about 20 minutes until sugar is dissolved and a light syrup is formed. Remove from heat and cool. Place in the refrigerator while fruit is being prepared.

Wash the blueberries and grapes well. Place all of the fruit into a very large bowl. Pour the chilled fruit syrup over the fruit. Mix gently.

Garnish with freshly whipped cream and mint leaves.

Serves: 6–8.

Company Carambola Fruit Salad

Although the exact origin of the carambola or "star fruit" is not known, it is thought to be indigenous to the Malayan region. It was brought to the Americas very early on, possibly by the Chinese sandalwood traders who brought trees with them to the Hawaiian islands. This beautiful, juicy fruit is now grown in numerous regions of the world, including southern Florida.

Carambolas can be sweet or tart. The sweet variety is the best one to use in this recipe. Try eating the fresh fruit out of hand—it's nice! More and more grocery stores are carrying the fruit now and they can be found fairly easily.

Chris Rollins, director of the magnificent Fruit and Spice Park in Homestead, Florida, gave me this prize-winning recipe.

2 cups water
1½ cups sugar
3 tablespoons fresh lime juice
2 tablespoons anise seed
½ teaspoon salt
1 small cantaloupe, cubed
1 small honeydew, cubed
1 small pineapple, cubed
2 nectarines, sliced into wedges
4 purple plums, sliced into wedges
4 oranges, peeled and sectioned
½ pound seedless green grapes, sliced in half
2 carambolas, sliced
3 kiwifruit, peeled and sliced
Mint sprigs for garnish

In a 2-quart saucepan, combine water, sugar, lime juice, anise seed, and salt. Cook over medium heat for about 15 minutes or until mixture becomes a light syrup. Refrigerate until cool.

In a large bowl, combine fruit and pour cooled syrup through a strainer over fruit. Cover and refrigerate until well chilled, stirring occasionally.

Serve in chilled glass bowls with a mint sprig for garnish.

Serves: 8–10

Bibb Lettuce with Honey-Lime Dressing

In the late 1800s Julia Tuttle was one of the two major Miami landholders with some 600 acres north of the Miami River (the other being the famed William Brickell, who owned 2,000 acres south of the Miami River). Many decades later, a dazzling restaurant was named after Julia and this delicious salad was served there. The restaurant is no longer operating, but the taste of this refreshing salad lingers on and reminds us of the pioneer spirit of our predecessors.

4 small heads Bibb lettuce, washed thoroughly, well chilled, and left whole
    to spread out like flowers
1 cup Honey-Lime Dressing (recipe follows)
½ cup chopped roasted pistachios or other chopped nuts
1 cup mandarin orange sections
Fresh mint, chopped

Place the individual lettuce heads on pre-frozen plates. Lace with about 3 ounces of the Honey-Lime Dressing. Garnish with pistachios, oranges, and mint. Serve with frozen forks if you want to get extra fancy.

Serves: 4.

Honey-Lime Dressing

½ cup walnut oil (found in the gourmet sections of most supermarkets)
Zest* of 2 limes
¼ cup fresh Key lime juice or Persian lime juice
⅛ cup honey
⅛ cup chopped shallots
Salt and freshly ground pepper to taste

Place all dressing ingredients in the container of a food processor or blender and emulsify.

Yield: 1 cup

*See Cooking Terms.

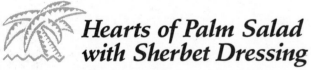

Swamp Cabbage* Salad

Between Fort Myers and Lake Okeechobee is the little town of LaBelle, Florida, which is famous for its annual Swamp Cabbage Festival. People flock from hundreds of miles away to taste the delights the Sabal palm has to offer. And most of them are sure to stop by Flora and Ella's Restaurant which is still recognized as the eatery with the best food in town. One of their popular salads is—well—the Swamp Cabbage Salad, of course.

1 head lettuce, torn into bite-size pieces
1 avocado
2 cups raw swamp cabbage soaked in strong salt water for 20 minutes
    and drained or 2 14-ounce cans hearts of palm (available in the gourmet
    sections of most supermarkets)
French dressing, your favorite recipe or bottled
Salt and lots of freshly ground pepper to taste

Peel and slice the avocado. Gently toss the salad ingredients together. Add the dressing and toss again. Add salt and pepper to taste.

Serves: 4–6

*Many counties in Florida regulate and protect the Sabal palm, the species from which the swamp cabbage comes. If you desire the raw cabbage, check with the local county government first on their regulations regarding the palm. See the Tropical Glossary for more information.

Hearts of Palm Salad with Sherbet Dressing

In order to claim you are a Floridian, you have to have eaten at one time or another, swamp cabbage, the terminal bud of the Sabal Palm or Cabbage Palm, as it is often called. While true "crackers" (those born and raised here) refer to the delicacy as Swamp Cabbage, the elite often refer to it as Hearts of Palm. The Captain's Table Restaurant in Cedar Key on Florida's west coast calls it Hearts of Palm in this very famous salad recipe.

1 14-ounce can of hearts of palm, sliced (available in the gourmet section
    of most supermarkets)
2 papayas, peeled and cubed*
2 bananas, sliced
1 fresh pineapple, cubed (May substitute 1 20-ounce can of pineapple
    chunks)
1 6-ounce box of dates, chopped

*To speed up ripening of papaya, cut very thin slits horizontally across the skin. Set fruit on the counter in a cool place and it should ripen faster.

1 pint Frozen Sherbet Dressing (recipe follows)
Lettuce for garnish

Mix the fruits together and place on individual lettuce-lined chilled plates. Top with a scoop of the Frozen Sherbet Dressing.

Frozen Sherbet Dressing

1 pint lime sherbet
1 pint pineapple sherbet
¼ cup mayonnaise
7 ounces extra-crunchy peanut butter
3 ounces lemon juice
1–2 drops green food coloring

Soften the sherbet while mixing the mayonnaise, peanut butter and lemon juice together. Whip the peanut butter mixture in with the sherbet. Return to the freezer until ready to serve.

Serves: 6–8

Renaissance Salad with Radicchio and Rose Petal Dressing

Florida's Bonaventure Hotel and Spa recently hosted a Great Chefs of Florida Weekend, a cooking seminar featuring the best of Florida cuisine. I was particularly impressed with this salad that was created by Chef Lisa Palermo.

1 head Bibb or Boston lettuce
1 head radicchio (red chicory)
32 orange sections
32 grapefruit sections
4 large ripe strawberries
¼ cup pine nuts
Rose Petal Dressing (recipe follows)

To prepare the salad, clean and rinse radicchio and lettuce separately, allowing radicchio to soak in lightly salted cold water. This removes any bitterness. Pat dry in towel.

Arrange lettuce leaves around each plate without allowing leaves to extend beyond the plate. Layer radicchio leaves in the center to create a flower effect. Then arrange citrus segments (8 of each fruit) in the center, alternating orange and grapefruit sections in a star formation. Place a strawberry in center. Sprinkle pine nuts over citrus sections. Pour Rose Petal Dressing over salad just before serving.

Rose Petal Dressing

4 leaves fresh basil
18–20 rose petals, washed
½ cup olive oil
Salt, freshly ground pepper, and lemon juice to taste
2–4 tablespoons sugar
½ cup raspberry vinegar

Cut basil and rose petals into thin julienne strips.* Mix all other ingredients well and add basil and rose petals. Mix well, chill and serve.

Serves: 4

*See Cooking Terms.

White Radish and Tomato Salad with Caper Dressing

Here's a very refreshing salad that you can vary by using different types of vinegars. I especially like the hint of capers along with the mildly zesty flavor of the white radish.

1 8-ounce package white daikon radishes, trimmed and sliced very thin
2 medium-sized very ripe tomatoes, chopped
2 tablespoons fresh minced parsley
½ cup chopped red Spanish onion
½ cup chopped green pepper
4 large leaves Romaine lettuce

In a clear glass bowl, gently mix all salad ingredients. Toss with dressing. Allow to marinate refrigerated for 15–20 minutes before serving. Serve on a bed of leafy green lettuce on ice-cold salad plates.

Caper Dressing

2 small cloves garlic, crushed
1 teaspoon Dijon-style mustard
Juice of ½ lime
⅔ cup olive oil or vegetable oil
2 teaspoons apple cider vinegar
Freshly ground pepper to taste
1 tablespoon chopped capers

Place the garlic in a small bowl. Mash well. Add the mustard and lime juice. Whisk in all the remaining ingredients except the capers. Slowly stir in the capers. Pour over salad ingredients.

Serves: 4–6

Art Deco Salad

When you don't feel like preparing a complicated meal for yourself, take 10 minutes to assemble this healthful salad. Use a food processor to prepare the ingredients.

1 cup shredded lettuce
½ cup shredded red cabbage
½ cup shredded carrots
½ cucumber with peel, very thinly sliced
½ cup thinly sliced daikon radish (available in most Oriental markets)
1 medium tomato, chopped
4 watercress sprigs for garnish
Salt and coarsely ground black pepper
Dill Dressing (see page 87)
Carambola slice for garnish

Using a medium-sized chilled salad bowl, arrange ingredients like wedges of a pie, grouping each ingredient in its own section. Add watercress in the center, with leaves rising flag-like, higher than the other ingredients.

Pour Dill Dressing over all. Center the carambola on top of the salad with a dollop of dressing in the center.

Serves: 1

Crippen Salad

Leonce Picot and Al Kocab, owners of the popular Down Under Restaurant in Fort Lauderdale, Florida, find this to be one of their most popular salads. I serve it as a separate course on clear chilled crystal plates and pretend I'm sitting in their restaurant, overlooking the Intercoastal Waterway, watching the glitzy yachts take turns parading by the well-dressed patrons.

4 tablespoons olive oil
1 tablespoon vinegar
½ teaspoon salt
½ teaspoon dry mustard
Freshly ground pepper
1–2 large bunches watercress, cleaned and stemmed
1 14-ounce can hearts of palm, sliced
1 cup thinly sliced mushrooms
½ cup almonds, sliced and toasted

Prepare the dressing by combining the olive oil, vinegar, salt, mustard, and pepper in a jar with a tight fitting lid and shaking vigorously.

Just before serving, toss all salad ingredients and place on chilled plates.

Serves: 4

Tomatoes with Garlicky Vinaigrette

Garlic is good for a lot that ails you: blood pressure, indigestion, and even hysteria. I bring a bowl of this salad with me to work when things start getting tense around the office. You know, I think it works!

Dressing

¾ cup olive oil
¼ cup red wine vinegar
2 tablespoons Dijon-style or Pommery mustard
½ teaspoon freshly grated pepper
3 cloves garlic, pressed
2 tablespoons bottled water

Salad

4 large red ripe tomatoes, sliced into eighths
3 tablespoons parsley, coarsely chopped

Mix all dressing ingredients in a food processor or blender for a few minutes until blended. Chill.

Slice the tomatoes and place in a medium-sized glass bowl. Add the fresh parsley and dressing. Toss and serve.

Serves: 4

Sweet 'n' Sour Cole Slaw

Whitey's Fish Camp in Orange Park, Florida, is a great hideaway to retreat to if you're looking for the ultimate in relaxin' and roughin' it. "Regulars" here are lots of fun. A trip just to meet some of these friendly folks is well worth the detour. The last time I visited Whitey's a foursome of "locals" neatly put away at least six dozen plates of raw oysters. They ordered this Sweet 'n' Sour Cole Slaw as a side.

1 small head green cabbage, shredded*
2 medium carrots, peeled and grated
½ cup chopped green pepper
1 cup sugar
1 cup vinegar
½ cup water
½ cup salad oil
1 tablespoon celery seed

*Sometimes Whitey's makes this dish with purple cabbage, which is also excellent.

1 tablespoon monosodium glutamate (optional)
Salt and pepper to taste

Mix all ingredients well. Let stand for 1 hour before serving.

Serves: 4–5

Pappas's Famous Salad

Louis Pappas left Sparta, Greece, in 1904 and settled in the Greek community of Tarpon Springs, Florida. He and his wife opened the quaint Riverside
Cafe in 1925. The restaurant clientele grew and today their sons continue
the traditions of their parents in a large modern cantilevered building on the
banks of the beautiful Anclote River. This legendary salad takes time to prepare, but makes an impressive and unique luncheon entrée. Be sure to make
the Potato Salad in advance and chill it well.

Salad

1 large head lettuce
3 cups Potato Salad (recipe follows)
12 roka leaves (Greek vegetable) or 12 sprigs watercress
2 tomatoes, cut into 6 wedges each
1 peeled cucumber, cut lengthwise into 8 fingers
1 avocado, peeled and cut into wedges
4 1-ounce slices Feta cheese
1 green pepper, cut into 8 rings
4 slices canned cooked beets
4 shrimp, peeled and cooked
4 anchovy fillets
12 black olives (Greek-style preferred)
12 medium hot Salonika peppers or other hot peppers
    (available in gourmet section)
4 fancy star cut radishes
4 whole scallions
½ cup distilled white vinegar
¼ cup olive oil
¼ cup vegetable oil
Oregano to taste

Prepare the potato salad and chill. Line the rim of large platter with lettuce
leaves. Place 3 cups of potato salad in the center. Shred the remaining lettuce
and cover the potato salad with lettuce. Arrange the roka or watercress on
top. Place tomato wedges around base of salad with a few on top. Place
cucumber wedges between the tomatoes. Place avocado wedges outside the
tomato and cucumbers.

Add the slices of Feta cheese on top, with green pepper rings over all. Place beet slices with a shrimp on each beet on top of all. An anchovy may top each shrimp. Place artistically the olives, pepper, radishes and green onions.

Sprinkle the entire salad with the vinegar, then oil. Sprinkle oregano over all. Serve at once.

Potato Salad

6 boiling potatoes
2 medium onions, chopped or ½ cup thinly sliced green onion
¼ cup parsley, chopped
Salt
½ cup salad dressing or mayonnaise (see page 59 for homemade)

Boil potatoes in jackets for approximately 30 minutes or until tender. Drain, peel, and slice into a bowl.

Add onions and parsley to potatoes. Sprinkle with salt. Fold in salad dressing lightly to hold everything together.

Serves: 4

 ## Fresh Watercress Salad with Olives

When her salad ingredients are eaten, my 12-year-old daughter "drinks" the remaining dressing from the bowl. The peppery taste is delightful—you'll want more right away.

2 cloves garlic, pressed
¼ cup capers, drained and chopped
3 tablespoons red wine vinegar
½ teaspoon Dijon-style mustard
¼ cup extra virgin olive oil
2 cups watercress, washed and long stems removed
2 cups ripe tomatoes, diced
½ cup pimento-stuffed olives
1 small onion, finely chopped
Freshly ground black pepper

Prepare dressing by combining the garlic, capers, vinegar, and mustard. Whisk in the olive oil. Chill well.

Combine watercress, tomatoes, olives, onion, and pepper. Gently toss. When ready to serve, shake dressing well. Pour over ingredients and toss again. Serve in chilled salad bowls.

Serves: 2–4

Yeehaw Junction Potato Salad

This recipe is a variation on a recipe by Bill and Jackie McCarthy, the last owners of the Desert Inn Restaurant, a once-popular establishment in Yeehaw Junction, Florida. The restaurant no longer exists, but fond memories of this potato salad still linger on.

The secret to fine potato salad-making often lies in the number of eggs included. Be sure to chill well.

    3 pounds potatoes, peeled
    2 cups mayonnaise
    ½ cup sour cream
    ¾ cup dill pickle relish
    2 scallions, finely chopped
    ¼ cup pimentos
    ¼ cup chopped onion
    ¼ cup prepared mustard (brown mustard will give a tasty zing)
    Salt and coarsely ground pepper to taste
    1 dozen hard-boiled eggs peeled and chopped
    Escarole and quartered tomato for garnish

Boil the potatoes whole until done. Cool. Cut into 1¼-inch chunks. Place in a large bowl. Mix together all remaining ingredients except the eggs, and combine with the potatoes. Add the eggs to the potato mixture and mix gently. Chill until ready to serve. Serve on a bed of escarole with a quartered tomato for garnish.

Serves: 8–10

Hot Fish Salad

Try this with leftover fish or with the fish that's on special at the market this week. It's quick and very good!

    2 cups cooked, flaked fish
    2 cups chopped celery
    ½ cup chopped green pepper
    ½ cup slivered almonds
    ½ cup mayonnaise
    ½ cup condensed cream of celery soup*
    1 2-ounce jar sliced pimento
    2 teaspoons grated onion
    2 teaspoons lemon juice
    ½ teaspoon salt
    3 cups crushed potato chips

*If you don't like canned soups, substitute a nice white sauce here with chunks of fresh celery.

½ cup grated New York sharp Cheddar cheese
Parsley, green pepper, or pimento slices for garnish

Preheat oven to 350°. Combine all ingredients except potato chips, cheese, and garnish. Mix well. Pour into a well-greased baking dish or into six well-greased scallop shells or ramekins. Bake for 20 minutes. Combine potato chips and cheese. Mix well. Sprinkle over fish mixture. Return to oven and continue cooking for 10 minutes or until thoroughly heated. Garnish with parsley, green pepper, or pimento slices.

Serves: 6

Fresh Tuna Niçoise

Mustard loses its flavor quickly after it is opened, particularly the imported brands. To help preserve the flavor of your mustard, cut a slice of lemon and insert it in the jar. Replace it every week or so—this will help to maintain the mustard's impact. Speaking of impact, it definitely exists in this perky Niçoise which could easily have come from Martinique in the French West Indies.

Dressing

½ cup olive oil
½ cup wine vinegar
3 tablespoons Dijon-style mustard
Freshly ground pepper to taste
Salt to taste
1 clove garlic, pressed
2 teaspoons chopped fresh thyme or 1 teaspoon dried thyme

Salad

2 cups fresh green beans, blanched and drained
Romaine and Bibb lettuce, torn into pieces, drained and chilled
1 pound fresh cooked tuna, broken into chunks
2 large tomatoes, quartered
½ cup ripe pitted olives, sliced in half
3 hard-boiled eggs, sliced
1 green bell pepper, cut into strips
1 red bell pepper, cut into strips
1 small can anchovies in strips, drained
¼ cup freshly chopped parsley

Prepare dressing by blending all the ingredients for a few seconds in the container of a blender or food processor. Pour over the cooked beans and let marinate for about 2 hours in the refrigerator. Drain dressing from the beans after it has marinated. Reserve the dressing.

Line a deep serving bowl with Romaine and Bibb lettuce. Add the tuna, tomatoes, olives, eggs, peppers, and anchovies. Place the marinated beans on top in the center. Cover with dressing and gently toss. Sprinkle parsley on top.

Serves: 2–4

Bajan Salt Fish Salad

"Bajan" is the local term given to the foods cooked Barbadian-style. The Bajan style of cooking is a blend of French, Creole, and hearty African style cooking.

Years ago, when refrigeration was difficult, many of the foods were heavily salted for preservation, cod being the most popular salted fish. West Indians still enjoy their salt fish very much, but are careful to soak must of the salt out of the fish, leaving just enough for a flavorful taste. Some of the islanders I spoke with enjoyed it very salty, but I preferred to give mine a rather lengthy soaking.

1 pound salted codfish (available in West Indian markets), soaked for 8
    hours or more.
2 scallions, finely chopped
1 green pepper, chopped
1 ripe tomato, chopped
½ cup vegetable oil
Coarsely ground black pepper
Pickled hot peppers and thinly sliced onion for garnish
Fresh leafy lettuce

In a large bowl, wash the salted codfish that has been soaked. Depending on taste, soak the cod up to 48 hours to remove saltiness, with several changes of water. Rinse. boil in a heavy pot for 1-1½ hours or more so that the salt will cook out. Taste for degree of saltiness desired.

Remove from the heat and drain. Once again, wash the fish in a large bowl of fresh water. Now, flake the fish into a separate bowl. Add in the scallions, green pepper, tomato, oil, and seasonings.

Arrange on a leafy bed of lettuce. Garnish with pickled hot peppers and onions.

Serves: 4

Shrimp Remoulade Salad

Here is a delicious shrimp salad that combines several interesting spices that give it a flavor all its own. Allow a few hours for the shrimp to marinate.

2 cloves garlic, finely chopped
2 tablespoons horseradish
2 tablespoons prepared mustard
2 tablespoons ketchup
1½ teaspoons Hungarian paprika
¾ teaspoon cayenne pepper
Salt to taste
⅓ cup tarragon vinegar
½ cup olive oil (may substitute salad oil)
½ cup chopped scallions
1 pound medium-sized, fresh shrimp, peeled, deveined, and cooked
Bibb lettuce
Black pitted olives for garnish

Combine all ingredients except the shrimp, lettuce, and olives. Shake well. Marinate the shrimp in the sauce for 2–3 hours in the refrigerator. Serve on lettuce with black pitted olives for garnish.

Serves: 4–6

Chilled Shrimp Salad in Tomatoes

If you use small shrimp, this dish can be quite economical for a luncheon party. Dress it up with a mixture of leafy greens and add lots of crudites on the side.

1 pound small shrimp, peeled, deveined, and cooked
1½ cups diced celery
1 cup drained cooked peas, chilled
⅓ cup sliced scallions
¾ cup mayonnaise
2 tablespoons ketchup
1 teaspoon cream-style, prepared horseradish
1 teaspoon lemon juice
¼ teaspoon salt
4 large tomatoes
Salad greens
Additional mayonnaise
Watercress or mint sprigs for garnish
Crudites

Combine the celery, peas, and scallions in a large bowl. In a separate bowl, combine the mayonnaise, ketchup, horseradish, lemon juice, and salt. Mix well. Pour over the vegetables and toss lightly. Fold in the shrimp.

Wash the tomatoes (choose very ripe ones) and remove the blossom end. Cut the tomatoes, not quite through, into 6 even wedges. Press the wedges open to form a "star" and place each tomato on a bed of salad greens. Fill each tomato with about 1 cup of the shrimp mixture. If desired, top with a dollop of mayonnaise. Garnish with watercress or mint sprigs.

Serves: 4

Dilled Shrimp

Fresh stone crabs dipped in butter, sweet Florida lobsters, and other seafood delights attract visitors from all over the world to the Colony Restaurant on Longboat Key in Sarasota, Florida. The Klauber family has long made the Colony a mecca for those who love to be pampered with extravagant culinary events and cozy, quiet dinners pool-side.

Take a luncheon plate of this delicious shrimp out to the pool and enjoy a nice rum punch.

2 pounds large shrimp, peeled, deveined, and cooked
2 cups blended oil (olive and vegetable)
1 cup wine vinegar
¼ cup freshly chopped dill
⅛ cup chopped shallots
⅛ cup freshly chopped parsley
⅛ cup freshly chopped scallions
¼ teaspoon Herbes de Provence
¼ teaspoon sweet basil
¼ teaspoon oregano
¼ teaspoon chopped garlic
¼ teaspoon salt
¼ teaspoon freshly ground white pepper
Leafy greens

Cut the shrimp in half lengthwise. Combine all other ingredients for marinade. Add the shrimp and allow to marinate overnight in the refrigerator. Drain. Serve well chilled on leafy greens with a scoop of Yeehaw Junction Potato Salad (see page 77) on the side.

Serves: 4–6

Salade Tropicale

On the penthouse floor of the magnificent Grand Bay Hotel in Miami's famous Coconut Grove section reigns Regine's, a favorite haunt of the "rich and famous." A private club, the restaurant is open only to members and guests of the hotel. A well-known French chanteuse, Regine has cleverly combined her culinary mastery with the Florida lifestyle to create "greats" such as this Salade Tropicale.

3 tomatoes peeled and seeded
Handful of fresh basil leaves, chopped
Salt and freshly ground black pepper
3 heads radicchio (red chicory)
2 heads Belgian endive (available at most gourmet shops)
3 heads Bibb lettuce
3 cooked lobster tails, shelled and cut into ½-inch pieces
6 1-ounce slices smoked salmon, cut into ½-inch pieces
6 slices fresh pineapple, core removed, cut into wedges
6 large mushrooms, thinly sliced
6 cooked artichoke hearts
Salade Tropicale Dressing (recipe follows)

Cut the tomatoes into ¼-inch cubes, and combine with the basil leaves, salt and pepper. Wash and dry the lettuce leaves. Cut up the lobster and salmon. Slice the pineapple and mushrooms. Prepare the dressing.

Arrange the lettuces on the plates, leaving the middle space open. Place an artichoke in the center of each plate and fill it with the tomato mixture. Arrange the lobster slices around the artichokes. sprinkle the smoked salmon pieces on top of the lettuce. Arrange the pineapple wedges and sliced mushrooms on top.

Spoon the Salade Tropicale Dressing on top and serve at once.

Salade Tropicale Dressing

2 tablespoons Dijon-style mustard
Salt and freshly ground black pepper
Juice of 2 fresh limes
3 tablespoons vinegar
2 tablespoons very finely chopped shallots
¾ cup olive oil
1 small bunch fresh marjoram, finely chopped
1 ounce parboiled ginger, peeled and grated

Combine the mustard, salt, pepper, lime juice, vinegar, and shallots in a heavy bowl. Gradually whisk in the oil, followed by the marjoram and fresh ginger. Add additional salt or pepper as necessary. Let the dressing stand at least 30 minutes before serving.

Serves: 6

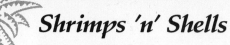

Shrimps 'n' Shells

Here's a perfect luncheon entree. Be sure not to overcook the shrimp or much of the flavor will be lost. Chill the plates and forks to add to your enjoyment.

At one time, radicchio was almost unknown in the United States. Most of it was imported from Italy, and what there was of it was quite expensive ($6 per pound was not unusual five years ago). It has become quite popular here, though, and it is more readily available and more reasonable in price. If you have never tried it, you should. It is a particularly flavorful and very attractive salad ingredient. When selecting radicchio, be sure that the white core at the base is unblemished and that there are no spots.

1 pound fresh shrimp, shelled, deveined, and cooked
12 ounces tri-colored pasta shells
½ onion, minced
2 celery hearts, chopped
2 teaspoons fresh dill
½ cup extra virgin olive oil
Freshly ground pepper to taste
½ teaspoon Vegit seasoning (available at most health food stores)
Radicchio (red chicory)
½ cup black olive slices
2 tablespoons chopped pimento

Prepare the shrimp.
Prepare the pasta according to package directions. Drain well. Mix it together with the onion, celery, dill, olive oil, pepper, and Vegit. Add the shrimp and toss lightly. Chill.
Serve on a bed of radicchio and garnish with black olive slices, chopped pimento, and more dill.

Serves: 4–6

Florida Spinach and Frog Leg Salad

Bon Appetit restaurant, beside St. Joseph Sound in Dunedin, Florida, is one of the Sun Coast's highway's highest-rated eateries, thanks to owners Peter Kreuziger, Karl Riedl, and Steven Farquhar. Arrangements can be made to dock your boat or yacht and dine waterside. Consider starting your meal with this Bon Appetit favorite. Try the Snapper Barbados (see page 143) for your main course, and the Strawberries Marguerite (see page 258) for dessert.

2 pounds Florida leaf spinach, washed and drained, stems removed
½ small onion, finely chopped
2 cloves fresh garlic, peeled and chopped
8 frog legs, washed
2 tablespoons butter
1 bay leaf
1 sprig thyme
Salt and freshly ground pepper
1 cup dry white wine
1 cup julienne* carrots
Dressing (recipe follows)

Drain the spinach thoroughly and pat dry. Tear the leaves into pieces and chill until they are crisp.

Sauté the onions, garlic, and frog legs in butter. Add the seasonings and white wine. Cover and simmer for 15–20 minutes or until tender. When cool, remove meat from bones.

Toss spinach, carrots, and frog leg meat with dressing recipe which follows. Serve on pretty glass plates.

See Cooking Terms.

Dressing

½ cup wine vinegar
Salt and freshly ground black pepper to taste
1 tablespoon Dijon-style mustard
¼ cup white wine
1 egg yolk
1½ tablespoons salad oil

Combine first 4 ingredients. Stir the mixture well with two forks. Add the yolk and oil. Beat dressing with forks until it thickens.,

Serves: 4.

Coconut Curried Chicken Salad

Use a good curry powder to create this dish. Kale makes for an unusually pretty bedding. Use the flowering kind if you can find it—it's a caterer's dream and a good source of Vitamin A.

4 cups boiled, skinned, and chunked chicken
2 teaspoons curry powder
1 cup mayonnaise
4 scallions, finely chopped
4 cloves garlic, pressed
½ cup peeled and finely chopped celery

2 tablespoons coconut shavings
Freshly ground pepper to taste
Bunch of kale or flowering kale
2 ripe tomatoes, chopped

Combine chicken, curry, mayonnaise, scallions, garlic, celery, coconut shavings, and pepper to taste. Mix well. Chill for at least 1 hour. Serve on a bed of kale with tomatoes for garnish.

Serves: 4–6

Easy Chicken Curry Salad

The chickens walk around in rural Jamaica much as the goats do in Grenada, West Indies—as if they were never going to end up on the dinner table. But they do and it's most often a dish to talk about, like this pretty chicken salad.

4 cups chicken chunks, freshly cooked with all fat removed
½ teaspoon curry powder, to taste
1 cup mayonnaise
4 scallions, chopped
2 cloves fresh garlic, pressed
½ cup finely chopped celery
1 teaspoon freshly grated green pepper
2 tablespoons coconut shavings
Bunch of kale or leafy greens
½ cup chopped ripe tomatoes for garnish
Freshly grated black pepper

Combine the first 8 ingredients (up to the kale). Toss well. Chill for at least 1 hour. Serve on a bed of kale. Garnish with tomatoes. Sprinkle with pepper.

Serves: 4

Conch and Avocado Salad

"Conch." To many, the word conjures up songs by Jimmy Buffet, visions of lanky palm trees and images of strong-muscled island men. But to aficionados of this sought-after delicacy, "conch" simply means "delicious". This recipe is from Mrs. Emily Wooley Goddard and the Key West Women's Club Cookbook, a best seller since its introduction in 1949. Try this island delicacy with several dashes of Old Sour (see page 239). Prepare using a good quality olive oil.

2 conchs, ground or pounded and finely minced
1 medium onion, finely chopped
1 green pepper, finely chopped
Juice of 3 Key limes (may substitute 3 tablespoons Persian lime juice)
1 clove garlic, peeled and mashed
1 teaspoon chopped fresh parsley
½ teaspoon thyme
½ cup olive oil
1 tablespoon vinegar
1 teaspoon curry powder
Salt, freshly ground pepper, and Old Sour to taste
2 avocados, halved and seeded

Combine the first 10 ingredients in a medium-sized bowl. Refrigerate, covered, overnight.

To serve, spoon the mixture into halved avocados. Add salt, pepper, and Old Sour to taste.

Serve chilled.

Serves: 4

Avocado-Crab-Grapefruit Salad

There's nothing like smooth, tasty avocados and sweet, ripe grapefruits to refresh you on a hot, humid afternoon. Add some crab meat and you'll have something quite special.

4 avocados
1 pound crab meat, picked through and diced
½ cup pecans
1 cup mayonnaise
2 teaspoons ketchup
dash of Worchestershire sauce
Lettuce
1 cup halved grapefruit sections
2 hard-boiled eggs, chopped
Black olives

Cut the avocados in half and remove the seeds. Combine the crab meat with the next 4 ingredients and spoon into the avocados. Serve on a bed of crisp lettuce surrounded by grapefruit sections and garnished with chopped eggs and black olives.

Serves: 4

Key West Conch Salad

The Pier House in Key West holds special memories for my husband and me since we purchased everything for our wedding reception at the popular Pier House Market—the roses, champagne, pâté, seviche, etc. You must try this conch salad, typical of the area. Allow two days for it to marinate. Be sure to pound the conch well or it will be tough.

    1 pound conch
    Juice of 6 Key limes or 2 Persian limes
    ½ red onion
    1 cucumber, peeled, seeded, and finely chopped
    ½ cup fresh cilantro* (coriander leaves)
    ½ red bell pepper, finely chopped
    1 cup olive oil
    1 level teaspoon leaf oregano
    1 level teaspoon sugar
    ½ level teaspoon salt
    ½ level teaspoon ground black pepper
    Leafy lettuce

Pound the conch and chop into ⅛-inch pieces. Cover with lime juice. cover and marinate for 24 hours. Drain.

Chop onion, cucumber, cilantro, and bell pepper finely. Combine all ingredients. Refrigerate for 24 hours. Serve chilled on a bed of leafy lettuce.

Serves: 4

*Also known as Chinese parsley. Since cilantro adds such a unique flavor, I do not feel that it can be satisfactorily substituted for.

Dill Dressing

It's fun dining gulfside at the Colony Beach Restaurant on Longboat Key in Sarasota, Florida. The owners, the Klauber family, have created a truly romantic and memorable setting. Their food is quite good, too, like this Dill Dressing, which is tangy but mild. Toss it with your favorite selection of salad greens.

    2 eggs
    4 tablespoons olive oil
    1 teaspoon minced garlic
    2 teaspoons minced Spanish onion
    1 teaspoon Dijon-style mustard
    2 tablespoons chopped fresh dill weed
    ¼ cup heavy cream

3 tablespoons red wine vinegar
1 teaspoon sugar
1 teaspoon salt
½ teaspoon white pepper

Mix all ingredients well with a hand mixer, or in the container of a blender or food processor. Beat for 10–15 minutes until creamy.

Yield: 1 cup

Joe's Vinaigrette Dressing

Jo Ann Sewitz, of Joe's Stone Crab Restaurant in Miami Beach, Florida, gave me this recipe for their special vinaigrette. It goes well with a stone crab dinner, of course, or with just about any salad. Jo Ann is the grand-daughter of Joe Weiss, a waiter who came to Miami Beach from New York in 1913 to start the original Joe's Restaurant. Now called Joe's Stone Crab Restaurant, this restaurant proves without a doubt that it is not necessary to have fancy decor in order to be an award-winning establishment. The simplicity of the interior, which is done in what you might call basic fish house style, adds a special touch that makes dining at Joe's not just a meal but an experience.

½ medium onion, finely chopped
3 tablespoons minced parsley
1 2-ounce jar diced pimentos
1 hard-boiled egg, chopped
¾ cup vegetable oil
⅓ cup wine vinegar, red or white
1½ teaspoons sugar
1½ teaspoons salt
2 tablespoons minced chives, fresh or dilled

Combine all the above ingredients and stir well. Place in the refrigerator in a covered jar for no longer than 24 hours. Shake thoroughly before serving.

Yield: About 1¼ cups

Passion Fruit and Walnut Vinaigrette

Although native to Brazil, the passion fruit is grown in the tropical areas of southern Florida. The name "passion fruit" originated with the diaries of early Spanish missionaries who recorded how the flowers, seen during church holiday seasons, reminded them of the passion of Christ.

The juice is best described as tasting like a blend of guava, pineapple, and citrus fruit juices. It is the primary flavor ingredient in many of the commercial tropical punch beverages on the market today.

Be sure to select passion fruits that are firm and free from brown spots. If you are unable to find the fresh fruit, substitute the bottled version that is available at most gourmet or health food markets. For best results, use a good quality olive oil.

¼ cup passion fruit juice
½ teaspoon salt
⅛ teaspoon ground pepper
¼ cup finely chopped walnuts
¾ cup olive oil
¼ teaspoon fresh ginger, minced
1 tablespoon anchovy paste
¼ teaspoon prepared "deli-style" mustard
1–2 sprigs fresh watercress, finely chopped

Combine passion fruit juice, salt, pepper, walnuts, olive oil, ginger, anchovy paste, mustard, and watercress in a shaker container. Shake to combine. Pour over your favorite tossed salad.

Yield: 1 cup

Poppy Seed Dressing

"New American Cuisine" is "hot" and so is Lunch on Limoges, a quaint yet elegant restaurant in Dade City, Florida, about 40 miles northeast of Tampa. It's unusual in that it's part of an exciting combination of fashion and cuisine—yes, clothes and dining available under one roof. Co-owners Phil Williams and Skip Mize have done an excellent job of creating a fashionable restaurant alongside a trendy clothing shop, where guests can enjoy a fashion show while they dine.

Their Poppy Seed Dressing is good served on a bed of assorted salad greens. I've tried it, too, on their fresh fruit bowl, which is absolutely teeming with the star-shaped carambola fruit.

¾ cup sugar
1 cup vegetable oil
⅓ cup cider vinegar
1 tablespoon onion juice or ⅛ teaspoon grated onion
1 teaspoon salt
1 teaspoon dry mustard
1½ tablespoons poppy seeds

Combine all the ingredients, except the poppy seeds, in the container of a blender. Process on high speed until well blended.

Stir in the poppy seeds. Chill thoroughly. Stir well before serving.

Yield: about 1¾ cups.

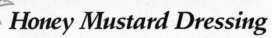

Honey Mustard Dressing

The Honey Mustard Dressing at the Historic Bryan Homes restaurant in Fort Lauderdale, known for its New Florida Cuisine, is one of my favorites. Serve it on crisp salad greens.

1 cup Dijon-style mustard
¼ cup white wine
¼ cup honey
Salt to taste
1 3½-ounce can green peppercorns, drained
Mayonnaise to taste

Mix all ingredients except mayonnaise together in a saucepan. Bring mixture to a simmer. Cook approximately 20 minutes. Refrigerate until cold.

Mix this base with ½ cups mayonnaise according to your taste. Thin with salad oil or water if it is too thick.

Yield: 1½ cups base; 2½ cups dressing

Soups

Cold Banana Soup with Cinnamon Croutons

Here's a taste of the tropics that one is not likely to forget. Be sure to serve with a little light reggae music and a lot of spirit.

It's a favorite of mine, created by Executive Chef Gerard Messerli of the Hyatt Regency Cerromar Beach Hotel in Puerto Rico.

4 slices ½-inch thick bread, crust removed
Melted butter for croutons
2 teaspoons cinnamon
3½ cups cold milk
6 ripe bananas, peeled and cut into small pieces
¼ teaspoon baking soda
Pinch of salt
1 teaspoon powdered ginger
1 tablespoon fresh lemon juice
1 pint banana ice cream*

Preheat oven to 375°. Cut bread slices into ½-inch cubes. Brush cubes with melted butter and place on a baking sheet and bake until golden. While still hot, sprinkle the cubes with 1 teaspoon ground cinnamon. Set aside.

In a heavy saucepan, bring milk to a full boil. Add bananas, soda, 1 teaspoon cinnamon, salt, ginger, and lemon juice. Cook for another 10 minutes or until bananas become soft. Let cool, then pour into the container of a blender or food processor. Add ice cream and blend until smooth and frothy. Add more milk or cream, depending on the consistency desired. Pour into chilled glass bowls and sprinkle with croutons.

Serves: 6–8

*I've also tried this with coconut ice cream—delicious.

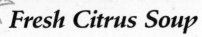

Fresh Citrus Soup

The garden is the perfect place in which to sit and enjoy this unusual soup from the Maison & Jardin Restaurant in Altamonte Springs, Florida. No wonder this eatery has garnered many awards such as the Holiday Fine Dining Award and a Mobil Four Star Guide rating.

3 oranges
3 grapefruit
1 cup sugar
¼ cup water
½ cup currant jelly
2 tablespoons brandy
Sour Cream

From the peel of the fruits, make julienne* strips for garnish and set aside.

Finish peeling the fruits, cutting out the sections carefully, removing the pits and seeds. Cut the grapefruit sections into smaller pieces. Place in a mixing bowl.

Cook the sugar, water, and currant jelly for about 15 minutes to make a syrup. Cool. Pour this syrup over the orange and grapefruit sections. Add the brandy. Stir and refrigerate for 2–3 hours.

To serve, pour in cups, top with dollops of sour cream, and garnish with julienne strips of peel.

Serves: 6–8

*See Cooking Terms.

Chilled Peach Soup Remy

This great-tasting soup recipe is from Sous Chef Eric Englund of the Bonaventure Hotel and Spa, Bonaventure, Florida, who is a graduate of the Culinary Institute of America. Eric shared this recipe at the Great Chefs of Florida Weekend which was sponsored by the hotel.

4 medium-sized ripe peaches, peeled, and seeded
½ cup club soda
½ cup white wine
¼ cup sugar (more or less, depending on sweetness of peaches)
Juice of ½ fresh lemon
¼ cup orange peel
1½ ounces Remy cognac (may also use Grand Marnier or brandy)

Put the peaches in the container of a blender. Add the club soda, white wine, sugar, lemon juice, and orange peel. Blend at medium speed to purée. Add a few ice cubes to chill. Just before serving, fold in the cognac. Serve in chilled long-stemmed wine glasses.

Serves: 4

Cold Star Fruit and Peach Soup

The carambola or star fruit has been grown in the United States for about 100 years now, primarily in Florida. It's as versatile as an apple and the average tree is quite prolific, producing 300–600 pounds of fruit per year—almost enough for an owner to go into a small business. Carambolas can be sweet as well as sour, but the sweet ones seem to work best in most dishes, like this refreshing soup. By the way, its thin yellow skin is almost always eaten as is the core of the fruit.

2 pounds ripe peaches, skinned, pitted, and sliced
¼ pound carambola, sliced with seeds removed
½ cup fresh orange juice
1 teaspoon finely grated orange rind
½ cup Marsala or other wine
¼ cup sugar
3 tablespoons cornstarch
Lemon peel for garnish

Place all ingredients into the container of a blender or food processor. Purée thoroughly. Pour fruit mixture into a heavy medium-sized saucepan. Bring to a slow boil, then lower the heat. Simmer and stir soup for about 8–10 minutes, until clear and slightly thickened. Remove to refrigerator and chill until ready to serve. Serve in chilled clear glass bowls. Garnish each serving with a strip of lemon peel.

Serves: 4–6

Passion-ate Strawberry Soup

You can enjoy the cool flavor of a tropical rain forest by adding passion fruit juice to this wonderfully fruity soup. This recipe is from J. R. Brooks and Son, in Homestead, Florida, "passionate" growers and packers of great tropical fruits.

3 cups fresh strawberries, sliced
¼ cup sugar or light flavored honey
½ cup rosé wine
6 dried apricot halves, chopped fine
2½ tablespoons cornstarch
½ cup passion fruit juice (available in most gourmet shops)
1 tablespoon fresh lime juice
1 cup plain yogurt
Fresh sliced strawberries for garnish

Combine the fresh strawberries and sugar. In a separate bowl, combine the rosé wine and finely chopped dried apricots. Allow both fruit mixtures to stand for 3–4 hours. (If longer, store under refrigeration during standing process.) Pour the apricot mixture into the container of a blender and process for a "zip" or two until apricot pieces are finely shredded but not puréed.

Combine the cornstarch and passion fruit juice in a medium-sized saucepan. Drain the strawberries, saving liquid. Add the liquid from the strawberries, apricot and wine mixture, and lime juice to the passion fruit mixture. Bring the mixture to a boil, stirring constantly until it is thick and clear. Cool. Stir in the drained strawberries and yogurt. Serve chilled in chilled clear glass bowls. Garnish with fresh strawberry slices.

Serves: 6

Strawberry Soup

When the weatherman forecasts a hot day ahead, whip up this soup in the cool of the morning (it'll only take you 10 minutes) and pop it in the refrigerator. It's guaranteed to cool you down later, when the mercury rises. The recipe was given to me by Barbara Friedenreich, proprietor of the famous Klaus' Cuisine restaurant in Holly Hill, Florida.

1 pint fresh strawberries, washed and stems removed
1 cup sour cream
½ cup milk
½ cup ginger ale
6 tablespoons sugar
1 teaspoon vanilla extract
1 tablespoon fresh lemon juice
6 large strawberries for garnish

Combine all ingredients in the container of a blender or a food processor. Blend until smooth. Chill well.

Serve in frosted cups. Garnish with a strawberry or sliced strawberries.

Serves: 6

Avocado and Ginger Vichyssoise

Jamaican spices combined with native fruits and vegetables produce some of the world's most exciting and memorable dishes. Avocado and fresh ginger are the key ingredients in this most distinctive soup. And make no mistake, there is nothing quite like *fresh* ginger.

This recipe is prepared at the Hotel Inter-Continental in Ocho Rios, Jamaica, one of my favorite vacation spots.

½ cup butter or margarine
1 medium onion, finely chopped
1 ounce fresh ginger, peeled and grated
1 large avocado, peeled and mashed
2 cups chicken stock*
1 teaspoon black pepper
½ cup light cream
1 scallion, finely chopped

Melt the butter in a sauté pan. Cook the onions and grated ginger for about 2 minutes. Add the mashed avocado and chicken stock. Mix all ingredients thoroughly, using a wire whisk to eliminate lumps. Simmer slowly for about 10–15 minutes. Add salt, pepper, and cream. Stir and chill for at least an hour. Chill bowls before serving. Garnish each bowl with scallions.

Serves: 6

*See Cooking Terms.

Miss Grimble's Cucumber Soup

A stop at the Bal Harbour Shops in pricey Bal Harbour, Florida, is a necessity for any serious-minded shopper with a limitless budget. As you drive past the British-garbed parking guards, you'll enjoy the parade of Rolls Royces, Mercedes, and Jags just ahead of you. Have your Mercedes washed and waxed (why not?) while you shop and indulge yourself in a pleasant lunch at one of the elegant sidewalk cafes. After a few tastes of the haute cuisine, you'll be in the mood to browse through Cartier, Gucci, or maybe the Williams-Sonoma store for a selection of the latest in fashionable "gourmetware" by Chuck Williams. You may even bump into Miami Vice's Don Johnson in one of the fashionable men's shops.

Here's an easy recipe that will make your guests think you were in the kitchen all day when, in fact, you were out gallivanting in Bal Harbour. This cooling soup is from Miss Grimble's Cafe in Bal Harbour where I've enjoyed it many, many times.

6–7 scallions, coarsely chopped
¼ cup lemon juice
1 teaspoon salt
1 teaspoon white pepper
4–6 cucumbers, peeled, seeded, and cut into 1-inch pieces
2 cups heavy cream
2 cups half-and-half
6 cucumber slices
Chopped scallions
Hungarian paprika for garnish

Place the first 4 ingredients in the container of a blender. Fill the blender to the top with cucumber pieces. You will use 4–6 cucumbers, depending on their size. Add cream and half-and-half. With the blender on high speed, blend until mixture is creamy, chunky, and thick. Chill for at least 1 hour.

To serve, garnish each chilled bowl with a cucumber slice, chopped scallions, and a sprinkle of paprika, if desired. Serve with crusty french rolls.

Serves: 6

"Hot" Gazpacho

This island "pepper-hot" cold soup is a new world version of the famous old dish from Spain. The Scotch Bonnet is a volatile pepper that demands respect in this recipe.

Combined with your favorite rum drink, this soup would be a great way to cool off and warm up, simultaneously, for that afternoon barbeque.

1 cup whole wheat bread, cubed and crust removed
1 red bell pepper
2 large cloves garlic, peeled and quartered
½ small Scotch Bonnet pepper, chopped
1 medium red onion
2 cups very ripe tomatoes, blanched and peeled
Freshly ground black pepper to taste
¼ teaspoon cayenne pepper
4 tablespoons extra virgin olive oil
1 tablespoon red wine vinegar
2 tablespoons light rum
Tabasco sauce to taste (optional)
1 cucumber, peeled, seeded, and finely chopped
4 scallions

In a bowl, soak the bread in about ½ cup cold water for a few minutes. With your hands, squeeze excess water from the bread.

In the container of a blender or a food processor, purée the red pepper, garlic, Scotch Bonnet pepper, onion, and tomatoes in small batches. Do not purée completely. Add the bread, wine vinegar, oil, and black pepper. Blend until smooth. Transfer to a mixing bowl. Beat in the rum and Tabasco sauce. Stir in the cucumber and cayenne pepper. Cover and chill thoroughly.

Before serving, stir, taste, and correct seasoning. Ladle into chilled soup bowls or mugs. Garnish each serving with a crisp whole scallion.

Serves: 4

Cool Minty Cucumber Soup

You're going to love this one! The combinations of mint and cucumber together with the smoothness of the sour cream produces one of the most flavorful and cooling tastes you'll ever experience.

The recipe is another creation of Gerard Messerli of the Hyatt Regency Cerromar Beach Hotel in Dorado, Puerto Rico. I like to use a mango chutney and extra virgin olive oil. Be sure to serve in chilled bowls and garnish with a twisted slice of cucumber or mint leaf.

3 cloves garlic, minced
3 teaspoons olive oil
3 teaspoons chutney
1½ teaspoons salt or to taste
2½ cups sour cream
¼ teaspoon white pepper
½ cup chopped parsley, stems removed
½ cup (about ½ bunch) fresh mint leaves
Drop of Pernod
4 cucumbers, peeled and chopped
Sour cream and mint or cucumber slices for garnish

Put the first 9 ingredients in the container of a food processor or blender, and process well. Add the cucumbers and process until the mixture is very smooth and creamy. Chill well. When ready to serve, add a dollop of sour cream to each bowl and a piece of mint or a twisted slice of cucumber.

Serves: 8–10

Unicorn Black Bean Soup

This version of black bean soup is served at the Unicorn Village restaurant in North Miami Beach, Florida. The restaurant is noted for its fine, healthful cuisine cooked totally fresh with no additives, etc. The soup is light and delicious; the recipe was given to me by thriving entrepreneur Terry Dalton. The beans need a good 8-hour head start.

2 cups black beans
8 cups water or chicken stock
2 tablespoons olive oil
1 large onion, chopped
8 cloves garlic, crushed
1 teaspoon dried thyme
2 teaspoons ground cumin
2 teaspoons chili powder

2 teaspoons nutritional yeast (optional, available at health food stores)
2 ounces Burgundy
1 tablespoon tamari soy sauce
Salt and cayenne pepper to taste
2 medium tomatoes, seeded and chopped
2 bay leaves
Chopped raw onion

Soak beans in enough water to cover the beans for 8 hours. Discard water. Place beans in a pot with 8 cups fresh water or stock and simmer. As the beans cook, skim the foam from the top.

Heat the olive oil in a medium-sized saucepan. Sauté the onion until transparent. Then add the garlic, thyme, cumin, chili, yeast, Burgundy, soy sauce, salt, cayenne, and tomatoes. Simmer onion mixture for 10 minutes, adding a little water if needed to keep it from sticking. When the beans become soft and start to break, stir in the onion mixture and bay leaves. Simmer until thickened. Serve with chopped raw onion on the side.

Yield: 2 quarts

Columbia Spanish Bean Soup

The Columbia Restaurant in Tampa, Florida, was founded in 1905 by Casimirio Hernandez, Sr. His son-in-law, Cesar Gonzmart and wife Adela are the present owners. Cesar's flamboyant violin virtuosity and the lively floor shows highlight any evening spent at this restaurant. If you can't make it to the restaurant to enjoy the music while you eat, you can at least enjoy one of their most popular dishes. You will need to soak the beans overnight.

½ pound (about 2 cups) dry garbanzo beans
1 tablespoon salt
1 beef bone
1 ham bone
2 quarts water
4 ounces salt pork or white bacon, diced
Pinch of Hungarian paprika
1 large onion, chopped
¼ cup lard
1 pound (about 3 medium) potatoes, quartered
Pinch of saffron*
Salt to taste
1 chorizo, thinly sliced (Spanish smoked sausage—available in most
    Latin American markets)
Chopped white onions

*See Tropical Glossary.

Soak the garbanzo beans overnight in sufficient water to cover the beans, with 1 tablespoon of salt.

When ready to cook, drain the water. Place the beans in a large pot with the beef bone, ham bone, and 2 quarts of water. Bring to a boil, then reduce heat to low. Cook for 45 minutes.

In a separate skillet, fry the salt pork or bacon with the paprika and onion in the lard until the salt pork is rendered and onions are transparent. Add to the beans along with the potatoes, saffron, and salt to taste. When potatoes are tender (about 45 minutes), add the chorizo. Cook another 10–15 minutes and serve hot with chopped white onions, if desired.

Serves: 4

Broccoli-Mushroom Soup Limoge

Here's a tasty treat from Lunch on Limoges, a restaurant in Dade City, Florida, where Phil Williams and Skip Mize's past New York fashion merchandising experience combines with their adeptness in presenting colorful and beautifully garnished culinary delights.

1 cup sliced leeks
1 cup sliced mushrooms
3 tablespoons butter
¼ cup flour
3 cups chicken broth
1 cup chopped broccoli florets
1 cup light cream
1 cup shredded Swiss cheese
2 eggs

In a large saucepan, place the leeks, mushrooms, and butter. Sauté until tender, but do not brown. Mix flour with a little water and add to the mushroom mixture. Stir until bubbly. Remove from the heat and gradually add the chicken broth, stirring until mixed. Return to heat and cook while stirring until the mixture is thickened and smooth. Add the broccoli florets. Reduce heat and simmer about 15 minutes or until the vegetables are tender.

Mix the light cream, cheese, and eggs in a separate mixing bowl. Temper by adding small amounts of soup to the bowl until the ingredients are warm, stirring constantly. While stirring, slowly pour the tempered egg mixture into the pot. Simmer until heated through and cheese is thoroughly melted.

Serves: 8

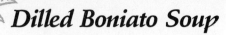

Dilled Boniato Soup

Boniato (batatas) is often referred to as the tropical sweet potato. Despite its rather buttery flavor, boniato contains no cholesterol or fat. It's much like a potato, so peel it in a similar manner. For a special treat, try this rather unusual soup. Boniato gets my vote for smoothness and great taste!

1 large boniato, peeled and cubed (available in most
    Latin American markets)
¼ cup butter or margarine
1 cup coarsely chopped onion
1 clove garlic, chopped
1 cup plain yogurt
1 cup skim milk
2 scallions, chopped
½ cup freshly chopped parsley
1 tablespoon fresh dill

Place the boniato in a medium-sized saucepan. Cover with water and cook covered until tender. Drain and add the butter, cup of chopped onion, and garlic. Sauté until the onion is translucent.

Stir in the yogurt and milk. Heat until warm. Add the chopped scallions, parsley, and dill. Heat thoroughly. Serve nice and hot.

Serves: 4–6

Calabaza Soup (Pumpkin Soup)

The calabaza (the word simply means squash in Spanish) is often referred to as the tropical pumpkin because it resembles the pumpkin in size and shape, and is widely grown in tropical and sub-tropical areas of the world. The calabaza pumpkin is frequently round, more commonly pear-shaped, and varies in color from solid green to traditional orange to a striped variation of both.

The history of its cultivation goes far back in time. It is thought to have been cultivated by the ancient Mayan and Aztec Indians. A wide variety was the mainstay of the Florida Indians.

The calabaza is a most versatile squash, but best when combined with other ingredients rather than used by itself. It's a welcome addition to many dishes, including this soup which is prepared at the Hotel Inter-Continental in Ocho Rios, Jamaica.

2 quarts cold water
1½ pounds soup meat
½ pound bacon slices, cut in half
2 cloves garlic, crushed
1½ teaspoons salt or to taste

2 pounds calabaza, peeled, seeded, and diced (available at most
   Latin American markets)
2 medium white potatoes, diced
½ green or red bell pepper, diced
1 medium tomato, diced
1 medium onion, diced
2 scallions, cut into 4 pieces each
2 sprigs thyme or 1 tablespoon powdered thyme

Put water in a large soup kettle. Add meat, bacon, garlic, and salt. Bring to a rapid boil. Lower heat and simmer about 1½–2 hours or until the meat is almost cooked, then add calabaza and potatoes. Stir and simmer for an additional 15 minutes. Add peppers, tomato, onion, scallions, and thyme. Stir well and simmer for about 20 minutes or until all ingredients are cooked. Adjust seasoning.

Serves: 6 or more

Elfreda's Calabaza Soup (Pumpkin Soup)

Here's another version of calabaza soup, this one a bit spicier than the preceding one. It is also different in that it contains chayote and yellow yams. The calabaza, or pumpkin squash as it is commonly called, is available in most supermarkets. Because the pumpkin is large, as with our yellow pumpkin, pieces are often sold in large chunks.

Yams are actually worshipped in some cultures and given ceremonial status in others, perhaps due to the huge size that they can often grow to. It is the honest-to-goodness truth that yams have been recorded to grow as large as 600 pounds. Now that's a yam!!!

In a good produce market, yams are often cut to show the interior. In the upscale Latin American markets, the produce man (the viandero) will split one to show the quality.

Elfreda Clarke, a Jamaican friend, showed me how to prepare this fantastic soup.

3 quarts water
1 pound beef soup bones
2 pounds calabaza*, peeled and cut into chunks
3 large carrots, peeled and chopped
4 stalks celery, finely chopped
1 chayote*, cut into small chunks
1 piece (about ½ pound) yellow yam*, scrubbed, peeled, and quartered
   (available in most Latin American or West Indian markets)
2 Irish white potatoes, peeled and cut

*See Tropical Glossary.

1 package dry Grace chicken noodle soup*
1 whole Scotch Bonnet pepper
2 scallions, crushed
1 clove garlic, crushed
1 piece fresh thyme

Into a large soup kettle, measure 2 quarts of the water. Add the beef bones and bring to a boil. After water boils for a few minutes, add the calabaza and cover. On medium heat, boil for 45–60 minutes or until tender. When tender (test with a fork), remove the calabaza from the liquid. Place the calabaza in a glass bowl and mash it with a fork. Return calabaza to the soup pot.

Now add the carrots, celery, and chayote. Stir and cook for about 30 minutes or until the vegetables are cooked. Add the yellow yam, Irish potatoes, 1 quart more of water, chicken noodle soup mix, Scotch Bonnet, scallions, garlic, thyme, and a little more water if a thinner consistency is desired (I like this soup thick). Cook for another 30 minutes or until all ingredients are cooked. Serve hot with buttered toast pieces.

Makes: About 3 quarts

*You may substitute other brands of dried chicken noodle soup mix. This one is the brand Elfreda Clarke likes best and is commonly found in Latin American or West Indian markets.

Sugar Reef's Callaloo Soup

The Sugar Reef restaurant in New York City first opened its doors in 1985 and has been serving Caribbean food to huge capacity crowds ever since. The six owners of the restaurant, all of whom had memorable experiences in the Caribbean islands, combined their ideas to create this very casual, lively eatery.

When I visited Sugar Reef, it was difficult for me not to order nearly everything on the menu. I limited myself to 6 items, convincing my sister Lee to try at least 4 of the offerings, including the delicious rum punch and this lovely Callaloo soup, one of the most popular soups in the islands.

2 pounds fresh callaloo* (available in most Latin American markets—
    may substitute kale or spinach)
¼ pound salt pork, cut in narrow strips
½ pound lean fresh pork, cubed
2 onions, peeled, cut in half and thinly sliced
Freshly ground pepper to taste
1½ tablespoons Jamaican red pepper sauce (available in most
    West Indian markets)

*See Tropical Glossary.

1 tablespoon Jamaican thyme*
6 cups well-flavored chicken broth
½ pound fresh white crab meat

Pull leaves off callaloo or kale stems. Discard stems and roughly chop the leaves. Wash very well.

Place salt pork strips in a large, heavy soup kettle. Sauté over medium heat for 10 minutes or until they are brown, rendering their fat. Discard all but 2 tablespoons of the fat. Add lean pork cubes and onions to the pan. Sauté over medium-low heat for about 5 minutes or until the cubes are brown and the onions are translucent.

Add half the chopped callaloo or kale, several grinds of black pepper and red pepper sauce. Roughly chop or crumble the Jamaican thyme and add to the callaloo. Add broth. When the first batch of callaloo has subsided, approximately 5 minutes, add remaining callaloo. Cover and simmer for about 2½ hours.

Remove the salt pork strips. Add the crab meat. Stir to mix well. Cover and continue simmering for 5 minutes more. May be served immediately, but it is better if made in advance and reheated before serving.

Serves: 6–8

*Sugar Reef brings their spices back from Jamaica and uses the spice in the form of dried sprigs. You may substitute any commercial brand of thyme, but dried sprigs can be found in most West Indian shops.

Ginger Kale Soup

There are some knowledgeable food writers who feel that kale is pretty and makes a nice garnish, but that it hardly has a prayer as an "edible" green. I am not one of them, though. Quite the contrary—I spent some time experimenting with the "flowering cabbage," as it is also known and came up with this delight—almost a meal in itself for a hot summer's day. The ginger in this soup appears to be having a love affair with the kale and succeeds in bringing out its best qualities.

4 cups kale, heavy stems removed, chopped
2 tablespoons water
1 tablespoon peeled and freshly mashed ginger
3 thin slices very lean deli ham
2 tablespoons extra virgin olive oil
2 tablespoons finely chopped onion
2 tablespoons flour
4 cups milk
¼ teaspoon cayenne pepper
Salt and freshly ground pepper to taste
Sherry
Freshly grated nutmeg

Pick over, trim, and wash the kale very well. Be sure to chop off the very thick parts of the stems. Place into a heavy saucepan, adding 2 tablespoons of water to the pot. Cover and cook on medium-low heat for about 5 minutes, stirring occasionally. Check to see if a little more water is needed to keep the kale moist and add more, if necessary. When the kale is almost limp, remove it from the pot. Place in the container of a food processor or blender along with the ginger and ham. Process for a few minutes until the kale and ham are very fine.

Heat the olive oil in a heavy saucepan. Add the onion and sauté for about 2 minutes. Whisk in the flour, being careful to keep the mixture smooth. Gradually add in the milk and continue to stir. Season with salt, pepper, and cayenne. Add the kale mixture. Heat the soup until almost boiling. Ladle into bowls. Just before serving, add 1 teaspoon of sherry to each bowl and mix gently. Grate fresh nutmeg over each bowl.

Serves: 4

Pepperpot Soup

My 12-year-old, Julie, just loves this soup. But when I told her I was going to put in the book, she said, "Mom, I don't think people will want to make it when they read pigs' tails!" She may be right. But, if you want to taste one of the best soups you'll ever have, you won't let the pigs' tails bother you at all—rather, you will want to try them in a variety of other dishes.

There are as many different varieties of Pepperpot soup as there are cooks. Here's my friend Elfreda Clarke's version which is popular in her native Jamaica. She uses a variety of locally-grown vegetables and tubers including a Scotch Bonnet pepper to heat it up a little. Allow time for the pigs' tails to soak overnight.

2 quarts water
2 pigs' tails, cut into 2-inch pieces, soaked overnight
½ pound salt pork, washed and cut into 2-inch pieces
1 pound fresh callaloo* (available in most Latin American markets—may substitute fresh spinach here or 1 18-ounce can of callaloo if added later)
12 small fresh okra, stemmed and thinly sliced
1 pound kale* or spinach
1 cup coconut milk*
1 medium-sized cocoyam*
½ pound yellow yam*, peeled and quartered
2 small sweet potatoes, peeled and quartered
3 scallions, crushed
2 cloves garlic, crushed
1 whole Scotch Bonnet pepper*
3 pieces fresh thyme
1 tablespoon monosodium glutamate (optional)

*See Tropical Glossary.

To a large soup kettle filled with 2 quarts water, add pigs' tails that have been soaked overnight (to remove excess salt), and salt pork. Cook for a few minutes. Then, add callaloo (add here, only if fresh), okra, and kale or spinach. Cook for about 1 hour or until vegetables are tender and seasoned. Add coconut juice to the mixture and cook about 15 minutes longer.

Now, add the canned callaloo (if you are not using fresh), the cocoyam, yellow yam, small sweet potatoes, scallions, garlic, Scotch Bonnet (if you desire your soup very hot, burst the pepper, and chop and mix it into soup), fresh thyme and monosodium glutamate. Add another cup or so of water if necessary and allow to simmer for 1½–2 hours.

Yield: About 1–1½ quarts

Cream of Tannia Soup*

Grenadians call it tannia, Cubans call it malanga, the Puerto Ricans named it yautia and it is known by at least five other names throughout the world. But, whatever you call this potato-like vegetable, its flavor is unlike most anything you have ever tasted before. And I can guarantee that you will love it.

I happened to enjoy it very much, especially in this nicely seasoned soup created by Chef Cicely Roberts of the Calabash Resort in St. George's, Grenada.

2 tablespoons margarine
1 pound tannia, peeled and chopped
1 onion, minced
1 tablespoon celery
1 tablespoon chopped green pepper
2 chicken bouillon cubes
1 tablespoon seasoning salt
Pinch of salt
3 black peppercorns
4 cups water
1 tablespoon evaporated milk
Freshly chopped parsley

Melt margarine in a sauté pan. Sauté tannia, onion, celery, and pepper. Add bouillon cubes, seasoning salt, salt, and peppercorns. Add water and boil slowly for 30 minutes. With a wire whisk, blend mixture well. Strain to remove lumps and peppercorns. Heat again. Add milk before serving. Serve nice and hot. Garnish with chopped parsley.

Serves: 4–6

*See Tropical Glossary.

Creamy Tomato Soup with Fresh Dill

You're going to enjoy this blend of fine fresh flavors. It is most important that you use tomatoes that are very red and dill that's perky and green. This is a rich soup, so it's fine for a late supper with a green side salad.

3 cups red ripe tomatoes, peeled* and chopped
½ cup finely chopped celery
¾ cup finely chopped scallions
2 tablespoons freshly chopped dill
1 clove fresh garlic, pressed
1 teaspoon sugar
1 tablespoon tomato paste
1 teaspoon Hungarian paprika
4 tablespoons butter or margarine
2 tablespoons flour
4 cups half-and-half
Salt and freshly ground pepper to taste

In a heavy saucepan, combine the tomatoes, celery, ½ cup of the scallions, dill, garlic, sugar, tomato paste, and paprika. Simmer for about 15 minutes, stirring occasionally.

In a separate heavy saucepan, melt the butter. Whisk in the flour and blend until smooth. Add the half-and-half and cook over medium-low heat for a few minutes.

Remove the vegetable mixture from heat and cool for a few minutes. Process this mixture in the container of a blender or food processor for about 5–8 seconds. Slowly add the processed vegetable mixture to the cream mixture. Blend well with whisk. Add salt and pepper to taste. Serve hot. Garnish each bowl with remaining scallions.

Serves: 4–6

*To peel, drop tomatoes in boiling water for a few minutes and skin will begin to fall off.

Caribbean Fish Stew

Ruskin, Florida, produces a most flavorful harvest of tomatoes. It's fun to spend the day pickin' your own, and it certainly saves on your budget, too. Combine fully ripe tomatoes with the day's "catch" for this interesting, easy-to-prepare stew from the Florida Tomato Exchange.

1½ pounds (about 3 cups) fully ripe tomatoes, coarsely chopped
1 cup chopped onion
1 teaspoon minced garlic
Salt and freshly ground pepper to taste
1 teaspoon crushed oregano leaves

2 cups unsalted chicken broth
2 cups diced celery
1 cup sliced carrots
1 pound fresh white fish fillets, cut in 1-inch chunks
2 teaspoons Hungarian paprika
½ cup dry sherry
1 tablespoon white vinegar

In a large saucepan, place the tomatoes, onions, garlic, salt, pepper, oregano, and chicken broth. Bring to a boil. Reduce heat and simmer, covered, for about 10 minutes.

Add the celery and carrots. Simmer, covered, for 5 minutes or until vegetables are almost tender. Add fish, paprika, sherry, and vinegar. Simmer, covered, about 3–5 minutes or until fish is opaque.

Serves: 6

Chayote Sea Chowder

Chayote is a tropical squash that looks much like a gnarled pear. It is one of the new squashes often available in many produce markets and is becoming quite popular due to its versatility. It is grown in many regions of the tropics including the southern part of Florida. This low-calorie vegetable is a great source of potassium.

Select firm chayotes that are smooth and free from bruises and decay. Since chayote belongs to the same family group as cucumbers and squashes, it can be substituted for them in many recipes. Here's a recipe clam and oyster lovers will enjoy.

¼ cup olive oil
1 large chayote, peeled and diced
¼ cup sliced celery
½ cup chopped onion
1 cup liquid from oysters and clams (add more water to make up the
     1 cup, if necessary)
1 cup heavy cream
2 tablespoons cornstarch dissolved in 2 tablespoons of water
1 cup fresh oysters, drained (reserve liquid)
1 6 ½-ounce can chopped clams, drained (reserve liquid)
¼ teaspoon fennel seed (may substitute ½ teaspoon
   Anisette liqueur)
Fresh parsley for garnish

Sauté the chayote and celery in olive oil until tender. Add the onion and cook all until the onion is translucent.

Drain the juices from the oysters and clams to equal 1 cup. Pour the liquid over the chayote mixture, setting the seafood aside. Add the cream and cornstarch mixture to the vegetable and drained juices. Stir constantly until smooth and glossy. Do not boil. Add the oysters, clams, and fennel seeds or Anisette. Heat to serving temperature. Garnish with freshly chopped parsley.

Serves: 4–6

Whitey's Catfish Chowder

Usually the only complaint one ever hears at Whitey's Fish Camp in Orange Park, Florida, is about the size of the catfish being served that day. Catfish run the gamut from being small to extremely large and most folks you talk to have a different opinion about which is best. Personally, I like the small channel ones.

Here's a simple chowder that's good for whatever's ailin' you.

1½ pounds fresh-water catfish
2 quarts water
¼ pound salt pork or bacon
2 medium onions, chopped
2 medium potatoes, diced
1 tablespoon monosodium glutamate (optional)
Tabasco sauce to taste
Salt and freshly ground pepper to taste

Clean and wash the catfish. Cook in water for 15–20 minutes or until the fish starts to come away from bone. Meanwhile, fry the salt pork until crisp. Chop and set aside with drippings.

Carefully remove bones from fish. Return the boned fish and all other ingredients including the salt, pork, and drippings to the pot. Bring back to a boil and simmer for 10–15 minutes or until potatoes and onions are tender.

Yield: 2 quarts

Caribbean Seafood Chowder

The Burgundy wine in this tasty chowder gives it a very unique flavor. Even though there are many ingredients, it is easy to prepare once you've got everything chopped. I was served this chowder on a visit to the Unicorn Village Restaurant in North Miami Beach, Florida, and return regularly for more. It's a thick and hearty soup.

The Unicorn was recently named one of the "top ten" health food restaurants in the United States by *Delicious Magazine*.

1 tablespoon vegetable oil
3 cloves garlic, crushed
1 medium onion, chopped

3 stalks celery, peeled and diced
2 medium carrots, peeled and diced
1 small potato, peeled and diced
2 medium tomatoes, blanched, peeled, and diced
1 16-ounce can (2 cups) tomato sauce
1 medium green pepper, diced
½ teaspoon basil
½ teaspoon oregano
½ teaspoon whole thyme leaf or crushed thyme
1 bay leaf
1 teaspoon Hungarian paprika
½ teaspoon celery seed
½ teaspoon dry mustard
1 cup clam juice
3 cups fish stock*
½ cup Burgundy
¼ pound small raw shrimp, peeled and chopped
½ pound fish fillets, cut into chunks
¼ pound clams
Salt and freshly ground pepper to taste

Heat the oil in a large soup kettle. Sauté the garlic and onion until the onions are translucent. Add the next 16 ingredients (up to, but not including the shrimp). Simmer about 30–40 minutes or until vegetables are tender. Add seafood and simmer until just cooked. Add salt and pepper to taste. Serve piping hot.

Serves: 10–12

*See Cooking Terms.

Easy Breezy Clam Chowder

Sometimes I'm in the mood for a simple soup, without a lot of frills and fanfare. This clam chowder, which I learned to make many years ago, has been a staple in my cooking repertoire.

1 quart fresh clams, liquor reserved
2-inch piece fat salt pork, finely chopped
1 onion, thinly sliced
4 cups diced potatoes, cut in ¾-inch squares
2 tablespoons butter or margarine
4 cups milk
1 teaspoon salt or to taste
⅛ teaspoon freshly ground pepper
8 soda crackers

Drain the clams and remove the pieces of shell or purchase clams already shelled at your local seafood shop. Retain the liquor.

Fry the salt pork slowly in a medium-sized saucepan until crisp. Add the onion. Fry for about 5 minutes or until the onions are translucent. Add the cubed potatoes, clam liquor, and enough water to cover. Stir well. Cook until nearly tender. Slowly add the butter, milk, salt, and pepper, and blend well. When the potatoes are completely tender, add the clams (whole or cut up) and the crackers. Cook about 3 minutes longer. Serve hot.

Serves: 4–6

Cream of Shrimp Soup

The famous Hyatt Dorado Beach Hotel was originally a Rockefeller playground. The quality of life there didn't change much when it became a public establishment. When the hotel opened in December, 1958, 150 millionaires and their spouses were invited to the festivities. They all went.

And you'll probably go too, if you are interested in sampling their luscious cuisine, like this soup created by Executive Chef Wilhelm Pirngruber for the guests at the Su Casa Restaurant. Simple but elegant.

1 pound medium shrimp, shelled and deveined
¼ cup butter
¼ cup finely chopped onion
¼ cup finely chopped carrot
¼ cup finely chopped celery
2 cups water
2–3 tablespoons lemon juice
⅛ teaspoon freshly grated nutmeg
Salt and freshly ground white pepper to taste
1 cup heavy cream
Freshly chopped parsley

Cut each shrimp into three or four pieces.

In a large saucepan, melt the butter and sauté the onion, carrot, and celery over medium heat for about 5 minutes or until tender. Add 2 cups of water, lemon juice, nutmeg, and salt and pepper to taste. Simmer 10 minutes. Stir in the shrimp. Cook just until shrimp turns pink. Add the cream and heat gently. Taste for seasoning, adding more lemon juice and nutmeg if needed. Sprinkle each serving with chopped parsley.

Serves: 4–5

Bahamian Conch Chowder

In the tropics, there are endless versions of conch chowder, but few are as easy to make or quite as delectable as the one served at Bernard's Restaurant in Boynton Beach, Florida. Several years ago, I helped the chef prepare this at a local department store demonstration and the demand for the fare was so great that eager eaters had to take part in a drawing to win a taste.

Bernard's was designed in 1929 as headquarters for the then famous Rainbow Tropical Gardens, created by horticultural expert C. O. Miller. Dining there is a relaxing and enjoyable experience. If you are unable to visit Bernard's and taste this soup first hand, try it in your kitchen and don't forget the sherry as it truly enhances the flavor.

6 cleaned conch pieces, pounded and ground*
1 large carrot, diced
1 green pepper, diced
2 onions, diced
½ cup butter
½ teaspoon thyme
½ teaspoon oregano
Salt and freshly ground pepper to taste
1 28-ounce can whole tomatoes
½ (6½-ounce) can tomato paste
1 quart fish stock**
3 tablespoons flour
6 tablespoons sherry

Sauté the conch, carrot, green pepper, and onions in half the butter. Add the thyme, oregano, salt, pepper, tomatoes, and tomato paste. (You may freeze the remaining paste in tablespoon portions for future use.) Stir in the fish stock. Bring to a boil for a few minutes, then simmer for 30 minutes.

Brown the flour, then mix in the remaining butter. Add a little stock from the hot chowder and then return mixture to chowder to thicken. Continue to simmer until ready to serve.

To serve, put a tablespoon of sherry in each bowl. Ladle in the chowder. Add more sherry, if desired.

Serves: 6

*The preparation of the conch is of utmost importance. With a meat mallet, beat for at least 10 minutes, or grind in a meat grinder or the container of a blender into small pieces. (Also see Tropical Glossary.)
**See Cooking Terms.

Good Oyster Stew

I think the best oyster stew is often the simplest. Keep it easy and keep it hot. Sprinkle it with your best Hungarian paprika. And use cream for a richer flavor.

1 pint oysters, liquor reserved
2 tablespoons butter or margarine
2 cups scalded milk, cream, or cream and boiling water, mixed
½ teaspoon salt
Hungarian paprika for garnish

Pour the oysters into a strainer over a saucepan. Reserve the oyster liquor. Remove any pieces of shell, then add the oysters to the strained liquor. In a separate skillet, melt the butter. Add oysters and liquor. Cook slowly for 3 minutes or until the edges of the oysters curl. Add milk or cream and salt. Cook about 1 minute. Sprinkle with paprika.

Serves: 1

She-Crab Soup

The Grand Bay Hotel in Coconut Grove, Florida, is the proud bearer of a five-star Mobil Guide rating. This soup, one of the restaurant's specialties, tastes best when made with backfin lump meat from a female crab, hence the name. You'll want to use the best paprika (imported from Hungary) in this soup; you can store it in the freezer once opened to preserve its flavor. Fresh clam broth is also best, but you may find the bottled variety more convenient.

2 tablespoons finely chopped shallots
⅓ cup sherry
1½ pounds Alaskan lump crab meat
3 tablespoons Hungarian paprika
2 pinches thyme
4 cups clam broth
2 cups heavy cream
2 teaspoons cornstarch
½ teaspoon cayenne pepper
Salt and freshly ground pepper to taste

Combine the shallots and sherry in a large saucepan. Simmer until reduced by half. Add the crab, paprika, and thyme. Simmer for 3 minutes. Add the clam broth and cream. Bring the soup to a boil. Dissolve the cornstarch in 1 teaspoon of water and whisk it into the soup. Simmer for 5 minutes, adding seasonings to taste.

Serves: 4–5

Duck and Black Bean Soup

When I tasted the first spoonful of this soup at Patriccio's restaurant in Coral Gables, Florida, I immediately called the chef to express my enjoyment. The combination of flavors is exciting, making this one of the best duck soups I've ever had.

There's a good deal of advance preparation involved in making this soup. The beans need to soak overnight, and you must roast a duck, first, too. (Actually, the duck can roast while the beans are cooking.) Use a Long Island duckling—it is definitely a superior breed.

1 4–5 pound Long Island duck
¼ fresh orange
2 tablespoons finely chopped onion
¼ teaspoon sage
¼ teaspoon cinnamon
¼ teaspoon allspice
Salt and pepper to taste
16 ounces dry black beans
1 large onion, chopped fine
3 tomatoes, diced
1 clove garlic, minced
1 tablespoon fresh cilantro (coriander) or ½ teaspoon dry
4 tablespoons butter
2 medium carrots, diced
5 scallions, chopped fine
½ cup pimento, chopped
¼ cup cognac
1 cup demiglace* or purchase bottled
2 tablespoons fresh dill, minced
2 teaspoons fresh basil, minced or ½ teaspoon dry
1 teaspoon fresh mint, minced
2 tablespoons Worcestershire sauce
Salt to taste
1 quart cream or more depending on desired thickness
Sour cream, fresh cilantro, and fresh pimento for garnish

Preheat the oven to 350°. Clean and pat the duck dry with paper towels. Place the orange and chopped onion in the cavity. Carefully place the duck on a rack in a baking pan. Season with sage, cinnamon, allspice, and salt and pepper to taste. Bake for about 1½ hours or until the joints move easily. Remove duck and cool. Remove skin from duck and dice the meat. Set aside.

Soak the black beans overnight, with enough water to cover. In the morning change the water. Add water to again cover beans. Add half the

*See Cooking Terms.

chopped onion, 2 diced tomatoes, garlic, and cilantro. Simmer 1–1½ hours or until beans are tender. In a skillet, melt butter and sauté diced carrots, remaining onions, scallions, remaining tomato, and pimento. Add the duck meat to the vegetables and sauté until vegetables are tender. Pour cognac over vegetables and carefully ignite. Add undrained beans. (If water cooked down too much, add water as needed.) Now add the demiglace, black pepper, dill, basil, mint, cilantro, Worcestershire sauce, and salt to taste. Cook over low heat for about ½ hour. Add cream and stir until blended. Cook 15 minutes longer.

Soup may be garnished with a dollop of sour cream, a sprig of cilantro, and a strip of pimento.

Serves: 4–6

Breads

Johnnycakes

Initially, the slaves in the Caribbean did not eat bread. Later, though, their masters taught them how to make bread and because they were not used to those light, yeast-leavened breads, they created a variety of heavier breads that they liked better, including the flat unleavened breads known as Johnnycakes. These little cakes are served at most meals. The recipe varies from island to island. Here's a baked version.

1½ cups flour, sifted
2 teaspoons baking powder
½ teaspoons salt
¼ cup lard, melted
¼ cup butter or margarine, melted
½ cup coconut milk*
3 tablespoons freshly grated coconut, peeled

Preheat the oven to 375°. Liberally grease a cookie sheet. Sift together the dry ingredients—the flour, baking powder, and salt. Add the lard and the butter very slowly to make a dough. Gradually add the milk and coconut, mixing well. Roll into small balls and flatten with a glass or rolling pin to about ½–¾ inches thick.

Bake until golden brown. Butter while hot and serve immediately.

Yield: 10–12 cakes

*See Tropical Glossary.

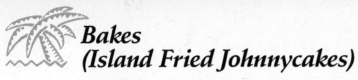

Bakes
(Island Fried Johnnycakes)

"Bakes" are an island favorite. Serve them up hot and crispy. The dainty size of the biscuit is a nice twist, sort of a Caribbean-style hush puppy.

2 cups all-purpose flour, sifted
2 teaspoons baking powder
1 teaspoon sugar
1 teaspoon salt
2 tablespoons lard
⅓ cup warm water
1 cup peanut oil or other vegetable oil for frying

Combine the flour, baking powder, sugar, and salt in a bowl. Add the lard and mix until the mixture is crumblike. Add water and mix until a smooth stiff dough is formed. Knead thoroughly but lightly, until all lumps have disappeared. Place on a floured board in a warm location and cover with cheesecloth or a towel. Let stand about 20 minutes.

In a heavy iron or aluminum skillet, heat oil to about 400°.

Roll small pieces of the dough mixture into balls, each about the size of a golf ball. Flatten with the bottom of a glass or with a rolling pin into small circles about ½-inch thick. Fry the "Bakes" until golden brown on both sides. Drain on paper towels. Serve warm.

Yield: 10–12

Cinnamon Banana Muffins

This recipe makes 12 extra-large muffins. Chef-creator Gerard Messerli insists that you use very ripe bananas in order to get the richest flavor. These muffins are served daily at the Hyatt Regency Cerromar Beach Hotel in Puerto Rico. They freeze well and can be stored frozen for up to one month.

2 cups all-purpose flour
2½ teaspoons baking powder
½ teaspoon salt
1½ cups (about 1¼ pounds) mashed very ripe bananas
¼ cup milk
½ cup butter, softened
1 cup plus 1 tablespoon sugar
2 eggs
1 teaspoon vanilla
½ teaspoon cinnamon

Preheat oven to 375°. Butter a 12-cup muffin tin.

On a piece of waxed paper, sift together the flour, baking powder, and salt. Set aside. Combine the bananas and milk. Set aside.

In a large bowl with an electric mixer at medium speed, cream the butter and 1 cup sugar until light and fluffy. Beat in 1 egg at a time. Beat in the vanilla. On low speed, stir the flour into the egg mixture alternately with the bananas, stirring until just combined. Spoon into muffin tins.

Combine the remaining 1 tablespoon sugar with the cinnamon. Sprinkle over the muffins. Bake 30 minutes or until a toothpick inserted in the center comes out clean. Cool in the pan for 5 minutes. Place muffins on wire racks to cool.

Yield: 12 muffins

Flora and Ella's Corn Meal Muffins

Flora Hampton and Ella Burchard's grandparents were probably the first white inhabitants in the area now called LaBelle, Florida. Before they settled there the Calusa Indians had lived there, but that tribe had been driven out in the Seminole Wars in the 1800's. A trip to Flora and Ella's Restaurant takes you back to those times. It's a place where pioneer images, tropical "tastes," and the very ambiance let you transcend time and place, and experience life as a Florida "cracker".

1 cup flour
1 cup corn meal
¼ cup sugar
¼ cup salt
4 teaspoons baking powder
Pinch of baking soda
2 large eggs
1 cup buttermilk
⅓ cup melted butter

Preheat the oven to 425°. In a medium-sized bowl, mix together the flour, corn meal, sugar, salt, baking powder, and baking soda.

Add the eggs, buttermilk, and butter. Blend until just moistened. Do not overmix.

Grease an 18-cup muffin pan or use a non-stick pan. Fill the cups ¾ full with the batter. Bake for 10–15 minutes.

Yield: 18 muffins

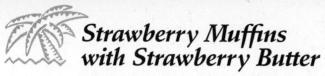

Strawberry Muffins
with Strawberry Butter

The proprietors of Lunch on Limoges Restaurant in Dade City, Florida, serve these mouth-watering muffins to thousands of customers a month. The butter can be served on these muffins or on a variety of other breads. For special occasions, serve the butter in tiny molded shapes.

   1½ cups flour
   ½ cup chilled butter, cut into 6 pieces
   ¾ cup sugar
   1 tablespoon baking soda
   ¼ tablespoon salt
   2 eggs
   ¼ cup milk
   2 tablespoons sherry
   ½ cup walnuts
   1 cup fresh strawberries, stems removed
   Strawberry Butter (recipe follows)

Preheat oven to 350°. Put the flour, butter, sugar, soda and salt in the container of a food processor. Process for 10 seconds.

In a small bowl, combine the eggs and milk. Beat well.

Add egg/milk mixture to the other ingredients. Process 10–15 seconds. Add the sherry, then turn the processor on and off for a few seconds. Add the nuts and process for 10 seconds. Add the strawberries and process another 10 seconds.

Bake in greased muffin pans for 18–20 minutes. Serve with Strawberry Butter.

Yield: 36 small muffins or 18 regular muffins.

Strawberry Butter

   1 cup fresh strawberries
   1 pound butter
   1½ cup confectioners' sugar
   1 tablespoon fresh lemon juice or bottled lemon juice

Purée the strawberries in a blender or food processor. Pour the puréed strawberries into a bowl and set aside.

Whip the butter in the food processor or blender until fluffy. Add the sugar and blend well. Add the strawberries and blend until the mixture is smooth. Add the lemon juice and blend again. Put the butter in suitable containers, cover, and refrigerate.

Yield: 2 cups

Mallard's Sweet Potato Muffins

The Mallard Beach Hyatt in Jamaica serves these mouth-watering muffins. To cook sweet potatoes, just boil them for 25 minutes or so

1 cup butter or margerine
1 cup sugar
6 eggs
1 teaspoon vanilla
2 cups milk
1½ cups flour
2 tablespoons baking powder
1 pound sweet potatoes, peeled, cooked, and mashed

Preheat oven to 350° and grease muffin tins very well.

Cream the butter and sugar together. Add the eggs, vanilla, milk, flour, baking powder, and sweet potatoes. Mix thoroughly to ensure that the ingredients are well combined. Drop the batter into the greased muffin tins. Fill about ⅔ full. Bake for about 30 minutes or until muffins are springy and golden brown.

Yield: 15–20 muffins

Carl's Cracklin' Corn Bread

Cracklings are made from the rind of ham or pork. You can buy them in the meat section of many supermarkets or make them yourself.

To prepare your own, cut the rind or fat into ½-inch squares. Place in a deep pan and bake at 300° until browned and all fat has been rendered. Drain and store in the refrigerator for use as needed.

This corn bread is a southern favorite given to me by owner Carl Allen of Allen's Historical Cafe in Auburndale, Florida. No need to add salt since the bacon grease and cracklings provide the flavor.

1½ cup white or yellow self-rising corn meal
½ cup self-rising white flour
1 teaspoon baking powder
4 teaspoons sugar
2 eggs
2 tablespoons bacon grease
½ cup cracklings
1 cup buttermilk or more

Preheat the oven to 350°. Mix all ingredients together except the buttermilk. Add enough buttermilk to form a pouring consistency, like cake batter. Pour into a hot, greased iron skillet or baking pan. Bake 20 minutes or until done.

Serves: 4–6

Mango Bread

This cake-like bread is served year-round at the home of Ettabelle Mann of North Miami, Florida. She moved here from Boston over 30 years ago and has been cooking with the fruit of her two backyard mango trees ever since.

Your mangoes must be ripe to prepare this very moist dessert-like creation.

½ cup margarine or butter
1½ cups sugar
3 eggs
½ cup vegetable oil
2 cups sifted flour
2 teaspoons baking soda
½ teaspoon salt
2 teaspoons cinnamon
½ cup raisins
¼ cup coconut flakes
2 cups peeled and chopped ripe mangoes*
1 teaspoon vanilla

Preheat the oven to 350°. Grease well two loaf pans. Cream the margarine and sugar until light and fluffy. Beat in the eggs. Add the oil. Set the batter aside.

Mix the flour, baking soda, salt, and cinnamon together. Dredge the raisins and coconut in a little flour. Add the remainder of the flour mixture to the batter. Fold in the raisins, coconut, and mangoes. Add the vanilla. Let stand for about 20 minutes.

Divide the batter into the two loaf pans. The bread will be done when a wire tester or toothpick comes out clean.

Yield: 2 loaves

*See Tropical Glossary.

Mango Nut Bread

Mangoes are often referred to as the tropic's peach. Grown in the very warmest regions of Florida, this very fragrant and juicy fruit tastes like a combination of pear, apricot, and pineapple. The flavors emerge victoriously in this nut bread recipe. Be sure that your mangoes are ripe. Sniff the stem end. There should be a pleasant scent—no perfume means no flavor.

1¾ cups sifted flour
2 teaspoons baking powder
¼ teaspoon baking soda

½ teaspoon salt
⅓ cup shortening
⅔ cup sugar
2 eggs
1 cup ripe mango, mashed
½ cup chopped nuts
½ cup raisins

Preheat oven to 350°. Grease a loaf pan. Sift together the flour, baking powder, soda, and salt. Set aside. Cream the shortening with the sugar. Add the eggs and beat until fluffy. Blend in the dry ingredients alternately with the mangoes. Mix until smooth. Add the nuts and raisins. Pour into the loaf pan. Bake 1 hour or until knife inserted in bread comes out clean. Cool 10 minutes before removing from pan.

Yield: 1 loaf

Orange Popovers

When making popovers, always be sure that your oven is very hot. Use heavy aluminum pans especially made for baking popovers if possible.

This recipe is from Klaus' Cuisine Restaurant in Holly Hill, Florida, just outside Daytona Beach. Prepare the batter a day ahead for best results.

12 eggs
3 cups milk
1½ cups orange juice
2 tablespoons grated orange rind
1½ teaspoons salt
4½ cups all-purpose flour

In the large bowl of an electric mixer or food processor, combine the eggs, milk, orange juice, orange rind, and salt. Mix at low speed until blended. Gradually add the flour. Mix at slow speed for 10 minutes. The mixture is best when prepared one day ahead and refrigerated.

When you are ready to bake, preheat the oven to 450°. Pour the mixture into cold, well-greased and floured popover or muffin pans to about ¾ full. Bake for 20 minutes, or until the popovers have risen. Reduce the heat to 300°. Continue baking 30–35 minutes. These popovers can be made ahead, cooled on a rack, and reheated in a 300° oven before serving.

Yield: 25–28 large popovers

Cranberry Nut Bread with Honey Butter

In 1985, Ken Dunn was voted one of the "Top 25 Hot Young Chefs in America" by *Food and Wine* magazine. *USA Today* has called him a "rising star of the New American cuisine." Since Chef Dunn has lived in Miami, we have become fast friends and I have been impressed with his emphasis on fine preservation and use of only the freshest products. He sums up his philosophy simply: "food must taste good and be beautiful at the same time."

This recipe reflects his Midwestern background as well as a tropical influence. For best results, wait a day before eating this bread.

2 cups sifted all-purpose flour
¾ cup granulated sugar
1½ teaspoons baking powder
1 teaspoon salt
½ teaspoon baking soda
1 large egg, beaten
1 teaspoon grated lime zest*
¼ cup Bogg's cranberry liqueur
¼ cup Kahlua liqueur
1 tablespoon fresh orange juice
2 tablespoons milk
2 tablespoons vegetable oil
1 cup coarsely chopped fresh cranberries
½ cup chopped roasted hazelnuts

Preheat oven to 350°. Sift together the flour, sugar, baking powder, salt, and baking soda. In a separate bowl, combine the egg, lime zest, liqueurs, orange juice, milk and oil. Mix well. Add to the flour mixture and mix thoroughly. Fold in cranberries and hazelnuts.

Pour batter into a greased 9×5×3-inch loaf pan. Bake for 1 hour or until done. Remove from the pan and cool. Wrap and store overnight.

Yield: 1 loaf

Honey Butter

½ cup fresh honey
1 cup unsalted butter, softened
Pinch of ground cinnamon
1 teaspoon fresh lemon juice

Mix all the ingredients together thoroughly. Serve on Cranberry Nut Bread. It's good on muffins, too.

Yield: 1½ cups butter

*See Cooking Terms.

Healthful Hush Puppies

If you're ever traveling through northern Florida, specifically the Gaines-villle area, be sure to visit the historic Marjorie Kinnan Rawlings home just outside of Cross Creek. Down the road from her celebrated hideaway is The Yearling Restaurant whose ancestry dates back to the 1930s when Mar-jorie's neighbor, Boss Brice, ran the place for the local fishermen to enjoy their catches. The Herman family runs the restaurant now, but you can almost picture Boss Brice cookin' up a feast for the hungry crowd. And, of course, the meal wouldn't be complete without a few hush puppies served on the side.

There is a wide variety of hush puppy recipes, but this one, made with grapefruit, is moist and delicious—one of the best.

2 onions, chopped
1¼ cups self-rising corn meal
2½-3 ounces grapefruit juice
1 tablespoon baking powder
1½ cups self-rising flour
¼ cup plus 1 tablespoon sugar
Light vegetable oil for frying

Mix all the ingredients together except the oil. The mixture will be dry. Coat the top with oil. Let rise 30 minutes to 1 hour.

Shape into walnut-sized balls. Fry in hot oil, taking care that the inside cooks and the outside is golden brown. Sprinkle with salt.

Yield: 3—4 dozen

Fish

Fish Escovitch

Fish is a staple food in the Caribbeans, and many islanders eat fish nearly every day. At one time, it was simply a matter of economics with the great abundance of seafood, but today it is a much sought after delicacy.

Here is one of my favorite fish dishes—freshly caught fish fried crispy so that the skin remains crunchy and the juices are sealed in, seasoned with a great mixture of herbs and spices.

My Jamaican friend, Elfreda Clarke, showed me how to prepare this dish. Although Elfreda *never* measures anything, she took the time to measure a little and showed me how she prepares this dish. Enjoy it cold, as it is often served, but is good hot, too. Allow at least 20 minutes for the fish to marinate.

4 small whole red snappers (about 2 pounds each), gills removed, cleaned, and scaled
2 fresh limes
2 onions, thinly sliced
3 stalks celery, peeled and chopped
1 green pepper, thinly sliced
3 scallions, finely chopped
1 Scotch Bonnet pepper*, seeds removed and chopped
2 cups vegetable oil
½ cup white vinegar or cider vinegar
12 allspice seeds
Salt and freshly ground pepper to taste

Cut the limes in half and rub a half over the whole fishes to remove any strong fishy taste. Wash the whole fishes well in water. Remove to a cutting board and pat the fishes dry.

With a sharp knife, slit the fishes diagonally on the sides in 4-inch long slices, about 3–4 cuts per side, so that the marinade will be able to penetrate well.

*See Tropical Glossary.

In a large bowl, mix together the onions, celery, green pepper, scallions, and ½ of the Scotch Bonnet pepper. Place the fishes in a long rectangular glass baking pan and rub the marinade over all. Be careful to wear rubber gloves while touching the peppers. Squeeze remaining lime halves over the fish and allow fishes to marinate, refrigerated, for about 20 minutes or more. Remove fish from bowl to a plate and reserve marinade.

To fry the fish, carefully heat the vegetable oil to a very hot temperature. Sprinkle a little flour on the fishes to keep them from sticking to the pan. Carefully add the fish to the oil and cook for about 8–10 minutes on each side. Pour off all but about 3 tablespoons of the oil from frying the fish. Pour the 3 tablespoons into a small 1-quart saucepan and add the vinegar. Add the vegetable marinade and cook until the vegetables are tender and translucent. Add the remaining ½ Scotch Bonnet pepper and allspice and cook another 10 minutes. Pour marinade over the fried fishes. Cover and place in refrigerator to chill, or serve hot.

Serves: 4

Ackee and Salt Fish

When my Jamaican friend, Elfreda Clarke, taught me how to make this dish, shopping for the ingredients at a local Cuban-West Indian market was almost as interesting as the cooking. The store stocked a huge variety of island foods including vegetables that I had never seen or heard of before—it was a true adventure for any gourmet or gourmand.

It is unlikely that you will ever find fresh ackee, but if you do, be cautious. Only ackee fruits that have been picked from the tree immediately after they have turned red and split open should be used because both immature and overmature fruits are poisonous. The part of the fruit used is the firm and oily white aril that surrounds the shiny black seeds and this is the only edible portion of the plant. The pink or purplish membrane near the seed should be discarded because this is also poisonous.

Which brings me to the reason for even including this recipe, even though the ingredients may be very difficult to find and there are no good substitutes. This is a book on tropical cuisine and it simply would not be complete without this recipe. It is the national dish of Jamaica and highly prized. When I talked to several Jamaicans about it, they became visibly excited as they described the delicacy.

The fruit is not easy to find in this country due to the strict import rules on the product. But, if and when you visit Jamaica, make it a point to sample it. I enjoy ackee very much, but it just may take getting used to, like, for instance, Scotch or sushi.

Elfreda says that this is her favorite dish.

1 pound boneless salted codfish, soaked overnight with several changes of
  water (available in most Latin American or West Indian markets)
1 quart water
½ pound (about 1 piece) salt pork
¼ cup coconut oil or vegetable oil
1 large onion, thinly sliced, then cut each slice in half
1 Scotch Bonnet pepper*, seeded and chopped
1 19-ounce (540 ml) can ackee* (available in West Indian markets)
1 tablespoon freshly ground black pepper

In a heavy pot, cook the salted codfish in water on medium heat. Add the
salt pork. Turn up heat and boil, covered, for about 30 minutes. This is done
to get the salt out of the fish. Remove the fish to a bowl of water. Rinse and
drain out water. At this point, fish will flake. Using your hands, flake any
chunks that remain. Remove the salt pork from the pot and cut into thin
slices about 1 inch square. Chop up the pepper, being careful to remove
seeds first before chopping.

Add the coconut oil or other oil to a preheated heavy saucepan and heat
until very hot. Carefully add the salt pork to the oil, browning nicely until
crisp. Now add the onions and the Scotch Bonnet pepper. Sauté until vegetables are tender. Add the fish to the mixture. Cook, covered, for about 15
minutes. Add the ackee and black pepper. Cook for a few minutes more
until nice and hot. Serve with greens and Johnnycakes (see page 115).

Serves: 4–6

*See Tropical Glossary.

Blaff

The name certainly does not do this dish justice. The blend of spices in
this very popular West Indian dish creates a taste that you will think about
days later. This recipe was given to me by Marina Polvay, a noted food consultant. It's from the island of Martinique in the French West Indies.

4 1-pound firm white fish, scaled, cleaned, and cut lengthwise into halves,
  or 4 10-ounce fish steaks, about 1-inch thick (red snapper is perfect, also
  yellowtail)
5 cups water
Juice of 1 lime
2 teaspoons salt
⅔ cup minced scallions
4 cloves garlic, minced
1–2 chili peppers (may substitute other hot peppers including jalapeño)
2 tablespoons minced fresh parsley

4 allspice berries
1 teaspoon minced fresh thyme or ½ teaspoon dry thyme
1 lime, quartered

Place fish in a glass or china dish. In another bowl, combine 2 cups of water, the lime juice, 1½ teaspoon salt, and 1 tablespoon scallions. Pour the marinade over the fish, and marinate in the refrigerator for 1 hour. Drain the fish and discard the marinade.

Place the remaining scallions, garlic, chili peppers, and parsley into a heavy pot (preferably cast-iron). With a wooden spoon, mash the mixture to extract the juices. Add the remaining 3 cups of water, allspice berries, and thyme. Cover the pot and place on high heat. Bring to a boil. Reduce heat and simmer for about 5 minutes. Add remaining ½ teaspoon of the salt and the fish to the broth. Cover and bring to boil again. Reduce the heat and simmer for about 10 minutes or until the fish flakes easily with a fork. With a slotted spoon, transfer the fish onto heated dinner plates. Boil the liquid on high heat for 2–3 minutes and spoon over the fish. Garnish with lime quarters.

Serves: 4

Fish with Green Peppercorns

I have enjoyed this dish many times at the Treasure Island Tennis and Yacht Club on St. Petersburg Beach, Florida, and I know you will, too. I make it with fresh grouper from Florida's waters, but any firm white fish will do.

Serve with a leafy green salad and fresh baby carrots. A Fume Blanc wine would be a nice accompaniment.

The recipe calls for crème fraîche, a rich soured cream, which you can easily make yourself if it is not available commercially-made in your area. Allow an extra day or two if you're making your own.

1 cup crème fraîche (or ¼ cup sour cream plus ¾ cup whipping cream)
1 firm white fish fillet
2 tablespoons green peppercorns, drained
Salt and freshly ground pepper to taste

Prepare crème fraîche by mixing the sour cream and the whipping cream together well. Let stand, unrefrigerated for 24–48 hours lightly covered. (If purchasing the crème fraîche, use 1 cup.)

Preheat oven to 350°. Bake the fish until nearly tender, about 5–8 minutes, depending on thickness. Remove the fish to a serving platter. Working now on the stovetop, add the crème fraîche, peppercorns, salt, and pepper to the liquid in the pan. Cook until thick and creamy. To serve, pour the sauce over the fish.

Serves: 1

Fish Pan Do

In 1498, Grenada (pronounced Gre-nay-da) was "discovered" by Christopher Columbus on his third voyage to the New World. He did not land there, however—just took a sighting and sailed off. More than 100 years later, a group of London settlers arrived and attempted to form a colony. But, unfortunately for them, they were quickly driven off by the fierce Carib Indians, who discouraged all other attempts at settlement until the French purchased the island from them, in 1650, for two bottles of brandy and a few trinkets.

The French tried to drive the Caribs from the islands but were halted in this campaign by a 100-year see-saw battle with the British for possession of Grenada. The island changed hands a few times, but was finally ceded to the British in 1783. It remained a part of the British commonwealth until it became fully independent in 1974.

The people of Grenada, in their customs and traditions have inherited the fine cooking expertise of the French along with the mannerisms and speech of the English. Chef/owner Terry Lampert of Delicious Landing restaurant in St. George's, with his cooking ability and traditions is testimony to Grenada's rich historical background.

You may think, as I did, that "pan do" is an exotic little-known culinary term. It simply means that you "do it in the pan."

2 tablespoons margarine
¼ cup sliced carrot
¼ cup sliced chayote
¼ cup sliced green plantains
¼ cup sliced mushrooms
¼ cup sliced cauliflower
¼ cup sliced broccoli
¼ cup garlic butter
1½ pounds fish fillets, cut into 8-ounce fillets
¼ cup fresh coconut milk*
¼ cup freshly grated Cheddar cheese
¼ cup celery
2 cups cooked rice

Heat the margarine in a fairly large skillet, and sauté the carrot, chayote, plantains, mushrooms, cauliflower, and broccoli until tender. Add the garlic butter and fish. Pour in the coconut milk, cheese, and celery. Simmer for about 8 minutes. Serve hot with rice.

Serves: 2–3

*See Tropical Glossary.

Sunshine Fillets

Sometimes the simplest recipes turn out to be the best. Use this recipe on any fish fillet. As always, the fresher the ingredients, the better the creation. Use a zester* to prepare the orange peel so that you will be sure to omit any of the bitter pith.

2 pounds fresh fish fillets
3 tablespoons melted butter or margarine
2 tablespoons fresh orange juice
2 teaspoons grated orange zest*
1 teaspoon salt
Dash of nutmeg
Dash of pepper
Orange twists and coils for garnish

Preheat oven to 350°. Cut the fillets into 6 portions. Place the fish in a single layer, skin side down, in a well-greased baking dish, 12 x 8 x 2 inches.

Combine the remaining ingredients. Pour the sauce over the fish. Bake for 15–20 minutes or until fish flakes easily when tested with a fork.

Garnish with orange twists and coils.

Serves: 6

*See Cooking Terms.

Fish with Parsley and Butter Sauce

The seafood dishes at the Calabash Resort at L'Anse aux Epines Beach in Grenada are second to none. The Calabash Resort, lauded for its great cuisine, serves this simple dish on an enchanting flower-covered terrace. The author is Chef Cicely Roberts who has been creating splendor in the kitchen for more than 13 years. She prepared it for me using a lovely fresh Kingfish which she broiled.

1 tablespoon flour
4 tablespoons butter
1 cup fish stock*
1 tablespoon freshly chopped parsley
1½–2 pounds firm white fish
1 teaspoon fresh lime juice
Salt to taste
Freshly cracked black pepper or white pepper to taste

Make a roux* with the flour and butter. Slowly whisk in the fish stock, parsley, and lime juice. Season with salt and pepper. Simmer for about 3 minutes.

*See Cooking Terms.

Wash fish with water and lime juice. Broil, grill, or steam the fish. Pour the sauce over the fish. Serve with a side dish of eggplant (aubergine) and a fresh garden salad.

Serves: 4

Fish Nostrand Avenue

The owner of the popular Caribe Restaurant (specializing in Caribbean, Spanish, and West Indian Cuisine) in New York City bills his eatery as a place with "Hot and Spicy Music and Hot and Spicy People." As the well-known food critic Bryan Miller of the *New York Times* has said, "Any restaurant that has the chutzpah to call a dish 'Fish Nostrand Avenue' can't be all bad."

By the way, Nostrand Avenue, which is in Brooklyn, is the one place you can find all the West Indian fruits and vegetables your heart would ever desire. As a matter of fact, most of the owners of New York City's Caribbean restaurants purchase their fresh fruits and vegetables from the street vendors there.

Enjoy this dish with Fried Green Plantains (see page 224) and a bowl of Unicorn Black Bean Soup (see page 97). And why not top it off with Jamaican Rum Punch (see page 33)?!!!

2 pounds firm fish fillets, salted to taste
1 cup ripe chopped tomatoes
1 cup chopped onions
1 cup chopped green peppers
2 cloves garlic, minced
1 teaspoon cayenne pepper
½ cup fresh lemon juice
1 tablespoon sugar
Lawry's Seasoning Salt to taste
¼ cup white wine
2 tablespoons butter or margarine

Place fillets on a steel baking platter that has been well greased. Combine all the ingredients except the butter or margarine and wine. Spread this "relish" over the fish fillets. Preheat oven to 350°

Sprinkle wine over all and dot with butter pieces. Bake for about 4 minutes. Then, place under the broiler for about 3 minutes or until done and nicely browned on top. Do not overcook.

Serves: 4–6

Lovely Lime Baked Fish

This is a perfect dish for those diet-conscious days as limes have only a few calories per squeeze.

For convenience's sake, limes can be squeezed and the juice frozen in ice trays for use throughout the year.

1 pound fresh fish fillets (4–6 fillets)
3 tablespoons butter or margarine
2 tablespoons fresh lime juice
Salt and freshly ground pepper to taste
1 teaspoon freshly chopped tarragon or ½ teaspoon dried
½ teaspoon freshly chopped chives
1 lime cut into thin wedges
½ teaspoon Hungarian paprika

Preheat oven to 350°. Melt the margarine in a shallow baking pan. Arrange fillets in the pan, turning well to coat both sides with the margarine. Drizzle lime juice over the fish. Combine the salt, pepper, tarragon, and chives. Sprinkle over the fish.

Cover with aluminum foil and bake for about 8–15 minutes, until the fish flakes easily. Do not overcook.

Garnish with lime wedges. Sprinkle wedges and fish with paprika.

Serves: 4

Fish with Lemon Relish

Here's an adaptation of a recipe I received from some friends at the Florida Department of Citrus. For best results, make the relish early so it has time to chill.

¼ cup crushed pineapple, drained
2 tablespoons peeled, seeded, and chopped lemon
2 tablespoons finely chopped green pepper
1 tablespoon finely chopped onion
1 tablespoon light brown sugar
1½ teaspoons grated lemon peel
¼ teaspoon dry mustard
¼ teaspoon celery salt
Dash of ground cloves

2 pounds fresh fish fillets
½ cup sour cream
Fresh parsley and lemon quarters for garnish

Combine the first 9 ingredients. Chill. About 20 minutes before serving, preheat oven to 350°. Cut the fillets into 6 portions. Place the fish in a single layer, skin side down, in a well-greased baking dish, 12 x 8 x 2 inches. Bake for 15–20 minutes or until the fish flakes easily when tested with a fork. To serve, pour the chilled sauce over the fish. Garnish with freshly chopped parsley and lemon wedges.

Serves: 6

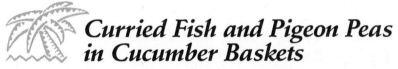 ## *Curried Fish and Pigeon Peas in Cucumber Baskets*

It's always fun to prepare something out of the mainstream. Islanders take life easier than most people do, leaving more time for enjoyable pursuits such as indulging in a little creative cookery—like in this decorative salad dish by Julie Walker, of Grenada, West Indies.

The pigeon peas used in this recipe are very popular in West Indian cooking, dried and fresh. They have a number of different names: the Spanish-speaking islands call them gandules; Trinidad recognizes them as gungo peas, pigeon peas, and arbar dahl; Jamaicans call them gungo, goongoo peas, and gunga. You can find them in most West Indian or Latin American markets, canned or frozen.

2 medium cucumbers, washed and peeled (reserve some of the peel)
1 cup pigeon peas or cooked fresh peas (available in West Indian
    or Latin American markets)
¼ cup mayonnaise
1½ teaspoons curry powder
1 cup cooked flaked fish (smoked flaked fish is delicious, too)
2 cups watercress, long stems removed
½ cup freshly chopped parsley
½ cup finely chopped red bell pepper
2 scallions, finely chopped for garnish
Freshly ground black pepper to taste
1 teaspoon fresh lemon juice

Carefully cut each cucumber into halves, vertically. Slice off ends so that ends will be flat. Cut each piece into 1½–2-inch pieces, being careful to cut straight. With a melon baller or small spoon, scoop out the inside of the cucumber pieces to form small cups. Set aside what you scoop out. Allow at least ½-inch of cucumber thickness on each base.

Heat the pigeon peas to boiling, then drain off water. Mix with mayonnaise and curry powder. Place 2 teaspoons of flaked fish into each cucumber cup. Place some pea mixture on top of the fish to fill the basket, allowing mixture to artistically overflow. Cut a thin slice of skin from the cucumber to form a handle for each basket.

Mix leftover pea mixture with scooped out cucumber filling. Place in a separate bowl and center on a platter with baskets ringed around bowl. Spread watercress around baskets. Garnish with parsley, scallions, red pepper, and black pepper. Chill for 10–15 minutes. Eat with knife and fork or serve as a finger-food appetizer.

Makes: 10–12 pieces

Fish Casserole with Plantains and Cheese

In the tropics the cooking banana, or plantain, is a staple in the diet of many. It's a versatile fruit that is used at all stages of ripeness: hard and green, soft and yellow, and also fully ripe at which point the skin will be black. One of the best ways to prepare the ripe fruit is to slit the skin and bake at about 350° until soft and then top with butter and brown sugar.

Here's a delightful way to prepare the green plantain. This is my variation on a dish by Grenadian resident Rhona Sylvester. It's a great dinner party dish.

2 pounds firm white fish fillets
2 cloves garlic, pressed
2 teaspoons fresh thyme or 1 teaspoon dried
1 fresh lime for seasoning fish
Salt and freshly ground pepper to taste
8 green plantains,* peeled and halved lengthwise
1 onion, finely chopped
2 teaspoons finely chopped celery
2 tablespoons margarine or butter
1 6-ounce can tomato paste
1 cup ketchup
2 eggs, well beaten
1 cup grated Cheddar cheese**

Preheat oven to 325°. Season the fish with 1 clove of garlic, 1 teaspoon thyme, and lime squeezed over and rubbed into the flesh of the fish. Salt and pepper the fish to taste.

Cook the plantains by dropping them into the boiling water to which a teaspoon of salt has been added. Cook for 20–25 minutes or until tender (a fork should glide softly into the plantain).

*See Tropical Glossary.
**I use a very sharp Cheddar cheese, but you may use any cheese that melts well.

Sauté the onion and celery in margarine until translucent. Add tomato paste, ketchup, remaining clove of garlic, and thyme. Add fillets and simmer uncovered until sauce becomes thick and fish is cooked through.

Grease well a long ovenproof baking dish. Place a layer of plantains on the bottom. Top with a layer of the fish with sauce and some of the beaten egg. Top with some grated cheese. Repeat to build about 3 layers, ending with the grated cheese. Bake for about 15 minutes or until everything is bubbly and cheese has melted. Serve with a steel serving wedge, being careful not to disturb the layers.

Serves: 4–6

Codfish Croquettes

The national dish of Grenada is flying fish prepared in any number of ways... boiled, stewed, sauteed in a delicate sauce, deep fried, as a sandwich, and baked. Flying fish is not available in many places, but you can substitute any firm white fleshy fish.

This recipe is from Theresa Baptiste of Grenada, West Indies, who is surrounded by a sea full!! Try it also with a smoked fish or salted codfish.

2 tablespoons butter or margarine
2 tablespoons all-purpose flour
¼ teaspoon of salt or to taste
Dash of white pepper
1 cup milk

2 cups (1 pound) cooked flaked codfish
1 teaspoon fresh lemon juice
1 cup fine bread crumbs
Vegetable oil for frying
½ teaspoon salt
1 beaten egg
Cocktail or Lime Marmalade Sauce (see page 245)

To make a medium white sauce, melt butter or margarine in a heavy saucepan. With a wire whisk or fork, blend in flour, salt and a dash of white pepper. Add all of the milk at once. Cook very quickly, stirring constantly until the mixture becomes thick.

Drain any liquid from the fish. Remove all bones and flake gently into small pieces, taking care not to break any bones.

Remove white sauce from heat. Add fish and lemon juice to the sauce. Gently shape the fish mixture into cone-shaped rolls or medium-sized balls. Carefully and gently roll into crumbs, then into beaten egg, then crumbs again. Refrigerate until very cold.

Heat oil on moderate to high heat in skillet about 1-inch deep. After fish rolls have become very cold, fry in the oil for a few minutes or until they turn a delicate brown color. Drain on paper towels or brown paper bags. Serve with cocktail or Lime Marmalade Sauce.

Serves: 4

Carol's Fishburgers

A visit to sunny St. Petersburg, Florida, demands a trip to Jack's Skyway Restaurant, a very casual diner managed by Jack Thomas, a fun-loving retired Navy cook. Breakfast or lunch at Jack's is an experience. Make this recipe by Jack's lovely wife Carol with any finfish, but a fresh firm catch works the best.

> 2–2½ pounds boneless and skinless fish
> 3 cups water
> 1 tablespoon salt (optional)
> ¼ cup minced onion
> ¼ cup minced celery
> ¼ cup minced green pepper
> ½ cup mashed potatoes
> 1 egg, beaten
> ¾ teaspoon Worcestershire sauce
> ⅛ teaspoon garlic powder
> ½ tablespoon monosodium glutamate* (optional)
> ½–⅓ cup breading mix
> Vegetable oil for frying
> Bakery buns

Bring the fish to a boil in salted water. Simmer only 10 minutes. Drain off water just until fish is slightly moist.

Crumble the fish. Mix it with the next 9 ingredients, using enough breading mix to hold everything together. Make into patties each about 4 inches in diameter and ⅜ to ½ inch thick, using about 4 ounces per patty. If more are made than needed, freeze the extras between sheets of waxed paper. Lay the remaining patties on a cookie sheet or similar tray and freeze (this may take several hours) until solid.

When ready to prepare, deep-fry the frozen patties until golden brown in oil heated to 350°. Drain on paper towels. Serve on buns with tartar sauce.

Serves: 5

*Monosodium glutamate, MSG, is a flavor enhancer and has been widely used for centuries, especially in Oriental food. The Food and Drug Administration considers MSG to be safe; however, some individuals who use it do have an allergic reaction.

Fish Rangoon

You'll find several versions of rangoon in the Florida Keys and Key West. This one is superbly flavored. It comes from the famous Marker 88 Restaurant, in Plantation Key, which is owned and operated by André Mueller. Be sure to use fresh fish when preparing this dish.

2 pounds of fillets of yellowtail, snapper, grouper, or similar firm white fish, with all bones and skin removed
1 teaspoon Worcestershire sauce
2 tablespoons fresh lemon juice
1 teaspoon salt
¼ teaspoon white pepper
2 eggs
¼ cup milk
1 teaspoon vegetable oil
½ cup clarified butter* or vegetable oil for frying
Flour for dredging
¼ teaspoon ground cinnamon
3 tablespoons currant jelly
Rangoon Sauce (recipe follows)

Season fillets with Worchestershire sauce, lemon juice, salt, and pepper. Beat the eggs together with the milk and 1 teaspoon of vegetable oil. Dip the fillets in the flour, then in the egg mixture.

Meanwhile, heat the butter or oil in a heavy skillet. Place the fillets in the skillet. Sauté until light brown. Turn the fillets over and continue to sauté until fish is cooked—just a few minutes. When the fillets are done, place them on a serving platter. Sprinkle with ground cinnamon and spread currant jelly over them. Keep warm. Discard butter or oil. Wipe out the skillet. Make Rangoon Sauce in this skillet.

Top each serving of fish with some of the Rangoon Sauce and serve.

Rangoon Sauce

½ cup each diced bananas, pineapple, mangoes, and papayas (may substitute peaches if mangoes or papayas are not available)
½ cup butter
1 tablespoon fresh chopped parsley
2 tablespoons fresh lemon juice

Using the skillet in which you prepared the fish, melt the butter. Add the fruit, parsley, and lemon juice. Shake skillet until everything is heated through. Be careful not to cook or heat too long.

Serves: 4

*See Cooking Terms.

Fish in Puff Pastry

Chef Wilfried Hausy, a popular chef in the Jacksonville, Florida, area, gave me the recipe for this moist fish entrée. Use frozen puff pastry, just like he does. When I prepare this, I often use red grouper, a member of the sea bass family. It's a valuable fish because of its excellent flavor, and is found on the South Atlantic and Gulf coasts from Virginia to Texas and southward to Brazil. Allow time for fish to marinate.

1 6-ounce firm white fleshy fillet
½ teaspoon lemon juice
½ teaspoon Worcestershire sauce
Salt and freshly ground pepper to taste
½ teaspoon thyme
½ teaspoon basil
½ teaspoon marjoram
½ teaspoon dry mustard
½ teaspoon curry powder
½ teaspoon coriander seed
¼ teaspoon ground ginger
2 Romaine leaves
6 ounces puff pastry (may be purchased in frozen foods section, use
       Pepperidge Farm brand)
1 clove garlic, mashed
1 tablespoon butter
Beaten egg and milk for brushing top
Olive slice, lemon wedges, and parsley sprigs for garnish

Mix together the lemon juice, Worcestershire sauce, salt, pepper, thyme, basil, marjoram, mustard, curry powder, coriander, and ginger. Marinate the fillets in this mixture for 4 hours in the refrigerator.

Preheat oven to 350°. Poach Romaine leaves for 30 seconds. Cool. Thaw pastry and roll into a thin square large enough to cover the fillet. Roll the fillet up in the Romaine leaves and place the roll in the center of the pastry. Spread with butter and garlic that have been blended. Fold the pastry over the fish, shaping it to resemble a fish. Seal well. Use an olive slice for the eye. Brush the top with milk or a beaten egg-and-milk mixture.

Bake for 20 minutes or until the pastry is golden brown. Garnish with lemon wedges and parsley sprigs.

Serves: 1

Flounder Scampi

Whip up the scampi butter a day ahead and reserve leftovers for other fish or shellfish. This recipe is easy and simply delicious, and comes from the well-known Unicorn Village Restaurant in North Miami Beach. This restaurant does the largest volume of business per square foot of any restaurant its size in Florida! This is great with dolphin fish—not the "Flipper" variety—but a nice firm white finfish found in tropical waters.

Scampi Butter

8 ounces whipped butter
2 teaspoons basil
½ teaspoon oregano
6 cloves garlic, crushed
¼ teaspoon white pepper
½ teaspoon salt (optional)
2 tablespoons dry white wine

8 8-ounce fresh flounder fillets or any firm white fish
2 tablespoons extra virgin olive oil

Preheat oven to broil, 550°. Allow the butter to sit at room temperature until soft. Add the next 6 ingredients and whip with a fork until well blended.

Place the fish in a shallow pan. Coat with olive oil. Add about ⅛ inch of water to cover the bottom of the pan. With a knife or rubber spatula, spread the scampi butter over the top of the fish. Broil until just done.

Serves: 8

Grouper with Mango and Peach Sauce

The Historic Bryan Homes Restaurant in Fort Lauderdale features dishes containing ingredients indigenous to Florida. Dining here is a treat and a truly "tropical" experience. The restaurant is located in two stone houses that date back to the early 1800s. The two houses have been joined together and beautifully decorated, inside and out, to capture the mood of Florida's early settlers. This dish is prepared using native Florida grouper.

4 6–8 ounce grouper fillets or other white firm-textured skinless fillets
¼ cup flour
⅓ cup vegetable oil or less
Lemon and fresh parsley for garnish
Mango and Peach Sauce (recipe follows)
Lemon slices and parsley for garnish

Preheat oven to 375°. Dust the grouper with flour on both sides. Heat the oil in large heavy skillet and sauté the fish until golden brown, about 4–5 minutes per side.

Place the fish on a heat-proof platter in the oven to finish cooking, about 7–10 minutes or less depending on the thickness of the fish. Do not overcook the fish. It should remain moist.

Place fish on a serving platter and top with the warmed Mango and Peach Sauce. Garnish with lemon slices and parsley.

Mango and Peach Sauce

¾ cup fresh mango, pitted and peeled (about 1 large mango)
¾ cup fresh peaches, pitted and peeled (about 3 medium peaches)
¼ cup melon-flavored liqueur

Purée the prepared mango and peaches in the container of a blender or a food processor. Place the mixture in a saucepan and bring to a boil. Stir in the melon liqueur, then reduce heat to low to keep the sauce warm until the fish is ready.

Serves: 2

 ## Whole Broiled Pompano

Just ask any of the locals in Panama City Beach, Florida for the best seafood restaurant in town, and the answer will most probably be "Captain Anderson's, of course." The pompano there made my mouth water, and I'm sure you will have the same reaction.

1 whole pompano (about ½ pound), cleaned
⅓ cup plus 2 tablespoons olive oil
⅔ cup butter
¼ cup fresh lemon juice
Salt and freshly ground pepper to taste
3 tablespoons chopped scallions for garnish
3 tablespoons chopped parsley for garnish

Rub 2 tablespoons of olive oil over the fish. Charcoal-broil the fish for about 7 minutes on each side. Do not overcook.

Blend the butter, lemon juice, and ⅓ cup olive oil over heat. Place the fish on a platter. Pour the sauce over it. (The fish should be swimming in sauce.) Salt and pepper to taste. Sprinkle with scallions and parsley.

Serves: 1

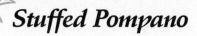

Stuffed Pompano

I've used this recipe with a variety of firm-textured fish and it's a winner every time. The milk removes any semblance of fishiness in the pompano. This is one of my favorites from the Dining Galleries at the popular Fountainbleau Hotel in Miami Beach—another winner.

2 1½-pound pompano fillets, skinned
2 cups milk
4 ½ tablespoons butter
2 shallots, peeled and chopped
1 clove garlic, chopped
¼ cup mushrooms, quartered
½ cup Alaskan king crab meat or other crab meat
1 cup heavy cream
½ teaspoon chopped chives
Pinch each of basil, tarragon, salt, and white pepper
Juice of 1 lemon
¼ cup flour
2 eggs, lightly beaten

Preheat oven to 350°. Soak fillets in milk for a few minutes. Melt half of the butter and add the shallots, garlic, and mushrooms. Sauté for 30 seconds. Stir in the crab meat and cook until just heated through. Add the heavy cream and chives. Simmer until thick. Season with basil, tarragon, salt, pepper, and lemon juice.

Remove from the heat and let cool. Sandwich the mixture between the fillets. Coat it with flour (shake off the excess), then dip it in egg. Melt the remaining butter and sauté the fish until brown on both sides. Put in the oven for 10–15 minutes.

Serves: 2

Red Snapper with Sauce Vierge

The meat of the snapper is juicy, white, and very flavorful. Well-laden snappers with high food value are the pink, mangrove, yellow eye, mutton, yellowtail, and the red varieties. Red snapper is among the most delicious deep sea delicacies in the market.

Here's an easy, habit-forming fish dish with a verdant herb dressing.

2 pounds fresh red snapper fillets
Mayonnaise to coat
Salt and freshly ground pepper to taste
2 tablespoons butter
2 cloves garlic, minced
Sauce Vierge (recipe follows)
Watercress and lemon slices for garnish

Spread mayonnaise well to coat both sides of the fish. Place the fish on a broiling pan. Season with salt and pepper. Melt the butter with the garlic and drizzle it over the fish. Place the fish under the broiler, until it is browned (brown it on one side only) or until the fish flakes when tested with a fork. Do not overcook.

Coat broiled fish with sauce or serve a bowl of Sauce Vierge alongside. Garnish with watercress and fresh lemon slices.

Sauce Vierge

1½ cups mayonnaise
1½ tablespoons chopped dried chives
1 teaspoon chopped dried tarragon or tarragon blend
1 teaspoon chopped dried dill
¼ cup chopped dried parsley

By hand, mix all ingredients well.

Serves: 4–6

Ruby's Baked Stuffed Snapper

How nicely the skin keeps the moisture in the fish! This is guaranteed to absolutely melt in your mouth. The recipe is Ruby Brown's from Grenada, West Indies, where there is *never* a seafood shortage!

1 whole red snapper (about 2½ pounds)
Fresh lime juice
2 tablespoons Kitchen Mate
2 medium onions, finely chopped
2 green peppers, finely chopped
2 scallions, finely chopped
2 stalks celery, finely chopped
2 cloves garlic, finely chopped
Pinch of powdered cloves
2 tablespoons ketchup
2 tablespoons fish stock*
1 cup bread crumbs
2 tablespoons margarine or butter, melted
Freshly chopped parsley for garnish

Preheat oven to 325°. Have your fish market do this or do it yourself—scale the fish, remove all the fins, slice through the back and remove the center bone and insides.

*See Cooking Terms.

Wash the fish with water and fresh lime juice. Dry the inside of the fish and sprinkle it with Kitchen Mate. Combine the next 9 ingredients and mix well. Stuff the fish with this mixture, securing it with toothpicks or string. Place the fish in a heavy roasting pan. Pour margarine over the fish. Cover with aluminum foil and bake until the fish is just cooked. Do not overcook. Remove toothpicks or string.

If desired, serve with melted butter or margarine to which freshly chopped parsley has been added.

Serves: 4

Snapper Barbados

The Unicorn Village Restaurant in North Miami Beach, Florida, does one of the largest dollar volumes per square foot of any restaurant in the state of Florida. Owner Terry Dalton attributes his success to fine quality, healthful foods and a reasonable price.

Everything in the restaurant is fresh, made from scratch with absolutely no additives. All fruits and vegetables used are organically grown. Because of Terry's total dedication to healthful eating—the restaurant being named in the top ten of *Delicious!* magazine's favorite restaurants in the United States—he is able to produce such mouth-watering, yet totally healthful dishes as this Snapper Barbados. A part-owner of a Caribbean restaurant, Terry knows what he's doing when blending island herbs and spices.

1 10-ounce snapper fillet
3 tablespoons lime juice
2 tablespoons fresh chopped parsley
1 tablespoon thyme
1 tablespoon marjoram
1 tablespoon freshly chopped shallots
1½ teaspoon freshly minced garlic
½ teaspoon cayenne pepper
1 teaspoon Hungarian paprika
⅛ teaspoon salt
Dash of hot pepper sauce, preferably a "natural" brand without additives
2 tablespoons olive oil or margarine

Blend all ingredients together very well. Cover the fillet with the mixture being careful to coat the entire fillet. Broil for a few minutes or until the fish flakes when tested with a fork.

Serves: 1

Red Snapper Tortuga

Enter Chadwick's popular eatery in Sanibel Island, Florida, and you are taken aback by the exciting montage of exotic colors splashed beautifully about in this tropical setting.

Just on the very tip of Captiva Island off the coast of Fort Myers, Chadwick's was named for Clarence Chadwick, who bought Captiva and the north end of Sanibel Island back in the 1900s as a Key lime plantation. It's an exciting place to visit, as I have done each year for the past 12 years. If you can't arrange a visit to the island, you can at least experience the joy of its cuisine. Here's my variation on a recipe that's one of the favorites there.

2 pounds red snapper fillets
3 ripe tomatoes, cut into 4 slices each
2 teaspoons basil
2 pieces fresh thyme, chopped
¾ cup freshly grated Parmesan cheese
½ cup dry white wine
4 tablespoons butter or margarine, melted
1 tablespoon fresh lime juice
1½ cups Shrimp Sauce (recipe follows, make ahead)
Freshly chopped parsley and lime wedges for garnish

Preheat oven to 350°. Rub fillets with lime juice. Grease well an ovenproof baking dish. Place the fillets, skin side up, in the dish. Place tomato slices on top of fillets. Sprinkle basil, thyme and Parmesan on top. Add the wine to the melted butter and pour over all. Bake for about 8 minutes or until fish flakes easily. Do not overcook. Remove from dish to warmed plates. Pour Shrimp Sauce over all. Garnish with freshly chopped parsley and lime wedges.

Shrimp Sauce

4 tablespoons butter or margarine
½ cup flour
2 cups fish stock*
½ cup heavy cream
¼ cup tiny shrimp or peeled and chopped shrimp

In a heavy saucepan, melt the butter. Whisk in the flour to make a roux.* Cook over medium-low heat for about 5 minutes or less. Add fish stock slowly to the roux. Bring to a simmer and cook for about 5 minutes more. Then, remove from heat. Add the shrimp. Cook for a few minutes or until shrimp turns pink and is cooked. Add heavy cream. Heat and serve over fish.

Serves: 4

*See Cooking Terms.

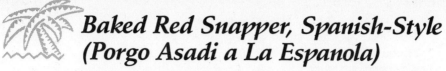

Baked Red Snapper, Spanish-Style (Porgo Asadi a La Espanola)

Here's a delightful recipe that was given to me by Lali and Glenn Fulqueira, chef/owners of the Lincoln Restaurant on Columbus Drive in Tampa, Florida, a street so filled with Hispanic eateries that it is often referred to as "Boliche Boulevard." (Boliche is a popular Spanish roast beef dish.)

6 snapper fillets, about 6–10 ounces each
Salt and freshly ground pepper to taste
1–2 medium onions, sliced ¼-inch thick
1–2 green peppers, sliced into ¼-inch thick rounds
1 14-ounce can whole tomatoes in juice, crushed
1 clove garlic, pressed
¾ cup fresh lemon juice mixed with 1 cup water or with ¾ cup orange juice
Hungarian paprika
¼ cup olive oil

Preheat oven to 350°. Arrange fillets in a heavy baking pan. Season with salt and pepper. Place the onions, green peppers, and tomatoes on top of the fillets.

Mix together the garlic and lemon juice mixture or orange juice, and pour over the fillets. Sprinkle with paprika. Using a pastry brush, coat the fillets with olive oil.

Bake for 20–25 minutes or until the fish is done.

Serves: 6

Grilled Swordfish with Mustard Sauce

The Hyatt Dorado Beach Hotel in Puerto Rico is situated on what once was the site of a pineapple and grapefruit plantation. It's loaded with coconut palms and even today coqueros—men who bind burlap around their bare feet—shinny up the trees with machetes to hack down the coconuts for two good reasons: one, so they don't fall on the guests' heads; and two, so they can be used as containers for the tropical drinks and desserts served there.

Enjoy a rum-based beverage with this easy-to-prepare dish created by Executive Chef Wilhelm Pirngruber of the Su Casa Restaurant. Follow the meal with Coconut Drop Cookies and some Coconut Cream to truly get the tropical "feel."

1 tablespoon butter
2 tablespoons finely chopped shallots
⅓ cup dry white wine
½ cup heavy cream

¼ cup coarse-grained Dijon-style mustard
4 6-ounce swordfish steaks
Lemon juice
Worcestershire sauce
Salt and freshly ground pepper to taste

Preheat the broiler or grill. Heat the butter in a small saucepan. Sauté the shallots for about 5 minutes or until tender. Add the wine and cook until most of the liquid is evaporated. Add the cream. Simmer until slightly thickened. Beat in the mustard. Remove from heat, cover, and keep warm while preparing fish.

Sprinkle the swordfish with a few drops each of lemon juice and Worcestershire sauce. Add salt and pepper to taste. Broil or grill 2–5 minutes per side, depending on the thickness of the fish. Spoon a little of the mustard sauce in the center of each of four plates. Top with the fish steaks. Add more sauce as desired.

Serves: 4

Florida Swordfish Stuffed with Lump Blue Crab

Mark Millitello of Max's Place in North Miami, Florida, is one of the most brilliant chefs in the sub-tropics. He likes to experiment with a variety of ingredients in many interesting ways. This recipe calls for the lump meat which are the solid lumps of white meat from the backfin of the body of the crab. Blue crabs can be found along the Atlantic and Gulf coasts from Massachusetts to Texas. Delicious!

2 slices bacon, chopped fine
1 tablespoon butter
2 ribs celery, peeled and diced
¼ cup diced onions
½ cup sliced wild or regular white mushrooms
4 ounces lump blue crab meat*, drained and picked through
Salt and freshly ground pepper to taste
1 teaspoon chopped fresh thyme
1 teaspoon chopped parsley
1 egg
2 8-ounce, 1-inch thick swordfish steaks
Caper Butter (recipe follows)

Sauté the bacon in butter until golden brown. Add the celery, onions, and mushrooms. When nearly tender, add crab meat, salt, pepper, and herbs. Remove from heat and mix in egg. Set aside to cool. Cut a pocket in each

*May use other varieties of crab meat, but blue crab is especially good in this dish.

swordfish steak and stuff it with the crab mixture. Grill until the steaks flake easily. Serve with Caper Butter.

Caper Butter

½ cup butter or margarine
2 tablespoons chopped capers
1 tablespoon chopped shallots
2 tablespoons fresh lemon juice
1 teaspoon freshly chopped dill
1 teaspoon Dijon-style mustard

Soften the butter at room temperature and mix it with the other ingredients until smooth. When the swordfish is cooked, place 2 dollops of Caper Butter on top of each steak. Serve additional Caper Butter on the side.

Serves: 2

Kon Tiki Shark Seaport

This recipe comes from the Seaport Inn in Port Richey, Florida—an interesting dish from a great seafood restaurant. Come on now, try it—it's not like you have to catch it!

Some features of shark meat that make it especially appealing are its firm texture, economical price, lack of bones, and pleasant taste.

1 cup fresh fruit such as: peaches, apples, plums, strawberries,
    grapes, or kiwifruit
2 pounds shark fillets (fresh, if possible)
Salt to taste
Flour for dredging
4 eggs, beaten
3–4 teaspoons clarified butter*
Shredded coconut (about ½ cup)
½ cup fresh lemon juice

Wash the fruit and slice into ¼-inch pieces. Pat dry.

Wash the fillets thoroughly and slice horizontally into ¼-inch thick fillets. Flatten each fillet with a mallet and lightly salt. Dip into flour. Then, dip into egg batter.

Heat the clarified butter in skillet to 400°. It must be very hot. Place the fillets in the skillet and cook until brown. Turn once and brown the other side. Remove the fillets to a serving platter. Add coconut to the remaining butter in the skillet. Place the fruit in the skillet and sauté very quickly. Add lemon juice to the mixture and heat through. Pour the sauce over the fillets. Serve with potatoes and fresh vegetables.

Serves: 6–8

*See Cooking Terms.

Curry Tuna Creole

A good number of my childhood meals consisted of tuna noodle casseroles and dried-out fish sticks... which were regularly served on Friday nights in my Roman Catholic household. When the Friday meat ban was lifted and we were allowed to eat meat on Fridays, we still ate tuna casseroles and dried-out fish sticks, although somehow it seemed to taste better! But it wasn't until several years later that I experienced the joy of fresh tuna—"You mean tuna doesn't grow in a tin?"—that I began to fully appreciate seafood.

Now I know there's hardly anything better than fresh tuna—it's heaven! Here's a nice Creole way to fix fresh tuna that was given to me by Terry Lambert, chef extraordinaire of Delicious Landing in St. George's, Grenada, West Indies. Allow time for the fish to marinate overnight.

1 10-ounce, 1-inch thick tuna fillet
½ cup soy sauce
1 tablespoon margarine or butter
¼ cup plus 1 teaspoon curry powder
1 medium onion, grated
1 onion, thinly sliced into rings
½ cup chopped celery
¼ cup chopped scallions
1 teaspoon thyme
2 teaspoons parsley
½ cup sliced fresh mushrooms
½ cup tomato juice
1 large tomato, sliced
2 tablespoons ketchup

To marinate the tuna, place it in a 2-inch deep pan. Mix together the soy sauce, 1 teaspoon curry, and grated onions, and pour it over the tuna. Allow the fish to marinate overnight, turning occasionally.

When ready to serve, remove the tuna from the marinade. Heat a sauté pan and add the margarine. Then, add the remaining curry, onion rings, celery, scallions, thyme, parsley, and mushrooms. In about 2 minutes, add the tuna. Cook for 2 minutes on each side. Then, add the tomato juice, tomato, and ketchup. Simmer for 4 minutes. Serve with Banana Grumby (see page 226).

Serves: 1

Fresh Tuna with Capers and Anchovies

Since I've been living in sub-tropical southern Florida, I find myself eating seafood three or four times a week—it's become a healthful and often economical habit.

Use the freshest tuna for this recipe from Laurenzo's Gourmet Italian Ristorante in North Miami Beach, Florida. Perhaps because I once lived in Rome, Italy, I treasure the pleasure of authentic Italian cuisine.

2 pounds tuna steaks, cut into 4 pieces
1 pound angel hair pasta*
¼ cup sliced garlic cloves
Extra virgin olive oil
8 basil leaves, finely chopped
1 small tomato, blanched, peeled, and chopped
½ cup pitted olives, chopped
½ cup capers, drained and chopped
½ cup (2 2-ounce cans) anchovies, chopped into medium pieces
1 tablespoon cognac
½ cup dry white wine

Prepare the angel hair pasta according to directions on the package. Sauté the sliced garlic in olive oil. When the garlic is browned, add all other ingredients except cognac and white wine. Cook a few minutes. Then, add the cognac and white wine. Add more or less depending on taste. Allow the sauce to cook on medium heat for about 10 minutes, being careful not to overcook the tuna.

Drain the pasta. Add a small amount of the sauce to a separate pan and toss the sauce with the pasta. Serve the tuna on a bed of pasta. Spoon more sauce on top. Double the amount of sauce if desired.

Serves: 4

*Angel hair pasta is a very finely-cut pasta. You may also use any other style of pasta.

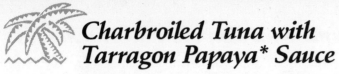

Charbroiled Tuna with Tarragon Papaya* Sauce

Papaya, which is known in the Caribbean as pawpaw, has a wonderfully sweet flavor whether it is cooked or eaten raw. Papayas are as common in the tropics as apples and oranges are in the United States. It makes wonderful sauces, as in this delicious version by Hermann Hiemeyer, Executive Chef at the Hyatt Regency Grand Cayman, British West Indies.

6 fresh tuna steaks, about 1-inch thick
Salt and freshly ground pepper to taste
1 fresh papaya
1¼ cups heavy cream
¼ cup dry sherry
Juice of ½ fresh lemon
1 bunch fresh tarragon, leaves only, chopped
Lime slices or fresh tarragon sprigs for garnish

Season the tuna with salt and pepper and broil it on medium heat (to avoid dryness) for about 2 minutes on each side.

Peel the papaya. Remove the seeds and blend the fruit to a fine purée in a blender or food processor. Now, push the purée through a fine sieve. In a small saucepan, reduce the heavy cream by ½ to thicken. Add in the papaya purée, sherry, lemon juice, tarragon, salt, and pepper. Boil for about 2 minutes. Then, place a layer of sauce on each plate. Set a tuna steak on the sauce. Serve with asparagus, carrots, and roasted potatoes. Garnish with lime slices or fresh tarragon sprigs.

Serves: 6

*See Tropical Glossary.

Shellfish

Lime Garlic Shrimp

Lime is a perfect fruit for the diet-conscious, as most of us are these days, it seems. It adds a nice zest to many dishes, without adding any calories to speak of.

Be careful not to overcook the shellfish!

2 pounds medium shrimp, cleaned, peeled, and deveined
¼ cup butter or margarine
4 cloves garlic, minced
1 cup minced scallions
¼ cup freshly squeezed lime juice
Coarsely ground black pepper
Tabasco or other hot sauce to taste
¼ cup freshly chopped parsley

Prepare the shrimp and set aside.

In a large sauté pan, melt the butter or margarine. Add the garlic and scallions and sauté until the scallions turn bright green. Add the shrimp and lime juice. Maintain the heat and cook just briefly, until shrimp turns pink. Stir in the black pepper, hot sauce, and parsley.

Serve over fluffy rice or on toasted, buttered rolls.

Serves: 4

Easy Scampi

Here's a nautical dining adventure that's as easy as 1 . . . 2 . . . Scampi!

Make the Scampi Butter ahead and your guests will be amazed at the speed with which you prepared the feast. You can also use the butter on other fish, or on escargot or chicken, too. The recipe was given to me by Stanley Pate of the famous Pate's restaurant in nautical Naples (Florida, not Italy!).

6 medium shrimp, cleaned, peeled, and deveined
Scampi Butter (recipe follows)
½ cup fresh bread crumbs
Sherry

Preheat oven to 475°. Lightly bread damp shrimp and place in a baking dish. Melt ⅓ of the scampi butter and pour over the shrimp evenly. (Reserve remaining scampi butter for future use!)

Bake for 8–10 minutes or until just done. Do not overcook. Sprinkle with sherry.

Serves: 1

Scampi Butter

1–2 cloves garlic, finely chopped
½ tablespoon finely chopped shallots
1 lemon, finely ground, including rind and pulp
½ teaspoon freeze-dried chives
2 dashes Tabasco sauce
1 dash Worcestershire sauce
¼ teaspoon salt
¼ teaspoon white pepper
½ cup butter, softened

Process the first 4 ingredients in a blender or food processor (or chop very fine). Add the remaining ingredients along with the softened butter. Mix well. Cover and refrigerate until ready to use.

Yield: ¾ cup

Shrimp with Mushrooms and Dill

Seafood is one of our most perfect foods, rich in minerals and vitamins, low in calories, and high in protein. Coupled with fresh vegetables and herbs, how can you miss? The dill in this recipe is great, but not over-powering.

1 pound medium-sized shrimp, cleaned, peeled, deveined, and butterflied
3 tablespoons butter or margarine
1 pound fresh mushrooms, sliced
3 cloves garlic, pressed
¼ cup flour
2 tablespoons dry white wine
1¼ cups milk
¼ cup heavy cream

2 teaspoons freshly chopped dill or 1 teaspoon dried
Salt and freshly ground pepper to taste
3 teaspoons brandy
Rice or toast points

Melt the butter on medium heat. Sauté the mushrooms and garlic for about 2 minutes. Gently add the shrimp. Sauté for a few minutes, until the shrimp turns white and is fully cooked. Gently remove the mixture to a bowl and cover it.

Stir the flour into the remaining pan juices. Cook until the mixture turns brown. While stirring, gradually whisk in the wine, milk, and cream. Cook, stirring constantly, until the mixture is very smooth and thick. Stir in the dill, salt, pepper, and brandy. Return the mushroom-shrimp mixture to the pan and heat well for a few minutes. Do not overcook.

Serve over rice or toast points.

Serves: 4–6

Peppered Shrimp

If you are able to visit Louis Pappa's famous Greek Restaurant in Tarpon Springs, Florida, you'll relish the scenic view and be surprised at the large crowds and fast service. If you can't visit the restaurant personally, you can at least try this popular shrimp entree at home.

1 cup vegetable oil
1½ cloves garlic, finely chopped
12 large shrimp, cleaned, peeled and deveined
3 ounces fresh lemon juice
3 ounces fresh lime juice
3 ounces dry vermouth
1 teaspoon salt
1 tablespoon freshly ground pepper or more, to taste
Lemon and lime slices for garnish

Heat oil and lightly sauté garlic until brown. Add the remaining ingredients and sauté, stirring occasionally, for 5–10 minutes or until shrimp are pink and slightly firm.

Serve with some of the pan juices. Garnish with lemon and lime slices.

Serves: 1

Cicely's Curried Shrimp

Grenada, the last jewel in the chain of Grenadine Islands, is a sleepy independent nation known primarily for its spices.

Cicely Roberts, chef for the past 12 years at the Calabash resort at L'Anse aux Epines, is master at blending spices and using just the needed amount. I was served this curried shrimp the first time I visited Calabash and haven't stopped thinking about it since. Be sure to use a good curry powder.

1 pound (10–12) large shrimp, cleaned, peeled, and deveined
Fresh lime juice
Salt to taste
Ve-tsin* (½ teaspoon or to taste)
1 clove fresh garlic, finely chopped or 1 teaspoon garlic powder
2 tablespoons curry powder
2 tablespoons olive oil or butter
1 medium onion, finely chopped
1 green pepper, finely chopped
½ cup chopped tomatoes
1 tablespoon freshly chopped celery
1 tablespoon freshly ground pepper
1 cup water or less
½ tablespoon cornstarch
Curry condiments: mango chutney, shaved coconut, chopped scallions,
    chopped tomatoes, and chopped peanuts

Season the shrimp with fresh lime juice, salt, and Ve-tsin.

Sauté the garlic and curry in a few tablespoons of olive oil for a few minutes. Add the onion, green pepper, tomatoes, celery, and ground pepper. Sauté until the vegetables are done. Add about 1 cup of water to the mixture and gently mix. Add ½ tablespoon of cornstarch to the mixture. Add more if necessary. Add the shrimp and cook about 1 minute or just until done. Don't overcook!

Serve with selection of curry condiments in small bowls or lazy susan.

Serves: 4

*Cicely uses Ve-tsin, an Oriental brand of seasoning from Hong Kong, but monosodium glutamate can be substituted. Because monosodium glutamte can cause an allergic reaction, some persons may wish to leave this seasoning out of the recipe. The back of the can of Ve-tsin reads, "A sprinkling of Ve-tsin will bring out the full natural flavor of your dishes and render them surprisingly delicious." OK!

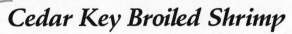

Cedar Key Broiled Shrimp

Here's a variation on a tasty little dish that is served at the popular Captain's Table restaurant in Cedar Key, one of the still relatively untouched areas left in Florida.

1 pound medium or large shrimp, cleaned, peeled, and deveined
½ cup olive oil
⅓ cup sauterne wine
⅓ cup fresh lemon juice
2 cloves garlic, finely minced
Hungarian paprika to taste
Salt to taste

Place shrimp in a broiling pan.

In the container of a food processor or blender, mix together the oil, wine, lemon juice, and garlic. Pour the mixture over the shrimp. Sprinkle paprika (about ½ teaspoon) on to each shrimp.

Broil for a few minutes until shrimp turns white. Turn at least once and baste with oil. Add salt to taste.

Serves: 2–4

Columbia Shrimp Supreme

A visit to Florida commands a trip to Tampa's historic Ybor City district and the Columbia Restaurant. This is one of their most popular dishes—perhaps, because the shrimp stay nice and juicy.

16 large shrimp, cleaned, peeled, and deveined
Juice of 1 lemon
1 teaspoon garlic powder
1 teaspoon salt
½ teaspoon freshly ground pepper
8 strips bacon
1 egg
½ cup milk
Flour
Vegetable oil for deep-frying

Pat the shrimp dry and marinate in lemon juice, garlic, salt, and pepper for 10 minutes.

Cut the bacon strips in half. Wrap a piece of bacon around each shrimp and secure with a toothpick. Beat together the egg and milk. Dip the shrimp in the egg mixture and roll in flour.

Deep-fry for about 5–8 minutes or until golden brown.

Serves: 2

Grilled Shrimp and Scallops with Salsa Picante

The Grand Bay Hotel in Coconut Grove, Florida, was recently awarded a Mobil five-star rating. After trying this simply delicious, flavorful and unusual salsa, you'll know why. A visit to the Miami area wouldn't be complete without a visit to their exquisite restaurant, the Grand Bay Cafe.

The leftover salsa can be kept for weeks and used as a dip for chips.

18 large shrimp, cleaned, peeled, and deveined
24 medium-sized sea scallops, cleaned
½ cup virgin olive oil
1 medium Spanish onion, chopped
2 cloves garlic, minced
2 red bell peppers, cut into ½-inch squares
2 green bell peppers, cut into ½-inch squares
6 green Mediterranean olives, chopped
12 black pitted olives, chopped
½ cup golden raisins
1 tablespoon tomato paste
4 whole beefsteak tomatoes or 8–10 Italian plum tomatoes, chopped
2 bay leaves, crushed
2 cups white wine
½ teaspoon cayenne pepper or to taste
Olive oil
Lemon slices for garnish
1 whole lemon, sliced
Salt to taste

Prepare the shrimp and scallops and set them aside.

To make the salsa: Heat the olive oil in a heavy medium-sized saucepan. Add the onion and the minced garlic. Let it brown. Add the red peppers, green peppers, olives, raisins, tomato paste, tomatoes, and crushed bay leaves. Cook for approximately 15 minutes. Add the white wine and cook for another 10 minutes. Season with salt and cayenne pepper.

Grill shrimp and scallops on an open barbecue grill, brushing with olive oil every couple of minutes. This should take no more than 7 minutes.

To serve, spoon the heated sauce on the middle of a serving plate. Place the seafood directly on top. Garnish with lemon slices.

Serves: 6

Shrimp Almendrina with Orange Mustard Sauce

The secret here is to be sure to use very large fresh shrimp. This recipe is from Pepin's restaurant in St. Petersburg, Florida. The owner, who everyone simply knows as "Jose," has created some of the most flavorful seafood dishes ever. Try this with Evander's White Sangria (see page 38).

2½ pounds jumbo shrimp, peeled and deveined, tails left intact
2 eggs
2 cups milk
2 cups flour
Salt and freshly ground pepper
4 cups sliced almonds
Vegetable oil for deep-frying
Orange Mustard Sauce (recipe follows)

In a medium-sized bowl, beat the eggs until light and fluffy. Stir in the milk. Gradually mix in the flour, blending well. Add salt and pepper to taste.

Holding the shrimp by the tail, dip into batter and allow excess to drip back into bowl. Do not cover tails with batter. Sprinkle all sides of batter-coated shrimp with almonds. Place on cookie sheet and refrigerate at least 2 hours before frying.

Heat oil to 375°. Deep-fry the shrimp a few at a time for about 2 minutes or until they turn pink. Do not overcook. Drain on paper towels and keep warm until all shrimp have been cooked. Serve immediately with Orange Mustard Sauce.

Serves: 6–8

Orange Mustard Sauce

¾ cup sweet orange marmalade
¼ cup chicken or beef stock
2 tablespoons fresh lemon juice
1 teaspoon dry mustard
Few drops hot pepper sauce

Thoroughly combine all ingredients.

Yield: 1 cup

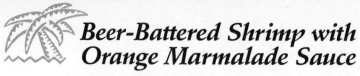

Beer-Battered Shrimp with Orange Marmalade Sauce

This is a light and natural tasting preparation for shrimp. Be sure to sift the flour well for a smoother coating. Try the batter with mussels and oyster, too. My girls, Julie and Christy, can't get enough of this dish which they like to indulge in while watching MTV.

1 cup flour, sifted
1½ teaspoons Hungarian paprika
Salt and pepper to taste
1 cup beer
1 pound jumbo shrimp (16–20 to the pound)
Flour for dredging
Vegetable oil for deep-frying
Fresh lemon juice (about 1 teaspoon)
Orange Marmalade Sauce (recipe follows)
Orange slices and fresh parsley for garnish

After sifting the flour well, combine it with the paprika, salt, and pepper. Gradually add the beer, stirring well with a wire whisk. The consistency of the batter should be that of rather thin pancake batter. Chill for 5–10 minutes.

Shell and devein the shrimp with a shrimp deveiner. With a sharp knife, cut the back nearly in half to form into a fantail shape. Sprinkle with fresh lemon juice and a little salt.

Holding the shrimp by their tails, dip them into the flour first and then into the beer batter. Deep-fry in vegetable oil at 350°. (Soybean oil works well and is virtually cholesterol free.) Be careful to place the shrimp one at a time into the oil so that they do not stick together. Fry until crisp and golden brown—a few minutes should do it. Serve with Orange Marmalade Sauce. Garnish the platter with orange slices and fresh parsley.

Orange Marmalade Sauce

1 cup orange marmalade
Juice of 1 large sweet orange
Pinch of ground ginger
1 teaspoon prepared horseradish

Put the above ingredients in the container of a food processor or blender and blend well for about 10 seconds.

Serves: 2–4, depending on the appetites

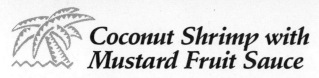

Coconut Shrimp with Mustard Fruit Sauce

It isn't often that a steak house serves great seafood, too. But there are exceptions to most rules as you'll see when you try this easy shrimp dish from Marty's Steak House in Tampa, Florida. Peanut oil is also good for frying the shrimp.

1 pound medium shrimp, cleaned, peeled, deveined, and butterflied
¾ cup milk
½ cup flour
2 eggs, well beaten
Shredded coconut
Vegetable oil for deep-frying
Coconut Amaretto liqueur
1 8-ounce can pineapple rings, drained
Mustard Fruit Sauce (recipe follows)

Dip the shrimp in milk, then very lightly dredge in flour. Dip into the beaten eggs, then, into the shredded coconut.

Heat the oil to 375° and fry the shrimp until golden brown. Sprinkle with more shredded coconut and lightly sprinkle with coconut Amaretto liqueur. Garnish the plate with pineapple rings. Serve with a cup of Mustard Fruit Sauce that has been warmed.

Serves: 4

Mustard Fruit Sauce

1 cup mustard fruits, chopped (available in most gourmet shops)
½ cup apricot preserves
2 teaspoons Grey Poupon mustard

Blend in a blender into a course sauce. Do not purée or liquify.

Yield: 1½ cups

Caribbean Coconut Fried Shrimp

When preparing this dish, the freshness of the coconut is of utmost importance. Select coconuts that "slosh" when gently shaken. And be sure to use only the freshest shrimp!

2 pounds large shrimp, cleaned, peeled, and deveined, tail section
   may be left on
2 cups all-purpose flour
1½ cups milk
1½ teaspoons baking powder

1 teaspoon curry powder
½ teaspoon salt
2 cups shredded coconut, preferably fresh
Vegetable oil for deep-frying

Measure ½ cup of flour and set aside. In a 1-quart mixing bowl, combine the remaining 1½ cups flour, milk, baking powder, curry, and salt. Place reserved flour and coconut in two separate shallow pans. Dredge the shrimp in flour, dip in batter, then roll in coconut. Fry in hot oil at 350° until coconut is golden brown. Drain on absorbent paper before transferring to warming tray. Serve hot with Lime Marmalade Sauce (page 245.)

Serves: 6

Curried Shrimp with Orange Rice

The orange is the cynosure of the citrus family, easily one of the most important fruits in the world. It is adaptable to a multitude of uses. In this recipe from the famed Chalet Suzanne restaurant in Lake Wales, Florida, the orange does wonderful things for the rice and nicely enhances the shrimp.

1 pound raw shrimp, cleaned, peeled, and deveined
1½ quarts water
2 tablespoons plus ½ teaspoon salt or to taste
¼ cup plus 1 tablespoon fresh lemon juice
⅓ cup butter or margarine
3 tablespoons unbleached flour
2 tablespoons curry powder
¼ teaspoon paprika
Dash of grated nutmeg
2 cups half-and-half
1 tablespoon finely chopped candied ginger (available in most
    Oriental markets)
1 teaspoon dry sherry
1 teaspoon onion juice
Dash of Worcestershire sauce
Orange Rice (recipe follows)
Assortment of condiments: chutney, chopped salted peanuts, chopped
    fresh parsley, crisp bacon bits, plain or toasted flaked coconut, chopped
    orange rind, or sliced apples dipped in lemon juice

Prepare the shrimp and set them aside.
Bring the water to a boil. Add 2 tablespoons of salt and ¼ cup of lemon juice. Drop in the shrimp and stir with a fork. Bring back to a rapid boil. Cook for 2 minutes or just until shrimp turn opaque. Do not overcook. Drain immediately. Put the shrimp in a glass bowl half full of ice water. Cover and refrigerate.

In a heavy saucepan or skillet, melt the butter. Blend in the flour, curry powder, ½ teaspoon of salt, paprika, and nutmeg. Cook and stir for about 3 minutes. Gradually add the half-and-half. Cook and stir until smooth and thickened. Add the ginger, 1 tablespoon of lemon juice, sherry, onion juice, Worcestershire sauce, and additional salt to taste. Remove the shrimp from refrigerator and drain the water. Stir in the shrimp and heat thoroughly. Serve with Orange Rice and condiments.

Orange Rice

1 cup raw long-grain rice
½ cup fresh orange juice
1 tablespoon freshly grated orange rind

Cook the rice according to your favorite method or package directions. Do not overcook. Add the orange juice and rind and stir. Reheat if necessary.

Serves: 4–6

Joe's Shrimp Creole

Bob Hosmon, a well respected food and wine reviewer in Florida, was recently quoted as saying "if the Sunshine State has two world-famous restaurants, one is Bern's Steak House in Tampa and the other is Joe's Stone Crab Restaurant in Miami Beach." Famous as Joe's is for its fresh stone crabs, they do a lot of other things well, too, like this Shrimp Creole.

2 pounds shrimp, cleaned, peeled, deveined, and cooked
½ cup chopped celery
½ cup chopped onion
¼ cup chopped salt pork
1 2½-pound can tomatoes
6 ounces chili sauce
2 ounces tomato paste
½ teaspoon thyme
1 teaspoon Maggi seasoning
2 cloves garlic, finely chopped
Salt and freshly ground pepper

Prepare the shrimp and set them aside.
Sauté the celery, onion, and salt pork until the salt pork is cooked. Add all the other ingredients, except the shrimp. Cook for 30 minutes over a low heat. Add the shrimp and warm through. Serve over rice.

Serves: 4–6

Lambi Dacali
(Sauced Conch)

Land crabs scurry about, lifting their heads as if to smell the spice-laden cooking at Delicious Landing in St. George's, Grenada. If you are anywhere near this restaurant managed by chef/owner Terry Lambert, you, too, may catch a whiff and suddenly change your sightseeing plans and head over for an early supper.

Floridians call it conch, but West Indians often refer to this spiral shellfish as lambi. By either name, you're sure to enjoy Chef Terry's wonderful sauced dish.

3 large lambi* (conch)
2 tablespoons brown sugar
1 onion, chopped
1 clove garlic, chopped
2 tablespoons chopped celery
1 tablespoon curry powder
1 teaspoon scallions
1 teaspoon thyme
2 tablespoons butter mixed with 1 garlic clove, minced
1 teaspoon cornstarch
2 tablespoons ketchup

"Beat the hell out of the lambi with a wooden meat tenderizer." Put the lambi in a large pot with enough water to cover, and boil for 45 minutes. Drain and reserve the liquid.

In a sauté pan, melt the brown sugar carefully. When melted, add the onion, garlic, celery, curry, scallions, thyme, and garlic butter. Blend well. Add the lambi and sauté until brown.

Add the cornstarch to ½ cup of the liquid left from boiling the lambi. Pour the cornstarch mixture and ketchup into the lambi mixture and mix well to thicken. Simmer for about 6 minutes.

Serves: 3

*See Tropical Glossary.

Scallops Singapore

You'll find that the fresh ginger root brings forth a distinctive, very addicting flavor. The oyster sauce is now available at most grocery stores, and is essential to recreating the famous Fort Lauderdale Mai Kai restaurant's popular dish. You may substitute sea scallops, but bay scallops are really "beautiful."

2 tablespoons peanut oil
¼ teaspoon salt
10 ounces bay scallops
1 1-inch slice fresh ginger root, smashed and chopped
7–8 large fresh mushrooms, sliced into thirds
½ tablespoon dry sherry
¼–½ cup chicken broth
1 tablespoon oyster sauce (may substitute soy sauce)
1 scallion, shredded
¼ teaspoon monosodium glutamate (optional)
1 tablespoon cornstarch

Heat 2 tablespoons peanut oil in a wok or frying pan over medium-high heat. Add salt. Add the scallops and ginger root and stir briefly. Add the mushrooms and sherry. Stir to prevent burning. Add chicken broth, oyster sauce, onions, monosodium glutamate, and enough cornstarch to slightly thicken the mixture. Remove immediately from heat and serve.

Serves: 2

Stone Crabs

Where else could I be certain to get the perfect stone crab recipe, but Joe's Stone Crab Restaurant in Miami Beach? As one would suspect, the house specialty is stone crabs, and they serve it with a magnificent mustard sauce. Freshest is best, so when you are purchasing your shellfish, be picky about just how long these fellows have been around. And fellows they are, as the fishermen select only the male crab. they remove one claw and throw the crab back in the water so that it will regenerate another claw.

5–6 fresh stone crab claws, about 1½ pounds per person
Ice
Lemon wedges
Hot melted butter
Joe's Stone Crab Restaurant Mustard Sauce (see page 241)

Store crabs in ice until ready to serve. To crack the claws for serving, place then on a cutting board and cover with a cloth. Crack the shell with a wide-headed mallet, starting at the knuckle of the crab and working toward the claw.

Pile the prepared claws in a pyramid shape on a platter, symmetrically arranged. Garnish with lemon wedges. Serve with hot melted butter and Mustard Sauce.

Note: Chilling firms up the flesh of the crab, so be sure to chill well. Joe's serves these with a variety of salted breads, Cottage Fried Sweet Potatoes (see page 229), and a nice selection of wines.

Serves: 1

Pan-Fried Oysters

A graduate of the Culinary Institute of America in Hyde Park, New York, Chef Michael Chiarello has created some wonderful dishes with ingredients indigenous to South Florida. He lives in California now, but the tastes of his cuisine linger on like in this oyster creation.

2 egg yolks
6 ounces Anchor Steam beer or other medium-dark beer may be
    substituted
2 tablespoons all-purpose flour
Pinch of salt
12 large oysters
Rock salt for bedding
½ bunch spinach
4 ounces Mango Remoulade (recipe follows)
½ cup corn oil
⅓ cup flour

Mix egg yolks and beer. Whisk in flour and salt. Set aside for 15 minutes.

Shuck the oysters and arrange the shells on a bed of rock salt. Wash the spinach and dry thoroughly. Roll the spinach leaves in bundles and slice thinly to make a chiffonade. Line the oyster shells with the spinach. Put 1 teaspoon Mango Remoulade in each shell.

Heat about ¼ cup corn oil in a large skillet on medium-high heat. Dredge oysters in flour and dust off excess. Dip in beer batter and fry on both sides until light brown. Drain on paper towels and place in shells. Drizzle with remaining remoulade and serve.

Mango Remoulade

1 very ripe mango, peeled and puréed
2 limes, seeded
1¼ cups olive oil
2 egg yolks, room temperature
½ bunch of cilantro (coriander)

Blend all ingredients in food processor or blender until smooth.

Serves: 2–4

Steamed Clams Minorcan-Style

About seven great-grandfathers ago, James Augustine Ponce's ancestors helped build the famous Castillo de San Marcos in St. Augustine, Florida. The Castillo is a huge fortress that was built by the Spanish in the late 1600s to protect the city from marauding pirates. And about 25 years ago, Ponce and his sons, Dave and Jim, built the famous Captain Jim's Conch

House where visitors are welcome and seafood selections are different from your everyday fare. While the restaurant will probably never reach the landmark status of the fort, it is certainly a favorite dining spot for the locals. This steamed clam dish is one reason why.

12 large clams for steaming
2 ounces butter
4 medium onions, thinly sliced
¼ cup Lea & Perrins Worcestershire sauce
2 stalks celery, chopped

Combine the butter, onions, Worcestershire sauce, and celery in a heavy kettle. Bring to a boil and add the clams. Steam for about 8–10 minutes or until all clams are wide open. Shake pan often. Discard any clams that do not open. Place steamed clams in a shallow dish and pour broth over all.

Serves: 1

Wakulla Springs Crab Imperial

In a tranquil forested setting just outside of Tallahassee, Florida, sits a beautiful lodge called Wakulla Springs. Chef Gerard Gowdy applies true southern hospitality to guests in his well-known dining room. Here's one of the specialties from his kitchen.

1 pound lump* crabmeat, picked through with cartilage removed
2 stalks celery, peeled and minced
⅓ cup mayonnaise
1 teaspoon fresh lemon juice
Salt to taste
¼ teaspoon monosodium glutamate (optional)
2 dashes Worcestershire sauce
2 cloves garlic, pressed
Butter or margarine for greasing casserole
Fresh cracker crumbs
Parmesan cheese

Preheat oven to 350°. Prepare a well-greased glass casserole dish. In a separate mixing bowl, combine all ingredients except the cracker crumbs and cheese. Mix well. Let sit for about 1 hour.

Place mixture into the buttered casserole dish. Top with cracker crumbs and Parmesan cheese. Dot with butter. Bake for about 20 minutes.

Serves: 4

*This is the choicest crabmeat, also called "backfin," which consists of while pieces of white meat from the body of the crab.

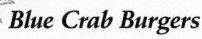

Blue Crab Burgers

Crab cakes, or burgers, are one the tastiest treats ever created. Served as a main course or between crusty Cuban bread, they're luscious!

1 pound blue crab meat, flaked (may substitute other varieties)
2 tablespoons butter or margarine
½ cup chopped celery
¼ cup chopped onions
1 small green pepper, chopped
Tabasco sauce to taste
Worcestershire sauce to taste
Salt and freshly ground pepper to taste
2–3 tablespoons evaporated milk
½ cup cracker meal or more

Sauté the crab meat in butter or margarine. Add the celery, onions, and bell pepper. Cook until soft. Season with Tabasco sauce, Worcestershire sauce, salt, and pepper.

Put the mixture in a bowl. Add the milk and enough cracker meal to bind everything together. Shape into flat burgers. Cook on a grill or in a frying pan to which a small amount of vegetable oil has been added. Serve with Tabasco sauce, for those who like it extra hot.

Serves: 2–4

Mama's Crab Backs

A five-minute excursion from St. George's, the capital city of Grenada, in an area called Belmont, the internationally-praised Mama's Restaurant serves 18–26 courses family style. There is no menu—just the best and freshest foods that Mama herself buys and prepares in her small kitchen. From Callaloo Soup to fresh fish to tattoo (armadillo) to chicken, it's a unique and memorable experience.

"Mama" is Insley Wardally, a happy and pleasantly plump woman whose determination to succeed has propelled her through many difficult times. She told me how she started her restaurant with "one table, six chairs, no fridge, no electric, and no lumps" (ice). And we complain about not having a food processor!

The night I visited Mama's, I was served 21 different courses. The incredible meal's finishing touch was exotic soursop ice cream and an invitation to view her homey Grenadian kitchen.

Here's her famous recipe for Crab Backs*. You can use most varieties of crab, although Mama uses the land crab from the island of Carricou.

*You may be curious as to why it is called "crab back." It's rather simple—it's because one stuffs the back of the crab!

1 cup crab meat, reserve shells (may use 4 land or sea crabs)
4–6 slices bacon
1 large onion, finely chopped
2 shallots, finely chopped
½ cup fresh bread crumbs
Pinch of thyme
Salt and freshly ground pepper to taste
Hot pepper sauce to taste

Preheat oven to 350°. Clean the crab shells well and set aside. Fry the bacon until crisp. Crumble. Reserve about 2 tablespoons of the bacon grease. Heat the grease, then fry the onions and shallots until just translucent. Add the crab meat, bread crumbs, thyme, crumbled bacon, salt, pepper, and hot pepper sauce and mix well. Stuff the crab shells. Bake for 15–20 minutes.

Serves: 4

Coconut Lobster

Because there is such an abundance of fresh seafood, Jamaican chefs are often given to experimentation with whatever the island waters have offered them for the day. For instance, here's a unique recipe for preparing lobster—it comes from the Mallard Beach Hyatt in Jamaica. Because I live in Florida, I generally use Florida spiny lobster, but any variety of lobster will do nicely.

Serve in the lobster shells, if desired.

Meat of 4 medium-sized cooked lobsters, shelled and cut into chunks
½ cup milk
1 cup cream of coconut*
1 small onion, finely chopped
2 scallions, finely chopped
2 springs thyme or 1 tablespoon powdered thyme
2 tablespoons curry powder
Salt and freshly ground white or black pepper to taste
Dash cayenne pepper
½ cup freshly grated Parmesan cheese
Fresh lime or lemon wedges

Preheat oven to 400°. Mix the milk and coconut cream together. Heat in a large saucepan over moderate heat. Add the onion, scallions, thyme, and curry powder. Stir and cook for about 5 minutes. Add the lobster chunks,

*See Tropical Glossary

salt, pepper, and cayenne. Cook slowly for 7–8 minutes so that all flavors are well blended. Remove to a baking dish and sprinkle with grated cheese. Bake for about 15 minutes or until lobster is browned. Serve with lime or lemon wedges.

Serves: 4

Lobster au Pan Do

How many times have you felt as if your vocabulary was possibly missing a few key words or your culinary lingo was not quite up to date on the latest in food trends? I gently queried Terry Lampert, chef/owner of Delicious Landing in Grenada, West Indies, as to how he would define the phrase "pan do." Expecting to hear some incredible intellectual explanation, he simply replied, "That's easy, you do it in a pan." So much for culinary intellectualism.

Here is Terry's very simple dish that was beautifully presented in his and partner Terry Dalton's popular restaurant. Be careful not to add salt or soy sauce to lobster (or to conch) as it toughens the flesh.

1 live spiny lobster
2 tablespoons butter mixed with 1 clove garlic, minced
2 tablespoons curry powder
1 onion, thinly sliced into rings
1 cabbage heart, chopped
1 chayote, diced*
1 large tomato, diced
2 tablespoons ketchup
1 teaspoon cinnamon
Pinch of nutmeg or to taste
¼ cup fresh coconut milk**

Boil the lobster for 20 minutes or less. Allow to cool, pull out the tail meat and cut it into chunks. Reserve the shell.

Melt the butter in a sauté pan. Add the curry and stir to combine well. Add the onion rings, chopped cabbage hearts, chayote chopped tomatoes, lobster chunks, and ketchup. Sauté for 4 minutes. Add the cinnamon and nutmeg. Pour in the coconut milk, mix, and simmer for 6 minutes. Serve in the lobster shell.

Serves: 1

*See Tropical Glossary.
**See Can Do.

Steamed Garlic Crabs

One of our most enjoyable family traditions is "crab night," when we steam huge amounts of local blue crabs. Then we sit, pick, and eat the delightful flesh of these delectable delicate creatures. My daughters, Julie and Christy like the crabs with loads of garlic, which can be increased or decreased, depending on your pleasure.

Have some hot wet cloths handy to wipe your hands because they're bound to get nice and greasy.

5–6 pounds blue crabs, back shells and apron removed, stomachs and
    lungs removed, and broken in half down the middle
1½ cups olive oil
5 whole bulbs garlic (not cloves!), peeled
2 teaspoons white pepper
2 tablespoons chopped fresh parsley

Add 1 cup of water to the bottom of a wok that has a steamer rack. Place the blue crabs on the steamer rack. Steam the crabs over high heat for about 5 minutes or until they turn red. Remove the crabs to a separate large bowl.

Remove the steamer rack and pour the water from the wok. Add the oil, garlic, and pepper to the wok and heat on medium setting. Add the crabs back and toss well to thoroughly coat with the garlicky oil. With steel tongs, lift the crabs out of the wok and place in a serving bowl.

Serve with crab "crackers" and a wooden mallet to break the claws. Be sure to have plenty of napkins and spread lots of newspapers on your table so shells can be discarded with minimum worry. Devour!

Serves: 4

Poultry

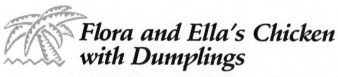

Flora and Ella's Chicken with Dumplings

Ella Burchard of the popular Flora and Ella's restaurant in LaBelle, Florida, features old-fashioned home cooking almost exactly as it was done in the 1940s. A dish of their famous Chicken with Dumplings will soothe any hungry tummy!

1 3–3½ pound chicken, cleaned
1–1½ quarts water
1 small onion, chopped
2 stalks celery, chopped
1 teaspoon salt
1 teaspoon black pepper
1 cup flour
Pinch of baking powder
1 large egg
¼–⅓ cup chicken broth
Salt and pepper to taste

In a large pot, place the chicken, water, onion, celery, salt, and pepper. Bring to a boil then simmer the chicken until done, about 1 hour. Remove chicken from the broth and allow to cool. Reserve the broth.

In a bowl, place flour and baking powder. Make a deep well in the center. Add the egg and ¼–⅓ cup of the chicken broth. Gently beat egg and broth together. Mix in surrounding flour. Form into a ball. Pinch small amounts of dough and roll on a floured board. Roll very thin. Cut in ½-inch strips and drop into boiling chicken broth. Cook slowly until tender.

Meanwhile, remove the bones from the meat. Cut the meat into bite-size pieces and return to the pot with the dumplings once they are tender. Add salt and pepper to taste.

Heat through and thicken with flour if necessary.

Serves: 6

Old-Fashioned Chicken Casserole

When the weather gets a little cool here in tropical southern Florida, around January or February, I like to fix one of Ma Hopkins's specials from the Hopkins's Boarding House in Pensacola, Florida. The regular bed-and-breakfast crowd finish every finger lickin' bit of this favorite dish. When I prepare it at home, my husband feels he's back home in Kentucky.

1 stewing chicken, cleaned and innards removed
1 8-ounce package flat egg noodles
1 16-ounce can tomato sauce
1 8-ounce can tomato paste
2 onions, chopped
1 green pepper, chopped
½ cup peeled and chopped celery
2 teaspoons oregano
Salt and freshly ground pepper to taste

Place the stewing chicken in a large kettle. Cover with water and simmer about 50–60 minutes or until tender. Remove the chicken from the broth and let cool on a plate. Set aside.

Cook the noodles in the remaining broth until they are almost tender. Add the remaining ingredients, cover and simmer until the vegetables are tender.

While the vegetables are cooking, remove the bones from the chicken. Return the chicken to the kettle just before the vegetables are done.

Serves: 6

Broiled Chicken with Tropical Barbecue Sauce

For an instantly delicious dinner, keep a jar of this tangy sauce in your refrigerator. It beats the bottled brands any day. You can almost taste the tamarind, one of the dominant flavors in the Worcestershire sauce. The sauce is better if prepared a day ahead.

1 4–6 pound broiler, cut up
1 cup molasses
½ cup apple cider vinegar
4 tablespoons Worcestershire sauce
2 tablespoons Dijon-style mustard
½–1 teaspoon hot sauce*
¼ cup fresh orange juice
Lime slices for garnish

Wash and dry the chicken pieces well. Prick the chicken with a fork so

*Pickapeppa brand is fine, or any homemade island hot sauce.

that marinade will seep in. Heat the broiler. Place the molasses, vinegar, Worcestershire sauce, mustard, and hot sauce in the container of a food processor or blender. Blend thoroughly.

Broil the chicken until nicely browned. Brush on the sauce with a pastry brush during the last 10–15 minutes, basting constantly.

Serve sauce on the side for dipping. Garnish chicken with slices of lime. Serve with chunks of Cuban Bread.

Serves: 4–6

Marinated Grilled Breast of Chicken

Dining at the Colony Beach Restaurant in Longboat Key is a truly romantic experience. They offer a fine selection of choice champagnes, including Dom Perignon, or a variety of vintage wines, such as a 1973 Château Lafite-Rothschild or a Château St. Jean Chardonnay, all served by the glass. I like a glass of Chardonnay with this easy-to-prepare entrée.

    1 large chicken breast, split
    2 tablespoons chopped shallots
    2 tablespoons fresh lemon juice
    ½ cup Chablis
    2 bay leaves
    1 teaspoon Herbes de Provence
    1 teaspoon fresh minced garlic
    ½ cup olive oil
    Chicken Sauce (recipe follows)
    Parsley for garnish

Put the chicken breast halves in a bowl or pan. Combine the next 7 ingredients and pour it over the chicken. Marinate for a minimum of 2 hours.

Grill the chicken for about 10–15 minutes. Top with Chicken Sauce and garnish with chopped fresh parsley.

Chicken Sauce

    1 onion, finely chopped
    1 carrot, finely diced
    1 stalk celery, finely diced
    2 tablespoons flour or more
    1 tablespoon butter

Simmer the onion, carrot, and celery in 1 quart of water for about 2 hours. Reduce* by ½ and strain. Make a roux* by mixing the flour with butter to form a paste. Use roux to thicken the sauce.

Serves: 2

*See Cooking Terms.

Chicken Roti

This chicken roti is a mixture of chicken and seasonings that is put into a piece of bread called a purie, and then eaten like a sandwich. The fillings vary from island to island in the Caribbean, depending on available ingredients and preferred seasonings.

In Grenada, I had lunch with one of the locals who preferred his roti served with the bones still in the chicken. He liked to pick the meat off the bones, which can be a time-consuming process. I prefer mine boned, like in this mouth-watering recipe that I begged from Chef Joseph Kissoonlal. He is of East Indian descent, and is the master behind the fine foods served at Granny B's Kitchen in Miami, a restaurant that features slow-cooked, fast food(!) Caribbean-style.

Dough

4 cups all-purpose flour
2 tablespoons baking powder
Pinch of salt
2 teaspoons vegetable oil
1½ cups lukewarm water

Chicken Curry

2½ pounds chicken, skinned, boned, and cut into 1½-inch cubes
1 small onion, finely chopped
1 teaspoon chopped garlic
1 scallion, finely chopped
½ teaspoon finely chopped Scotch Bonnet pepper*
1 teaspoon salt
3 tablespoons curry powder
1 tablespoon jira*, ground
½ tablespoon freshly ground black pepper
2 tablespoons vegetable oil for each purie
Scallions and finely chopped Scotch Bonnet pepper for garnish
½ cup water or more

To prepare the puries, combine the flour, baking powder, and salt in a mixing bowl. Pour the oil into the water, then add this mixture to the flour mixture to form a dough. Mix well. Knead for about 5 minutes until dough is very smooth. Divide into 6 balls of dough. Set aside for about 2 hours, covered with a damp cloth. Using a rolling pin, roll each ball into a thin flattened circle, a purie, about 9 inches in diameter. Set aside, covered.

To prepare the filling, combine the chicken and all the other ingredients except the oil and the garnish. Mix well and marinate for 2 hours or longer. When done marinating, add 2 tablespoons oil to a saucepan and heat to medium. Add the chicken mixture and cook, stirring constantly for about 5

*See Tropical Glossary.

minutes. Add the water and cook on low for about 5 minutes, or until chicken is tender. Keep warm.

Add 2 tablespoons of oil to a skillet or grill. Place the rolled puries on the skillet. Fry each side for about 2 minutes, or until lightly browned. Brush each side with margarine or oil. Wrap in clean towel to keep warm until ready to serve.

When ready to serve, fold about 2 tablespoons of chicken mixture into each round and serve. Garnish with scallions and Scotch Bonnet pepper.

Serves: 6

Chicken Florida

A popular department store in Florida held a statewide cooking contest for quick and easy, one-dish meals. Being chosen to act as a judge afforded me a great opportunity to sample some outrageously good creations. I especially like this winner from Bill Adams of Gainesville, Florida, perhaps one of the area's next great chefs.

4 chicken breast halves, boned and skinned, split again
1 cup Triple Sec
1 cup flour
Salt and freshly ground pepper to taste
2 eggs, beaten
1 cup freshly grated coconut
2 cups vegetable oil
2 cups orange marmalade
2 limes, seeded and juiced
½ teaspoon thyme
½ teaspoon rosemary
½ teaspoon cinnamon
4 oranges, sectioned
4 cups yellow rice, cooked
Fruit sections for garnish

Marinate the chicken in the liqueur for at least 2 hours refrigerated. Drain the chicken.

Dredge the chicken in flour to which salt and pepper has been added. Dip the chicken into beaten eggs and dredge in coconut.

Carefully heat the oil to about 375° and fry the chicken until golden brown. Do not overcook. Remove the chicken from the skillet. Pour off all oil except about 2 tablespoons. Add the marmalade, lime juice, and spices. Bring to a bubbly boil. Now add the chicken back into the pan and cook on each side for about 5 minutes. Just before the chicken is ready, add the oranges and heat.

Serve over hot fluffy yellow rice and garnish with fruit sections.

Serves: 4

Chicken with Coconut Curry Sauce

This recipe was given to me by Corinna Duczek, hostess at the Ti Paradis restaurant in Cap Haitien, Haiti. Together with owner David Woodard, a talented artist, they create a meal as pretty as any picture.

The quality of your curry will have a lot to do with the taste of the finished product, so be sure to use a very good curry blend.

   Salt and freshly ground pepper to taste
   Flour for dredging
   2 whole frying chickens, cut up
   ½ cup vegetable oil for frying
   Coconut Curry Sauce (recipe follows)

Place salt, pepper, and flour in a large paper bag. Place the chicken pieces in the bag 3 or 4 at a time, and shake vigorously until coated. Heat oil in a very large heavy skillet or two skillets. Carefully add the chicken so as not to splash oil. Cover and cook about 25 minutes or until tender, turning occasionally. Remove to a plate and set aside.

Coconut Curry Sauce

   2 medium onions, sliced
   3 ripe medium tomatoes
   1 green pepper, sliced
   1 tablespoon curry powder or to taste
   Pinch of saffron (may substitute Bijol*)
   Hungarian paprika to taste
   ½ cup peeled and grated fresh coconut
   3 cups chicken stock**
   4 cups cooked rice

Pour off all but 2 tablespoons of the leftover oil from the chicken. In the same pan in which the chicken was cooked, add the onions, tomatoes, and pepper. Add the curry, saffron, and paprika. Mix to coat the vegetables. Cook for a few minutes, then return chicken to the pan with the vegetables. Simmer gently.

In the meantime, simmer the coconut in the chicken stock for about 20 minutes. Let sit for another 15 minutes. Strain and discard coconut gratings.

Pour the coconut stock into the chicken and sauce. Blend well. Heat for about 10 minutes. Thicken with a little cornstarch if necessary. Serve with rice on the side or place chicken on a bed of rice. Pour sauce over all.

Serves: 4–6

  *See Tropical Glossary.
  **See Cooking Terms.

Chicken with Orange-Raisin Sauce

During the time of Spanish settlement, Florida Indians were great consumers of sour oranges. To sweeten the oranges, they would pierce the skin of the orange and fill it with honey.

Here is a simple but elegant recipe for chicken lovers. Use fresh Florida orange juice for best results.

3–4 pound chicken, cut up, skinned, and flattened
4 tablespoons flour
1 teaspoon salt
6 tablespoons extra virgin olive oil
1 medium onion, chopped
2 cups chicken broth*
1 cup fresh orange juice
½ cup fresh sour orange** juice
½ cup raisins
⅛ teaspoon ground cloves
3 tablespoons cornstarch mixed with cold water until smooth

Dredge the chicken in flour and salt. Sauté in the oil with the onion until the chicken is golden brown. Add the remaining ingredients, except the cornstarch, stir well, and cook for about 50–60 minutes or until chicken is tender. Add the cornstarch mixture and cook until sauce thickens.

Serve over rice with a nice leafy spinach salad.

Serves: 4–6

*See Cooking Terms.
**See Tropical Glossary.

Chicken with Scalloped Bananas

Just beyond the famous Skyway Bridge connecting Florida's St. Petersburg/Tampa area to Sarasota and Bradenton is a cozy little eatery, the Crab Trap, that serves some of the tastiest and freshest food in the area. I always make it a point to stop in for lunch or dinner whenever I'm en route to beautiful Sarasota. Try this simple tropical dish with a light fruity wine.

4 chicken breast halves, boned and skinned
4 tablespoons butter
Salt and freshly ground pepper to taste
8 Scalloped Bananas (recipe follows)
4 peach halves and juice

Sauté the chicken breasts in butter, until tender and browned. Season with salt and pepper to taste. Serve each with 2 Scalloped Bananas alongside and a peach half and juice on top.

Scalloped Bananas

4 medium ripe bananas, peeled
1 cup flour
½ cup milk
1 cup bread crumbs, unseasoned
Vegetable oil for deep-frying
5 tablespoons sugar
5 tablespoons cinnamon

Cut each banana into 3 or 4 1¾-inch chunks. Roll each chunk in the flour. Dip in milk, then roll in bread crumbs. Deep-fry in oil heated to 350° until golden. Combine the sugar and cinnamon. Roll the bananas in the cinnamon/sugar mixture. Serve warm, next to the chicken. These can also be served as a side dish with other entrees or as a dessert.

Serves: 4–6

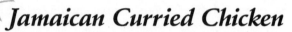

Jamaican Curried Chicken

Curry powder and fresh ginger combine forces to produce a flavorful curry that's easy to prepare. Enid Donaldson, a cuisine consultant for Jamaica, offered this lovely dish. I have also tried it without boning the chicken, and that's good, too.

2 medium-sized frying chickens, cut up and boned
Vegetable oil for frying (about 3 tablespoons)
2 cloves garlic, chopped
2 scallions, chopped
½ teaspoon pepper
1 tablespoon curry powder
1 teaspoon allspice
1 1-inch piece ginger, peeled and finely chopped
1 cup coconut milk*
2 large potatoes, peeled and diced
6–8 cups steamed rice
Mango chutney, coconut milk, and yogurt for garnish

In a stew pot, heat the vegetable oil. Add the garlic, scallions, pepper, curry, allspice, and ginger and cook for a few minutes. Add the chicken and simmer, covered, on low heat about 10 minutes. Add the coconut milk and potatoes, and continue to cook for 30–40 minutes.

Serve over hot steamed rice with a selection of condiments such as mango chutney, coconut milk, and yogurt.

Serves: 6–8

*See Tropical Glossary.

Ginger Chicken

Ginger, the spice lover's spice, adds a special zest to just about anything to which it is added. Caribbean cooks covet the spice and it's rarely absent from their meals.

This recipe was given to me by Cicely Roberts, head chef extraordinaire at the Calabash Resort in St. George's, Grenada. Allow time to marinate.

4 boneless skinned breasts of chicken, split
2 tablespoons minced onion
1 teaspoon minced garlic
1 tablespoon seasoning salt
1 teaspoon salt
1 teaspoon basil
1 tablespoon plus 1 teaspoon ground ginger
1 teaspoon Worcestershire sauce
2 teaspoons Ve-tsin* or monosodium glutamate (optional)
Corn oil for frying
1 tablespoon margarine
1 tablespoon flour
1 chicken bouillon cube
½ cup water
½ cup sherry
Fresh parsley sprigs for garnish

Season the chicken breasts with 1 tablespoon onion, garlic, seasoning salt, salt, basil, 1 tablespoon ginger, Worcestershire sauce, and 1 teaspoon Ve-tsin. Let stand in refrigerator for at least 1 hour or refrigerate to marinate overnight.

Preheat oven to 350°. Pan-fry the chicken in hot oil for 30 minutes or until golden brown. Remove chicken from frying pan and place in an ovenproof baking dish or casserole that has been well greased.

Pour off the leftover oil from the skillet in which the chicken was fried. Make a ginger sauce by adding 1 tablespoon margarine or butter and 1 tablespoon onion to the pan. Sauté the onion until it's translucent. Whisk in the flour and stir to make the mixture smooth. Add the chicken cube, 1 teaspoon ginger, 1 teaspoon Ve-tsin, and sherry. Simmer for a few minutes, stirring until it makes a nice sauce. Strain the sauce through a wire strainer over the chicken breasts. Bake for about 1 hour. Garnish with fresh parsley sprigs.

Serves: 4

*Ve-tsin is an Oriental "gourmet powder" used frequently in the Caribbean. It is made up of monosodium glutamate.

Lola's Caribbean Fried Chicken with Sweet Potatoes

Lola is a colorful restaurant on West 22nd Street in New York City that's known for its flamboyant Jamaican owner, Lola, and its nice touches of the Caribbean, including this chicken that has an added Oriental/Creole taste. Add more hot sauce if you like it spicy.

1 frying chicken, cut into small pieces
Juice of 1 large lemon
3–4 cloves garlic, minced
Hungarian paprika
Coarsely ground black pepper
Salt
Soy sauce
Louisiana hot sauce
2 cups flour
Crisco oil
½ cup butter
2 sweet potatoes

Marinate chicken pieces in lemon juice for 30 minutes. Rub garlic into each piece. Season each piece with generous amounts of paprika and black pepper. Salt each piece lightly. Then, sprinkle with soy sauce and hot sauce.

Pour flour into paper bag. Shake 2–3 pieces of chicken at a time in the bag, just to coat. Meanwhile, fill a frying pan half way with Crisco oil. Carefully, heat on high until the oil begins to smoke. Turn heat down to medium-low and add the butter. Put the chicken pieces in the pan. Cover and fry for about 15–25 minutes or until golden brown, turning at least once.

Meanwhile, peel the sweet potatoes and slice lengthwise to ¼-inch thick. Bake in buttered parchment paper at 250° for 15–20 minutes or until the slices are tender and intensified in color.

Serves: 2

Chicken Cacao with Avocado Salsa

Chef Michael Chiarello, who is only 26 years old, continues to gain recognition as one of America's up-and-coming food artists, winning kudos from a multitude of dining critics including *Food and Wine* magazine writer John Mariani. The special ethnic and regional touches Chef Chiarello creates are as exciting to the mind as to the palate.

"Cacao" comes from the scientific name of the cocoa plant, *theobroma cocao*. The seeds of the shrub or small tree are processed into chocolate which is then used in many ways, including the exciting combination in this dish.

   ¼ cup virgin olive oil
   2 pounds chicken breast fillets
   1 cup flour
   1 cup white wine
   ¼ cup minced shallots
   1½ cups chicken stock*
   ⅔ cup heavy cream
   Avocado Salsa (recipe follows)
   4 tablespoons minced cilantro (coriander leaves)
   1 ounce bittersweet chocolate, shaved
   ¼ cup butter
   8 blue corn tortillas, thinly sliced and fried (the flour is available at most
      gourmet shops)

Heat the olive oil in a sauté pan. Add the chicken fillets that have been dusted with flour. Sauté until light brown. Add the white wine and shallots. Reduce* by half. Add the chicken stock and cream. Simmer for 1 minute. Remove the chicken with tongs and arrange on a plate. Place a small cup of Avocado Salsa in the middle.

Reduce the cream sauce until thick. Remove from heat and swirl in the cilantro, chocolate, and butter. Pour over chicken and arrange fried tortilla juliennes* around the chicken.

Avocado Salsa

   3 avocados, peeled and diced in ¼-inch chunks
   ¼ bunch minced cilantro (coriander leaves)
   1–2 onions, diced
   1 teaspoon minced garlic
   Dash of Tabasco sauce
   Salt and freshly ground pepper to taste
   Juice of 2 limes

Blend all the ingredients together in the container of a blender or food processor until coarsley chopped.

Serves: 4–6

*See Cooking Terms.

Gingered Chicken with Mango

There are many varieties of mangoes, although the better varieties have a rich aromatic flavor. Be sure to prepare this recipe using nice, ripe mangoes. A mango is ripe when it gives off a rich, fruity aroma; squeezing it is usually not enough since some ripe mangoes will yield to the touch while others will not.

The invention of this recipe can be attributed to my devotion to the ingredients it contains.

¼ cup olive oil or vegetable oil
2 cloves fresh garlic, crushed
2 pounds chicken breast fillets, skinned
1 cup peeled and diced mangoes
¼ cup dark brown sugar
¼ teaspoon freshly ground cloves
2 teaspoons ginger
¼ teaspoon nutmeg
1 teaspoon soy sauce
Salt and freshly ground pepper to taste

Heat the oil in a heavy frying pan. Add the garlic and sauté for a few minutes. Then, add the chicken fillets. Cook for about 15–20 minutes until the chicken is cooked through.

Meanwhile, in a medium-sized bowl, combine the mango with the sugar, cloves, ginger, and nutmeg. Pour the mixture over the cooked fillets and gently mix to cover the chicken pieces. Add soy sauce, salt, and pepper to taste. Cook for about 10 more minutes.

Serve hot with a fresh green vegetable and a side dish of rice.

Serves: 4

Cinnamon Stir-Fry Chicken

Besides being totally impressed with the friendly charm of the Grenadian people, I am completely captivated by their food. This stir-fry, served at Delicious Landing restaurant in downtown St. George's, was the beginning of my love affair with the local cuisine.

1 chicken breast, skinned, boned, and cut into 1-inch cubes
2 tablespoons margarine, or more
2 green plantains, cubed
¼ cup sliced mushrooms
1 carrot, diced
1 cauliflower, trimmed of greens and chopped into 1-inch pieces
1 onion, sliced
1 head broccoli, chopped into 1-inch pieces
¼ cup soy sauce

2 teaspoons freshly ground cinnamon
½ teaspoon nutmeg
¼ cup finely chopped celery
1 teaspoon oregano
1 teaspoon cornstarch
¼ cup water
Caribbean-Style Rice and Peas (see page 237)
2 twists of orange peel for garnish
Cashew nuts for garnish

Sauté the chicken in the margerine, add plantains, mushrooms, carrot, cauliflower, onion, and broccoli, and cook on medium heat for about 8–10 minutes. Add soy, cinnamon, nutmeg, celery, and oregano.

Mix together the cornstarch and water to form a smooth mixture. Stir into chicken-vegetable mixture. Cook until mixture is thickened. Serve over Caribbean-Style Rice and Peas. Place an orange twist on either side of the plate and spread cashew nuts over chicken for garnish.

Serves: 2

Naples Beach Chicken and Scallops

After a full day of fun in the Florida sun, you'll be hungry for this delightful combination of chicken and scallops. It's served at the Naples Beach Hotel and Golf Club in Naples, Florida, but is easy enough for you to prepare right in your own home.

4 6-ounce chicken breasts, boned and skinned
Salt and freshly ground pepper
2 tablespoons butter or margarine
1 pound medium scallops
¼ cup dry sherry
4 teaspoons Dijon-style mustard
¼ cup cooked and chopped bacon bits
½ cup heavy cream
Fresh lemon juice to taste
Freshly chopped parsley

Season the chicken breasts with salt and freshly ground black pepper. Melt the butter or margarine in a large skillet. Add the chicken breasts and sauté until tender. Add the scallops and continue to sauté for approximately 2 more minutes. Add the sherry, mustard, and bacon bits. Simmer approximately 2 minutes. Then, add the heavy cream, lemon juice, and freshly chopped parsley. Reduce* on low heat to a creamy consistency.

Serve with fresh green asparagus with a herb butter sauce

Serves: 4

*See Cooking Terms.

Shooter's Hill Chicken

New York City's famous Jamaican caterer, Rennie Smith, prepared this nicely spiced chicken for Mayor Koch's Caribbean Day Festival in 1986. I tried the recipe, which I had found in a popular national magazine, but it seemed to be missing the zip. Some time later I had the good fortune to meet Rennie in New York. I asked him if he might have left something out of the recipe. Sure enough, he exclaimed, "I can't believe I left out the Pickapeppa sauce!" I tried the recipe again and it was great!

1 3-pound chicken, cut into serving pieces
1½ tablespoons dried thyme
1 medium onion, chopped
½ Scotch Bonnet pepper*, seeded and finely diced
1 tablespoon whole allspice berries
Salt and freshly ground pepper to taste
½ bottle Pickapeppa sauce (available at most supermarkets or
      gourmet shops)
Water

Wash the chicken well and pat dry with towels. Place the pieces in a shallow, glass ovenproof dish. Mix together the thyme, onion, Scotch Bonnet, allspice, salt, pepper, and Pickapeppa sauce. Pour over the chicken and coat each piece using a pastry brush. Refrigerate overnight. If the mixture becomes too dry, add a little water.

Preheat oven to 350°. Mix the chicken well with marinade. Bake for about 1 hour or until the chicken is done.

Serves: 4–6

*This pepper is very hot, so increase or decrease according to taste. For extra kick, leave the seeds in. Be sure to remember to wash hands in soapy warm water after working with hot peppers as they can cause irritation to the skin. If you happen to get too much hot pepper and need to cool your mouth, Rennie advises you to eat some yogurt.

Hot Chicken Salad Soufflé

February is the time to visit Brooksville; that's when the flowering dogwood trees and azaleas transform the area into one of the most picturesque places in Florida. Just two blocks west of Roger's Christmas House, where you can shop for Christmas decorations year round, is the Blueberry Patch Restaurant, where everything is prepared with lots of care and many of the recipes have been carried down from four generations of great cooks.

This recipe may take a little time to prepare (it must be refrigerated overnight before baking), but it's bound to remain in your cooking file for many years; it's a good one for pot-lucks or covered-dish suppers.

1 2½–3 pound whole chicken (may substitute 2 cups cooked diced chicken)
1 stalk celery, chopped
1 small onion, chopped
Salt to taste
6 slices white bread
½ cup finely chopped celery
½ cup finely chopped onion
½ cup finely chopped green pepper
½ cup salad dressing (white)
½ cup shredded Cheddar cheese
3 slightly beaten eggs
1½ cups milk
1 10-ounce can cream of mushroom soup

Cook the whole chicken with the celery, onion, salt, and enough water to halfway cover the chicken. Cook until done, turning the chicken over halfway through the cooking. Cool and dice 2 cups of the chicken. Use the rest for soup.

Trim the crusts from the bread slices and place the trimmed bread in the bottom of a 9 x 13 x 2-inch baking dish. Reserve the crusts.

Combine the chicken, celery, onion, and green pepper with the salad dressing. Carefully spread the mixture over the bread slices. Crumb or cube the reserved crusts and use as a topping over the chicken mixture. Sprinkle cheese over the crusts.

Mix the eggs and milk together. Pour over all ingredients in the baking dish. Refrigerate overnight. Before baking, spoon a can of mushroom soup over the top. Bake in a 350° oven for 1 hour.

Serves: 6–8

Lali's Chicken and Yellow Rice (Arroz con Pollo)

In Tampa, Florida, the locals who frequent the Lincoln Restaurant often dine there two or three times a week. Owners Lali and Glenn Fulqueira provide excellent meals at low prices without sacrificing quality or portion size. I feel that their version of Chicken and Yellow Rice is one of the best.

You may have trouble locating the dried stigmas of the saffron plant recommended in this recipe used to color the dish. If you can't find a Latin American or Oriental market, try substituting Bijol, also known as ground annatto seed or achiote. If all else fails, use a few drops of yellow food coloring.

¼ cup olive oil or lard
2 Spanish onions, chopped
1 green pepper, chopped
1–2 cloves garlic, crushed
2 bay leaves
Pinch of oregano
2 teaspoons salt
½ teaspoon freshly ground pepper
½ teaspoon Hungarian paprika
1 tomato, diced (may substitute 2 whole canned tomatoes, diced)
4 large chicken pieces
2 cups water
1 cup long-grained rice
4–5 stigmas saffron, toasted then crushed between fingers
Canned peas and pimentos for garnish

Heat the oil in a Dutch oven or large kettle that is ovenproof. Add the next 9 ingredients. Sauté until tender. Add the chicken pieces and sauté until firm. Add the water and bring to a boil. Add the rice and saffron. Bring to a boil again. Stir.

Cover and bake in a 375°–400° oven for about 20 minutes, or cook on the stovetop on medium-low heat for 20 minutes. Garnish with peas and pimentos.

Serves: 4–6

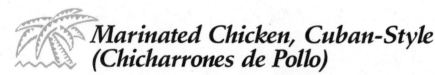

Marinated Chicken, Cuban-Style (Chicharrones de Pollo)

Marina Polvay, a noted food consultant from Miami Shores, Florida, shared this Cuban delight with me. Thanks, Marina, for one of the best marinated chicken dishes that I have ever had.

1 3½-pound frying chicken, cut into 16–18 pieces
¼ cup strained fresh lime juice
¼ cup dark rum
2 cloves garlic, mashed
2 tablespoons annatto oil*
2 teaspoons dark soy sauce
1 cup flour
½ teaspoon salt
¼ teaspoon freshly ground black pepper
2 cups vegetable oil
Rice or fried plantains

*See Tropical Glossary.

In a large glass bowl, mix together the lime juice, rum, garlic, annato oil, and soy sauce. Add the chicken pieces and turn until thoroughly coated with the mixture. Refrigerate for 2–3 hours.

Mix the flour, salt, and pepper together and spread in a shallow dish or on foil. Remove the chicken from the marinade and pat dry with paper towels. Discard marinade. Dredge chicken in flour mixture. In a large, heavy skillet, heat the oil until a haze appears. Fry the chicken pieces, turning occasionally until brown on all sides. Serve hot with rice or fried plantains.

Serves: 6–8

Chicken, Island-Style

Grapefruit is such a versatile and healthful fruit that it's a shame to confine it to the breakfast table. Here it's combined with juicy orange and tangerine sections to give a delightful taste to a chicken casserole.

This recipe is from the experts in the field—the Florida Citrus Commission.

2½-pound frying chicken, cut-up
Flour and salt for dredging
1 stalk celery, chopped
1 medium onion, sliced into rings
⅓ cup sauterne or other white wine
¼ cup soy sauce
2 tablespoons brown sugar
6 ounces frozen concentrated orange juice, thawed
Pinch of thyme
½ cup fresh grapefruit sections, pink or white-fleshed
½ cup chopped fresh pineapple
½ cup fresh orange sections
½ cup fresh tangerine sections
Coconut for garnish

Preheat oven to 350°. Dredge the chicken in the flour and salt mixture. Heat about ½ inch of oil in a frying pan. Fry the chicken until golden brown. Remove from the frying pan to a large ovenproof casserole or platter. Pour off some oil. Add the celery and onions to the chicken drippings. Sauté slowly until the onions are soft and translucent. Remove from heat.

Add the wine, soy sauce, juice, and thyme. Return to heat, stir, and bring to a boil. Pour the mixture over the chicken. Add the fruit. Bake, covered, for about 35 minutes.

Remove from the oven and garnish with coconut.

Serves: 4

Doretha's Fried Chicken

This dish is served to thousands of customers each month at the family-owned Doe-Al Country Cookin' restaurant in South Pasadena, Florida. They serve it "homestyle" with lots of Southern favorites like squash and collard greens, and the best darned cookies in town.

1 3-pound frying chicken, cut into 6–8 pieces
Salt and coarse black pepper to taste
2 cups self-rising flour
1 cup buttermilk
Vegetable shortening for frying

Season the fryer with salt and pepper to taste. (Doretha adds lots of black pepper). Let stand for about 3 hours in a cool place. To bread, dip the individual pieces in the flour, then in the buttermilk, and then back in the flour. Fry, covered, in a heavy black skillet at 350° with enough vegetable shortening to cover the chicken pieces at least halfway up.

Turn continually until done, about 20–25 minutes. By covering the skillet, enough steam and moisture is created to make this chicken "just right."

Serves: 4–6

Sugar Reef's Fried Chicken (Chicharrones de Pollo)

Here's another great *chicharron* recipe. I tasted this at the Sugar Reef restaurant in New York City. My reaction—I returned the next day for more. Enjoy this with a tall glass of Spiced Rum Punch (page 35). Allow time to marinate overnight.

1 3 or 4-pound frying chicken
3 cloves fresh garlic, crushed and minced
1 teaspoon salt
¼ cup olive oil
1 tablespoon malt vinegar
1 teaspoon garlic powder
½ teaspoon freshly ground black pepper
1 tablespoon sweet, mild paprika
Juice of ½ lemon
Juice of ½ lime
1 packet Sazon Goya brand seasoning with cilantro and achiote* (available
    at most Latin American markets)
Vegetable oil for frying

Cut the chicken into at least 16 pieces. Cut the wing tips from the chicken

*See Tropical Glossary.

pieces and discard along with the extra fat. Put next 10 ingredients into the container of a blender and purée. Marinate the chicken overnight in this mixture.

Bake the marinated chicken at 400° for 30–40 minutes. Remove the chicken from the marinade and deep-fry it in light vegetable oil heated to 350°. Fry for 3 minutes. Serve.

Serves: 4

 ## Baked Chicken (Pollo Asado)

Each year the Wolfson Campus of Miami-Dade Community College hosts the Miami Book Fair International, the largest consumer book fair in the country. In 1986, a special feature of the book fair was started, Epicure Row, where leading cookbook authors such as Jeff (The Frugal Gourmet) Smith, Maida Heatter, Bert Greene, Ernest (*White Trash Cooking*) Mickler, Phillip Schultz, and June Roth have demonstrated recipes from their cookbooks. Since I was chairman of Epicure Row, it was my duty to see that all authors were well fed, so I took them around Miami for some "tastes." Of all the restaurants we enjoyed together during their four-day stay, La Esquina de Tejas in Little Havana, a popular Cuban-American section of town, was one of their very favorites. It's been one of mine for a long time and it's the same restaurant President Reagan once enjoyed while in Miami. He tried this dish along with a plate of hot fried plantains and a cup of strong Cuban coffee.

3 chickens, cut into quarters
2 teaspoons salt
2 cloves garlic, chopped
Juice of 5 bitter oranges* (available at most Latin American markets)
Salt to taste

Preheat oven to 400°. Wash the chicken pieces and pat dry. Sprinkle with the salt and pat in gently. Place the chicken in a single layer in a large pan. Bake for about 1 hour. Remove from the oven.

In a jar, combine the garlic, orange juice, and a little more salt to taste. Shake well and pour over the chicken. Return to the oven for another 30 minutes and occasionally baste with the juices.

Serves: 4–6

*See Tropical Glossary.

Chicken in Lime Sauce

Two types of limes are grown in Florida: the seedless Persian lime and the seedy Key or Mexican lime. This recipe is excellent with either variety, although the Key lime definitely has a unique tart flavor all its own. The chicken needs to be marinated overnight.

3 pounds chicken pieces, skinned and boned
1 cup Persian lime or Key lime juice
2 teaspoons honey
⅔ cup water
2 teaspoons salt
1 teaspoon coarse black pepper
1 teaspoon thyme
2 tablespoons vegetable oil
1 tablespoon fresh ginger, peeled and finely chopped
Slices of Persian lime or Key lime for garnish

Place all ingredients except chicken and garnish in the container of a food processor or blender. Cover and process until ingredients are combined. If done by hand, be sure to blend well. Pour this marinade over the chicken pieces. Cover and let marinate in the refrigerator overnight. In the morning, drain and reserve the marinade.

Bake at 325° for about 1 hour and 20 minutes, basting with the reserved marinade every 20 minutes. Garnish with fresh lime or Key lime slices.

Serves: 4–6

Chicken with Yellow Rice, Cuban-Style (Arroz con Pollo)

I don't prepare this dish at home often because I can have it very inexpensively at any of the many great Cuban restaurants near my home in Miami Beach. But, when I do cook it at home, I use this recipe which I begged from the *Miami Herald*. I'm sure you will agree that it is *bueno*—very good!

1 3–3½ pound frying chicken, cut into serving pieces
¼ cup bitter orange* juice (available at most Latin American markets)
3 cloves garlic, crushed and minced
2 teaspoons salt
3 tablespoons lard, olive oil, or vegetable oil
1 large onion, chopped
1 large green pepper, chopped
2 cups long grain rice
4 cups chicken broth or water

*See Tropical Glossary.

1 bay leaf
4–5 stands saffron or 2 teaspoons Bijol*
1 16-ounce can tomatoes, drained and chopped
1 10-ounce package frozen petit pois (small peas), defrosted
1 4-ounce jar whole pimentos, drained and sliced
3 tablespoons dry sherry

Place the chicken in a single layer in a glass dish. Mix the bitter orange juice with the garlic and salt. Sprinkle over the chicken. Let marinate 30 minutes and drain, reserving any accumulated juices. Melt the lard in a paella pan or deep, heavy, ovenproof frying pan. Remove the chicken from glass dish and place in frying pan. Brown the chicken lightly on all sides. Remove chicken from the pan and set aside. Sauté the onion and pepper over medium-high heat just until the onion is transparent. Stir in the rice, coating the grains with the oil. Add the chicken broth to the pan and stir. Then, add bay leaf, saffron or Bijol, tomatoes, and reserved marinade. Bring to a boil and cook 5 minutes. Then, return chicken to the pan and stir. Cover and bake at 350° for 30 minutes or until the rice is tender and the chicken is cooked through. Just before serving, garnish with peas and pimento. Heat through. If desired, sprinkle with sherry.

Serves: 6

Roast Chicken with Bananas and Coconut

Just a short drive from the beautiful Tryall Golf and Beach Club in Jamaica are some of the island's most beautiful sights, including beautiful Negril Beach and one of my favorite places in the world, the Dunn's River Falls. It's fun to make a day of it by climbing the falls, lying on the beach, and then feasting on this delicious entrée by Executive Chef Thomas Phister of Tryall.

2 medium-sized chickens
Salt and pepper to taste
3 large ripe plantains or bananas
Vegetable oil for frying
6 tablespoons butter or margarine
¼ cup shredded coconut

Preheat oven to 325°. Season the chicken with salt and pepper to taste. Bake in a heavy roasting pan for about 45–60 minutes. Slice the chicken off the bones into thin slices. Pick the remaining meat off with your fingers. Carefully arrange the chicken on a serving plate.

Cut the plantains or bananas lengthwise into halves. Fry for about 4–5 minutes in about ½-inch oil until they are light brown and soft. Place them seed side up on top of the sliced chicken. Keep plate warm, but do not dry out the chicken. Prepare coconut mixture quickly by melting the butter in a sauté pan. Add the shredded coconut. Sauté until the coconut turns golden brown. Spoon mixture on top of the plantains or bananas and chicken.

To serve, carefully lift each portion with a steel spatula, keeping fruit on top of chicken pieces.

Serves: 6–8

Mango Maniac's Chicken Livers

"Mango mania" is slowly driving lovers of this peachy pineapply-flavored fruit to add mangoes to just about everything that's edible! I've had them in omelets, on ice cream, in breads and chutneys, and even with fried chicken livers! Its versatility is exciting.

Here's a moist dish that will easily soothe the "mango maniac's" taste buds. The recipe was given to me by Janell Smith of J. R. Brooks and Son, Inc., a packer and grower of tropical fruits located in Homestead, Florida. You may use garlic salt instead of fresh garlic, although it will never have the nice flavor of the real thing.

½ pound fresh select chicken livers
1 egg, well beaten
¼ cup flour
1 clove garlic, mashed
½ teaspoon rubbed sage
½ teaspoon Hungarian paprika
¼ cup melted butter, margarine, or corn oil
1 cup coarsely chopped onion
1 cup freshly sliced mangoes, peeled
Rice or toast points

Pour the beaten egg over the chicken livers. Combine the flour, garlic, sage, and paprika. Dredge the chicken livers in the flour mixture. Then sauté gently in melted butter or oil until brown, turning once.

Remove the livers to a heated serving dish. Place chopped onions in the frying pan and sauté until wilted. Add the mango slices and continue to cook until mangoes are heated throughout. Return livers to the pan to reheat.

Serve over rice or as a hearty brunch item over toast points.

Serves: 2

Meat

 ## Country Fried Steak

Plant City was named for Henry Bradley Plant, the great railroad and steamship entrepreneur, who, in the 1800s, built a railroad between Tampa and Stanford, Florida. Until then, Tampa was virtually isolated from the rest of the world. His actions transformed Tampa into a noted city. He was also responsible for the development of many towns along the branched railroad lines.

Plant City, Florida, was one of those towns on the railroad line. Buddy Freddy's Restaurant in Plant City has been a part of Plant City's history for over 30 years. The locals gather at the restaurant to reminisce on the past over a hefty plate of Country Fried Steak.

6 5-ounce choice top round cube steaks
1 cup plus 1 tablespoon flour
1 teaspoon salt
1 teaspoon black pepper
1 cup vegetable oil
½ teaspoon Lawry's Seasoned Salt
1 tablespoon fresh chopped onion
1 large clove fresh garlic, chopped
1 cup water

Combine 1 cup of flour, salt, and pepper. Roll the steaks in this mixture and fry in oil until done. Remove the steaks and set aside. Save half of the oil, and discard the rest.

Combine 1 tablespoon of the flour, the seasoned salt, onion, and garlic, and add it to the oil. Stir over medium heat until brown. Add water and steaks. Simmer, covered, about 15 minutes or until tender. Serve steaks covered with gravy.

Serve: 6

Captiva Rouladen of Flanken Steak

Dining in the Bubble Room Restaurant on tropical Captiva Island, Florida, is an experience one does not forget. Remember the bubble lights your grandma used to decorate her Christmas tree with? They surround the dining area along with wonderful bits of nostalgia that make dining here like a trip into the past. Be prepared for a wait during the season, as much as two hours, but chatting with bartenders dressed in "early" Boy Scout uniforms in the cozy upstairs makes waiting a hoot.

1 large flank steak (approximately 2–2½ pounds)
1 clove fresh garlic, minced
1 8-ounce package cream cheese, softened
½ cup drained chopped pimento
1 cup thinly sliced mushrooms
1 cup cooked spinach leaves, drained
4 5-ounce slices parma ham or other ham
16–20 whole peeled baby onions (approximately 1–1½ inches in diameter)
2 cups beef broth
2 cups red wine, medium dry to dry
1–2 bay leaves
Salt and coarsely ground pepper to taste
Flour for thickening

Preheat oven to 350°. To butterfly the flank steak, lay the flank flat on the counter with the length away from you. Using a long fillet knife, horizontally slide the blade through the side until it almost reaches the opposite side. Carefully split the meat half and half by slowly working the knife away from you. Lay the flanken open so you have one large piece of meat.

Rub the meat with garlic. Spread cream cheese over the entire fillet of meat. Sprinkle pimento over the meat. Sprinkle mushrooms over the pimentos. Lay cooked leaves of spinach over the entire surface (2–3 leaves thick). Lay ham slices over surface.

Carefully roll the meat and layered ingredients beginning at the narrow end. Continue rolling and secure the end with toothpicks. Place the rouladen in the center of a 9 × 12-inch pan. Surround the rouladen with the onions. Pour broth and wine over the meat and submerge 1–2 bay leaves in the broth. Bake for 1 hour.

Drain the cooked broth from the meat and onions. Set the rouladen and onions aside and keep warm. Thicken broth into a thin gravy. Salt and pepper to taste. Slice the rouladen into medallions. Ladle gravy over the top and serve onions on the side.

Serves: 4

Orange Beef

You can purchase preserved orange peel for this delicious recipe in most Oriental markets or you can make you own by peeling the skin from a nice fresh orange. Cut it into julienne strips about ¼-inch wide. Allow to dry for a few days in a warm, dry place.

Low Li, the chef at Wah Shing restaurant in Dadeland Plaza located in South Miami, Florida, created this recipe. It takes a little time, but it is worth the effort.

1 pound flank steak or trimmed sirloin steak
4 tablespoons rich chicken broth
2 tablespoons cornstarch
1 teaspoon kosher salt
¼ teaspoon white pepper
1 teaspoon sesame oil

2 tablespoons soy sauce
3 tablespoons pale dry sherry
¼ cup rich, unseasoned chicken stock (low-sodium canned is fine)
Pinch of white pepper
1 teaspoon hoisin sauce (available at Oriental markets)

6 cups vegetable oil
10–15 pieces preserved orange peel, each about ¼-inch wide
2 shallots, minced
2 cloves garlic, minced
8 inches of scallion, white part only, cut into ¼-inch pieces
6 whole dried chili pods*

Cut the steak against the grain into pieces 2 inches long by ½ inch wide. Pound lightly. Combine chicken broth, cornstarch, salt, pepper, and sesame oil. Marinate beef overnight in this mixture.

Combine the next five ingredients and set aside

Heat vegetable oil in a wok or frying pan to 350°. Fry the beef until well done and crispy. Remove from oil and place in a colander to allow excess oil to drain off. Remove all but 1 tablespoon of oil from the wok. Stir-fry the orange peel until well done and lightly browned. Add shallots, garlic, scallions, and chili pods. Stir-fry for an additional 20–30 seconds. Add sauce and reduce** by ⅓. Add beef and stir-fry for about 1 minute more.

Serves: 4

*If you like this dish fiery hot, crush the chili pods rather than using them whole.

**See Cooking Terms.

Tropical Tenderloin

They served this dish at the grand opening of the Pavillon Grill, an award-winning restaurant located in the Hotel Inter-Continental in downtown Miami, Florida. It was and is "tropically tremendous!" If tenderloin is tough on your budget, use another grade of beef.

Marinade

1 papaya, peeled, seeded, and finely chopped
Juice of 2 limes
1 tablespoon canned green peppercorns

2 pounds (enough for 8 4-ounce portions) beef tenderloin
Salt and freshly ground pepper to taste
2 papayas, peeled, seeded, cut in half lengthwise and sliced
2 tablespoons vegetable oil
3 tablespoons green peppercorns
Juice of 4 limes
½ cup Tio-Pepe dry sherry
2 cups demiglace*
¼ cup butter (optional)

Mix the marinade ingredients together in a pan large enough to hold the meat. Salt and pepper the beef and add to the marinade mixture. Marinate for 2 hours, turning now and then.

Preheat oven to 450°. Rub the papaya slices with oil. Roast for about 5 minutes. Remove and reserve.

Sear and sauté the meat in vegetable oil until desired doneness is achieved. Remove meat from the pan and pour off excess fat. In the same pan, toast 3 tablespoons of peppercorns for about 1 minute. Deglaze* with lime juice and then the sherry. Reduce* by ⅔. Add demiglace to this mixture and reduce until a good flavor is present. Adjust seasonings. If desired, to smooth out "flavor edges," whip in the butter.

Slice the tenderloin to desired thickness. Place alternating slices of beef and papaya on a platter, fanning the slices out into a circular pattern. Pour sauce around edge of plate.

Serves: 8

*See Cooking Terms.

Ropa Vieja
(Spiced Beef Strips)

Ropa Vieja, meaning "old rope," is one of the most popular traditional dishes from the Spanish-speaking islands of the Caribbean. The blending of flavors is magnificent in this recipe which I borrowed from Marina Polvay, a cookbook author who lives in Miami Shores, Florida.

There are many versions but this Cuban one is great.

1 flank steak (2½–3 pounds) trimmed
4 medium onions, chopped
2 bay leaves
Salt and freshly ground pepper to taste
4 quarts water or more as needed
3 tablespoons annatto oil* (available in Latin American markets)
3 cloves garlic, minced
1 green pepper, finely chopped
¼ teaspoon or more hot red pepper flakes
1 large carrot, peeled and coarsely grated
2 cups peeled, seeded, and finely chopped ripe tomatoes
⅛ teaspoon ground cinnammon
2 tablespoons capers, drained
1 cup chopped canned pimento for garnish
2 tablespoons minced fresh cilantro for garnish

Place the flank steak in a heavy 4-quart casserole and add half of the onions, 2 bay leaves, and salt and pepper to taste. Add water and cover the casserole. Bring to a boil on high heat. Reduce heat. Simmer for about 2 hours, or until the meat is very tender. Remove the steak from the casserole and place on a plate to cool. Strain the cooking liquid into a bowl and set aside. Discard onions and bay leaves.

Pour annatto oil into a clean 4-quart casserole and heat until sizzling. Add the remaining onions, garlic, green pepper, red pepper flakes, and carrots. Reduce heat. Cook, stirring frequently for about 7 minutes, or until the vegetables are soft but not browned. Add tomatoes and cinnammon. Cook on medium heat, stirring until most of the liquid evaporates and the mixture is very thick. Add the reserved cooking liquid and capers. Stir well. Add more salt and pepper if needed. Slice or shred the meat and add to the mixture, stirring constantly. Place meat and sauce on a serving platter and sprinkle with pimentos and cilantro. Serve immediately with Fried Green Plantains (see page 224) and Black Beans and Rice (see page 235).

Serves: 6

*See Tropical Glossary.

Barbecued Honey Steak

This recipe was given to me by a gentleman who sells honey for a living; his sales efforts immediately increased my yearly honey purchases. A superb taste for such little effort.

Allow 7–8 hours for the steak to marinate.

1 siroin steak, 5–6 pounds, the juiciest you can find
2 tablespoons crushed red pepper
1 teaspoon fresh ground black pepper
2 cloves fresh garlic, finely minced
1 large onion, very thinly sliced
1 cup honey*

Combine all ingredients well. Marinate the steak for 7–8 hours. Remove the meat from marinade and grill over a very hot fire. To serve, heat the leftover marinade and pour over the grilled meat.

Serves: 4

*The gentleman, whose name I can't remember, said to be sure to use Power's brand honey which is made in Florida, but you may substitute other brands.

Gourmet Barbecue Ribs

I always use my steamer to get rid of excessive fat. The beer enhances the flavor of the meat—the better the beer, the nicer the flavor. The Barbecue Sauce has a great tangy flavor—with just enough, but not too much spice. It's great over chicken, too.

4–6 pounds baby back ribs
1 teaspoon marjoram
1 teaspoon thyme
1 teaspoon rosemary
2 cans beer
Barbecue Sauce (recipe follows)

Mix together the marjoram, thyme, and rosemary. Crush the herbs with your fingers. Rub the mixture over the ribs, evenly coating each slab.

Steam the ribs at 250° in a steamer or electric wok, using beer in place of water, for about 1 hour. While waiting for ribs to cook, prepare Barbecue Sauce.

Barbecue ribs on grill until almost done. Brush sauce on for the last 5 minutes and serve sauce on the side.

Serves: 4–6

Barbecue Sauce

1 cup ketchup
1 10¾-ounce can tomato purée
½ cup water
1 tablespoon soy sauce
2 tablespoons Worcestershire sauce
2 tablespoons deli-style dark brown mustard (Boar's Head, if available)
2 cloves fresh garlic, minced
1 teaspoon Lousiana hot sauce
½ teaspoon Tabasco sauce, or to taste
2 medium shallots, finely minced
2 tablespoons wine vinegar
¼ cup extra virgin olive oil
½ teaspoon cayenne pepper
1 tablespoon fresh lime juice
½ cup warm beer

In a medium-sized saucepan, combine all the ingredients except the lime juice and beer over medium heat. After the sauce warms, add the lime juice and beer. Bring to a boil and cook for 15–20 minutes. Stir well.

Stuffed Party Beef, Jamaican-Style

It was a hoot listening to Rennie Smith, the famous New York City "Caribbean" caterer, describe how he prepares this dish. He was so enthusiastic! Rennie suggests using a top round roast, but you can use a variety of cuts if you like. I made it with a sirloin butt roast and it was tremendous. But, if you'd prefer a smaller roast, reduce the ingredients accordingly.

This dish is spicy and hot, so use a smaller amount of the Scotch Bonnet pepper if you'd like a milder variation.

1 10-pound top round roast at room temperature
3–4 cloves garlic, minced
Salt and freshly ground pepper to taste
1 cup (about 1 bunch) finely chopped scallions
1 large white onion, finely chopped
1 medium red bell pepper, seeds and stem removed, finely chopped
1 medium green bell pepper, seeds and stem removed, finely chopped
1 medium yellow bell pepper, seeds and stem removed, finely chopped
1 medium Scotch Bonnet pepper*, seeds removed, finely chopped
½ cup fresh chopped thyme
1 cup beef stock for basting

Preheat oven to 550°. Trim excess fat from the roast. Slit the roast horizontally in the center to form a nice deep pocket or have the butcher slice it for

*See Tropical Glossary.

you. Season the meat generously by rubbing the garlic into the roast, both in the cavity and on the outside of the roast. Salt and pepper the roast to taste.

Mix together all the other ingredients, except the beef stock. Stuff the mixture into the cavity (the stuffing will look dry unless the peppers are very juicy). Tie the roast together with string in several places so that the stuffing will not fall out. Place the roast, fat side up, on a rack in a pan in the oven. Reduce the heat immediately to 350°. Add the beef stock to the bottom of the roasting pan and baste the roast frequently. Cook about 18–20 minutes to the pound for medium rare.

To serve, remove the strings. Slice thinly and serve with the sauce to the side or poured over the meat.

Serves: 15–20

Boliche Relleno
(Spanish-Style Eye of Round)

Tampa, Florida is a city bursting with Spanish tradition. There is a quaint Latin Quarter in Tampa called Ybor City, a sort of town within the town, where Flamenco dancers and guitarists will put you in the mood for a Spanish feast. Just west of Ybor City is a stretch of Spanish restaurants. There you will find the Lincoln Restaurant, where Lali Fulqueira and her husband, Glenn, prepare thousands of authentic Hispanic dishes. Lali sent me this recipe just recently, noting that white rice, black beans, and fried plantains would dress up the meal quite nicely.

3–4 pounds eye of round (boliche)
1 strip (about ½ pound) salt pork
½ pound ham
3 chorizos (Spanish sausages)
4 tablespoons pure lard
2 large onions, chopped
1 large green pepper, chopped
3–4 cloves garlic, chopped
2 tablespoons oregano
4 tablespoons Hungarian paprika
4 bay leaves
3 cups water
2 tablespoons salt or to taste
Sliced potatoes and carrots (optional)

Preheat over to 325°. Pierce a hole through the length of the eye of round (some meat markets will do this for you). Stuff the hole with salt pork, ham, and chorizo sausages.

Heat 1 tablespoon of lard in a heavy pot. When hot, place the eye of round into the pot and braise until brown. Remove meat and place in a heavy roasting plan. Add the onions, peppers, garlic, oregano, paprika, bay leaves and 3 tablespoons of lard to the roasting pan. Cook for a few minutes on the stovetop. Add about 3 cups of water to the roasting pan.

Roast, uncovered for 1 hour. Baste frequently with juices. Cover and cook for another 2 hours or more until it is tender when fork is inserted. Baste several times more. If desired, add sliced potatoes and carrots during the last hour.

Serves: 6–9

Picadillo

This traditional Cuban dish is usually served with black beans, white rice, Cuban-style deep-fried eggs, and fried ripe plantains.

The recipe for this tasty beef stew was given to me by Marina Polvay, a food consultant and cookbook author who lives in Miami Shores, Florida.

3 pounds lean boneless chuck, cut into cubes
2 teaspoons salt
½ teaspoon coarsely ground black pepper
6 tablespoons annatto oil*
1 large mild onion, finely chopped
4 cloves garlic, finely chopped
4 green peppers, finely chopped
1–2 chili peppers, finely chopped
6 large tomatoes, peeled, seeded, and finely chopped (may substitute 2
    16-ounce cans of peeled Italian tomatoes)
¼ teaspoon ground cloves
½ cup stuffed green olives
½ cup raisins
3 tablespoons wine vinegar

Place the beef into a large pot. Add salt and pepper, and enough water to cover. Cook on low heat for about 1½ hours, or until very tender. Remove from heat and cool. Drain the beef, reserving the liquid for sauces or stock. Grind or chop the beef. Set aside.

In a heavy, large skillet, heat the annatto oil. Add the onions, garlic, green pepper, and chili pepper. Cook, stirring constantly on medium-high, until most of the liquid has evaporated. Add the olives, raisins, vinegar, and beef. Cook, stirring, until the beef is thoroughly heated. Taste for seasonings. Add more pepper or salt if desired. Serve immediately.

Serves: 6

*See Tropical Glossary.

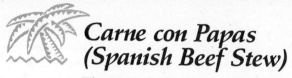

Carne con Papas
(Spanish Beef Stew)

There are many variations on this mainstay of Spanish cookery. This one, from the Lincoln Restaurant in Tampa, Florida, is economical as well as flavorful. Enjoy this with a leafy green salad and rolls.

1 pound top round, cut into cubes
Olive oil for sauteing
2 teaspoons salt or salt substitute
1 teaspoon freshly ground pepper
1 clove garlic, peeled and crushed
1 28-ounce can whole tomatoes, crushed
1 large Spanish onion, chopped
1 large green pepper, chopped
2 tablespoons oregano
3 bay leaves
4 carrots, peeled and sliced
2 medium potatoes, peeled and cubed
1 1-pound can string beans
3 tablespoons flour
¼ cup water

Put some olive oil in a large, deep skillet or Dutch oven along with the meat, salt, pepper, and garlic. Brown well. Add the tomatoes, onion, and green pepper. Cook for a few minutes longer. Add oregano and bay leaves. Bring to a boil. Reduce the heat to a slow simmer. Cook for about 30 minutes. Add the carrots and potatoes. Cook until tender or about 30 minutes longer. Add the beans. Mix the flour and water together and add it to the stew. Stir carefully until thickened. Serve with hard rolls. Use the rolls to sop up the delicious juices.

Serves: 4

Betty Mascoll's Pepperpot Stew

On a casual drive along the northern coast of beautiful Grenada in the British West Indies, I arrived at Douglaston Estate in the lovely market town of Gouyave. I was taken on a tour of the spice factory there, where nutmeg, cocoa, mace, cinnamon, and cloves are prepared and sorted by the local women. It was fun exploring and learning from the women how the spices grow and their various uses.

Then it was on to Sauteurs, on the northernmost tip of Grenada, where lunch was awaiting me at Betty Mascoll's plantation. The old plantation home, Morne Fendue, is a beautiful structure built of hand-chiseled colored stones and mortared with lime and molasses. In the coolness of the great house dining room, I was served a huge lunch. I feasted on callaloo soup, stewed chicken, sautéed pumpkin, baked bananas, salad with watercress—you get the idea—and this lovely Pepperpot Stew.

1 pound pork, cut into 2 or 3–inch cubes
1 pound oxtails*
2 onions, minced
½ cup minced scallions
2 tablespoons chopped fresh thyme
Salt and freshly ground pepper to taste
2 tablespoons cooking oil
3 tablespoons cassareep syrup* (available in most West Indian markets)
Rice

Season the pork and oxtails with a mixture of onions, scallions, thyme, salt and pepper to taste. Allow to marinate for at least 1 hour in a covered pot in the refrigerator.

Heat up in a heavy iron kettle. Add the oil and brown the meat well. Add water if necessary, but the meat should cook in its own fat. Cover and cook on a low simmer for several hours or until meat is very tender.

Serve over rice.

Serves: 4–6

*See Tropical Glossary.

Vee's Meat Patties

Meat patties are a popular snack throughout the West Indies. You can buy them on the streets from vendors who carry whole trays of them on their heads, or from snack shops everywhere. You'll find this tasty treat at Vee's Snack Bar at the Port Saline Airport in Grenada. If you happen to visit, try her Mauby drink and Sea Moss, too.

1½ pounds minced pork or beef with juices
1 tablespoon vegetable oil
½ cup finely minced celery
2 scallions, finely minced
1 tablespoon fresh thyme
4 cloves garlic, mashed
Salt and freshly ground black pepper to taste
1 tablespoon hot sauce or chopped chillies to taste
2 tablespoons curry powder
1 egg yolk
¼ cup evaporated milk (or more)
Yellow food coloring
Johnnycakes (see page 115)

In a skillet, brown meat in the oil. Add the next 7 ingredients and simmer until vegetables are tender. Drain off grease.

Mix up a recipe of Johnny cakes. Roll out the dough and cut into circles with a biscuit cutter or a glass that has been dipped in flour. Place about 2 tablespoons of the meat mixture in the center of each circle. Brush water on the edge of the circle and fold dough over. Seal the edges with the tines of a fork. To make the patties "shine," brush the crust with an egg wash made with an egg yolk and a little evaporated milk. Add a little yellow food coloring to the mixture. Brush thoroughly over each patty. Place on a cookie sheet and bake at 350° for 25–30 minutes.

Yield: About 12 patties or 20 small ones.

Miami Veal-Mango

Emilio Laureano Gonzalez was born in Buenos Aires, Argentina, and began cooking in his father's restaurant when he was 11 years old. He now lives in Miami and was head chef at Laurenzo's Gourmet Italian Ristorante in North Miami Beach, Florida. I requested this recipe after my first bite—it was *that good.*

12 veal scaloppini
2 tablespoons butter
2 pounds fresh mangoes, peeled and sliced
1 cup champagne
½ cup heavy cream
Fresh parsley for garnish

Place the veal escalopes between sheets of waxed paper and tenderize by beating them flat with a meat hammer or rolling pin. Heat the butter in a skillet. When sizzling, add the scaloppini and sauté for a few minutes until golden brown. Remove the veal to an attractive serving dish.

Add the mango and champagne to the pan in which the veal was cooked. Mix and then add in the cream. Let the sauce thicken under high heat. Pour sauce over the veal and serve while hot. Garnish with fresh parsley.

Serves: 4

Veal with Lemon

A wonderfully versatile seasoning, lemon adds flavor and "zest" to most any dish. To store lemons, place them in a plastic bag in the vegetable crisper; they will keep for at least four weeks.

Try fresh lemon on veal in this enjoyable creation by Chef Paul Girard and Edwin Sanchez of cozy Cafe Sorrento in Miami Beach, Florida.

1 pound veal cutlets cut into 4 pieces, thinly sliced
1 cup all-purpose flour
4 eggs, beaten
Vegetable oil or Crisco for frying
3–4 tablespoons margarine or butter
½ teaspoon chopped fresh parsley
1½ fresh lemons, squeezed
½ cup white wine
Carrot curls and fresh parsley for garnish

Pound the veal slices well with a meat mallet. Dip the veal in flour. Dip into beaten eggs. Dip in flour and in egg mixture once again. Heat oil until very hot. Fry the cutlets on both sides until golden, for a couple of minutes. Drain the cutlets on a brown paper bag or on paper towels.

Squeeze the lemon into the juices of the pan. Add the parsley and white wine. Cook, stirring for about 2 minutes.

Serve over spaghetti or linguini. Ladle sauce over the cutlet and the pasta. Garnish with carrot curls and fresh parsley.

Serves: 4

Curried Meat Patties

Meat patties are as popular in the islands as hot dogs and hamburgers are on the mainland. These beauties take a little time, but if you make a nice batch, you can reheat and serve again—that is, if there are any left!

Although the Venezuelan-style corn meal used in this version is similar to Mexican corn meal, the flavor is decidedly different so don't try to use a substitute. You can easily find a variety of brands at a Latin American market.

Patty Mixture

1½ cups Venezuelan-style masa harina (precooked cornmeal—available at
    most West Indian markets)
1½ cups boiling water
1 teaspoon sugar
1½ cups all-purpose flour
1 egg
3 tablespoons melted butter
⅓ cup freshly grated gouda cheese

Filling

2 tablespoons butter or margarine
1½ pounds finely ground beef
2 cloves garlic, mashed

1 onion, finely chopped
2 tablespoons finely chopped celery
½ green bell pepper, finely chopped
½ red bell pepper, finely chopped
½ Scotch Bonnet pepper*, seeded and finely minced
1 14½-ounce can tomatoes, drained and crushed
Salt and freshly ground pepper to taste
2 teaspoons curry powder
1 egg, beaten, mixed with a few drops of yellow food coloring
Parsley flakes
Vegetable oil for deep-frying

In a large bowl, add boiling water to the masa harina, and mix lightly. Cool. Add the sugar, flour, and egg. With your hands, mix well and form into a large ball. Flour a board. Knead the ball until it becomes very smooth. Return to the bowl. Add the butter and cheese and mix well until smooth. With a heavy rolling pin, roll the dough out until very thin. Using a large coffee can or cookie cutter, stamp out circles of dough. Do this all at one time and pile up circles ready for filling.

To prepare the filling, heat the butter or margarine in a heavy frying pan. Sauté the beef, garlic, onion, celery, and peppers until tender, or about 10 minutes. Drain off the fat. Add the tomatoes, salt, pepper, and curry. Cook about 5 minutes more. Cool for a few minutes.

To fill the circles, place about a tablespoon of the meat filling in the center of each circle. Fold over, forming a half-moon shape. Using the tines of a fork, press down on the outer part of the circles to seal well. Brush beaten egg mixture over the entire patty. Sprinkle with parsley flakes and fry in hot vegetable oil until golden brown.

These are delicious reheated the next day. Serve with a nice hot sauce like the Haitian Hot Sauce (page 240).

Yield: About 2 dozen patties

*See Tropical Glossary.

Breaded Veal with Lemon and Caper Garnish

Florida bookstore owner Joanne Hamburger is talented, not only in her trade, but in the kitchen as well. Since I'm an avid fan of anchovies and capers, I especially like her recipe for Breaded Veal with Lemon and Caper Garnish.

12 veal scaloppini (each about 1–1½ ounces)
2 eggs, lightly beaten
3 tablespoons water
Salt and freshly ground pepper to taste

1 cup bread crumbs
Flour for dredging
¼–½ cup vegetable or corn oil
4 thin lemon slices
4 flat anchovy fillets
¼ cup drained capers
6 tablespoons butter
1 hard-boiled egg for garnish
Capers for garnish
¼ cup finely chopped parsley for garnish

Place the veal escalopes between sheets of waxed paper and beat them flat with a meat hammer or rolling pin. They should be no less than ⅙-inch thick. Beat the eggs with water and season with salt and pepper. Put the bread crumbs in a second bowl.

Pour flour into a medium-sized paper bag, drop in the veal slices and shake until coated. Dip the veal in the egg mixture, then in bread crumbs and set aside on a separate plate. Heat oil in a large skillet. Fry the meat until browned on both sides (this should take just a few minutes).

Put 1 lemon slice on each of four plates. Shape each anchovy fillet into a round band and arrange a band on each lemon slice. Fill each anchovy band with a caper. Now, arrange the veal on plates.

Heat the butter in another skillet until it foams and becomes hazelnut-brown. Pour a little over each veal slice. Chop the egg white; force the yolk through a fine sieve. Garnish the veal with chopped egg white and yolk, more capers, and parsley.

Serves: 4

Grilled Veal Roulades with Finger Bananas and Tamarind Sauce

The ripe tamarind fruit is a brown pod, about 2 to 6 inches long, that contains large seeds surrounded by a pasty, date-like pulp. This pulp is the part used to prepare the tamarind nectar. Both the nectar and dried pulp can be purchased in many localities.

The tamarind sauce in this recipe is very tart and makes a pleasing contrast to the richness of the grilled veal and bananas. Miniature finger bananas are especially sweet and tasty, but larger bananas can be substituted. Chef Willi Pirngruber of Hyatt Dorado Beach Hotel, Puerto Rico, serves this dish accompanied by wild rice and steamed baby vegetables.

2 cups tamarind* nectar (available in Latin American or
    West Indian markets)
2 ounces dried tamarind pulp (available in Latin American or
    West Indian markets)

*See Tropical Glossary.

2 cups beef broth
¼ cup rum
1 pound veal cutlets, flattened, and cut into 16 pieces
8 finger bananas or 2 medium-sized ripe bananas

In a medium saucepan, combine tamarind nectar and pulp over medium heat. Reduce to a simmer and cook, stirring occasionally, for 20 minutes. Add the broth and rum. Cook for 25 minutes more. Strain the sauce, discarding the tamarind pulp. If the sauce is too thin, return to the saucepan and simmer until reduced* to 1½ cups.

Prepare the grill or preheat a broiler. Cut finger bananas in half lengthwise or cut medium bananas in half crosswise, then cut halves into quarters lengthwise. Wrap a piece of veal cutlet around each piece of banana and thread roulades on four metal skewers. Grill or broil 4 inches from heat source for 4 minutes on each side or until veal is lightly browned. Serve immediately with tamarind sauce on the side.

Serves: 4

*See Cooking Terms.

Pork Chops Negril

Negril, on the western tip of the island of Jamaica, has some of the most beautiful beaches in the world. It's fun to kick back there and sip a Red Stripe beer or tasty rum punch. After a few rounds, why not mosey over to the Negril Beach Village for a taste of their superb island cooking?

4 large shoulder or loin pork chops
Salt and freshly ground pepper to taste
Vegetable oil
2 medium green peppers, diced
1 medium onion, sliced
1 cup sliced apples
1 tablespoon brown sugar
1 tablespoon vinegar

Season the chops with salt and pepper. Brown lightly in a small amount of vegetable oil in a medium-hot skillet. Remove the chops from skillet and set aside. Saute the peppers, onion, and apple for about 5 minutes. Add the sugar and vinegar. Simmer for an additional 5 minutes. Add chops to the mixture. Simmer slowly, covered, for 2–3 minutes or until pork is properly cooked.

Serves: 4

Kingston Baked Ham

Jamaicans believe that there can never be too many cooks in their island kitchens, so at any big celebration, there are likely to be more helping hands than there are pots. That may account for a good deal of the experimentation that goes on in Jamaican kitchens. Here's a case of a traditional holiday dish getting a little something extra. Enjoy it with a not-too-heavy red wine such as a Beaujolais or Bordeaux-Médoc.

1 15- to 20-pound precooked ham
¾ cup brown sugar
4 tablespoons cherry brandy
½ cup apricot brandy
2 tablespoons dry mustard
Maraschino cherries for garnish

Place the ham in a large roasting pan. Place the pan, uncovered, on a rack in the oven. Bake at 325°, until it is within ½ hour of being done. (Allow approximately 25 minutes to the pound.) The meat is done when the meat thermometer registers 160°. Remove from oven. Score top of the ham. Sprinkle with brown sugar. Pour the cherry brandy over the sugar. Mix the apricot brandy with the mustard and add it to the pan. Return to oven and complete baking. Baste frequently with pan syrup. Slice and serve hot, garnished with maraschino cherries.

Serves: 30–40

Christmas Ham, Island Style

Rennie Smith, a Jamaican caterer who believes in spicy west Indian cuisine, has an interesting following. New York's Mayor Koch, the Dance Theatre of Harlem, and Bloomingdale's are just a few of his customers that enjoy savoring his fabulous cuisine of the tropics.

On a visit to the Big Apple, where I had the good fortune to speak with Rennie, I asked him what Christmas was like in Jamaica. He told me that it was a most treasured occasion and that the food was festive with some nice island touches. Then, he gave me this recipe for Christmas Ham.

Add some fresh orange juice to the basting juices for an extra fruity taste.

1 10- to 15-pound smoke processed ham
Ground allspice
White granulated sugar
Water
Callaloo or kale leaves*
Fresh whole strawberries
Watercress sprigs

*See Tropical Glossary.

Preheat oven to 425°. Unwrap and wipe the ham with a damp cloth.

With a very sharp knife, strip off the thick skin. Slice off most of the underlying fat, leaving just a thin layer of fat around the ham. Generously coat with allspice until none of the white fat shows through. Coat with a second layer of granulated sugar.

Place the ham in a large roasting pan. Place the pan, uncovered, in the oven, and immediately lower the heat to 325°. Add about 1 inch of water to the bottom of the pan. Cook the meat until it reaches an internal temperature of 160°, allowing about 20 minutes to the pound. Baste occasionally with pan juices, adding more water to the pan if needed.

Place on an attractive platter lined with callaloo or kale leaves and garnish with strawberries and watercress.

Serves: 20–30

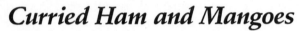

Curried Ham and Mangoes

When you prepare this dish, be sure the mangoes you choose are ripe. With mangoes, smelling—and not squeezing—is the indicator when selecting a ripe fruit. Conduct your test by sniffing at its stem. You're looking for a very full, fruity aroma.

Increase the amount of the curry if you prefer a stronger taste.

1 pound cooked lean ham, cut into 4 pieces
2 cups peeled and sliced ripe mango
2 tablespoons butter or margarine
¼ cup packed brown sugar
1 teaspoon curry powder

Put the ham in a baking dish. Place the mango slices on top of the ham. Combine the butter, sugar, and curry powder. Sprinkle the mixture on top of the ham and mangoes. Broil until the curry powder bubbles.

Serves: 4

Jamaican-Style Stewed Peas
with Dumplings

My Jamaican friend, Elfreda Clarke, showed me how to make this dish early one morning before I left for work. I hurried home a few hours later to enjoy the feast for lunch. The beans (called peas in the islands), salted pork, and pigs' tails need to soak overnight.

You can serve this as a side dish or as the meal itself.

3 cups dried red kidney beans, soaked overnight
1 pound salted beef* (available in West Indian markets), soaked overnight
1 pound pigs' tails (available in West Indian markets), soaked overnight
1 cup coconut milk*
2 cloves garlic, minced
1 medium-sized onion, chopped
2 scallions, chopped
1 small Scotch Bonnet pepper*, seeds removed, chopped
coarsely ground black pepper to taste
2 tablespoons dried thyme leaves
1 cup flour
4 cups cooked white rice

The salted beef and pigs' tails must be soaked overnight or for at least 8 hours to reduce the saltiness. Change the water 3 or 4 times to help remove the salt. Soak the beans separately in a heavy kettle with enough water to cover.

Bring the beans to a strong boil. Add the salted beef and the pigs' tails (which have already soaked) to the kettle. Reduce heat some but keep on a medium-high boil and cook for about 1 hour. Add the coconut milk and stir. Mix the milk with a little water to dilute if it is thick. Cook for another 45–60 minutes or until beef and beans are tender. Add scallions, Scotch Bonnet, ground pepper, and thyme. Cook for another 10–15 minutes.

To make dumplings, combine the flour with enough water to form a light dough. Form into very thin, finger-like dumplings. Drop into the kettle and cook a few minutes until done.

Serve with white rice.

Serves: 4–6

*See Tropical Glossary.

Curried Goat

When Jamaican native Elfreda Clarke showed me how to make this spicy dish, (that I thought I would not have the courage to taste —but it's great!!!) there were no notes or recipe files. I even had to slow her down to measure the ingredients because that's something she never does!

This will be too spicy for some, but that's the way it's usually made by the Jamaicans who rarely party without preparing a large pot of this goat stew. Serve with rice, pigeon peas, fried plantains and a heavy-duty rum punch.

5–6 pounds goat meat, cut into 1-inch cubes (available in West Indian markets)
5 scallions, very coarsely chopped
3 large onions, chopped

3 Scotch Bonnet* peppers, seeds removed, and minced or chopped
1 teaspoon ground allspice (pimento)
2 tablespoons freshly ground black pepper
4 tablespoons curry powder or more if desired
1½ tablespoon salt or to taste
2 tablespoons margarine or butter
¼ cup coconut oil or ¼ cup plus 2 tablespoons vegetable oil
2 tablespoons curry powder
1 large clove garlic, minced

Using your hands, mix the goat together with the next 7 ingredients, blending well.

Now, as the Jamaicans would say, "put it down overnight." Translated, this means "let marinate in the refrigerator for about 8 hours to season."

In a large kettle, heat the margarine and add the coconut oil or vegetable oil. Add 2 tablespoons curry powder and mix well. Add the garlic and brown. Now add the seasoned goat to the hot mixture. Mix well. Cover and leave on a low boil for about 2–3 hours (depending on toughness of meat) or until meat is tender. Add a little water if needed.

Serves: 8–10

*These are fiery hot peppers. You may wish to reduce the amount here to 1 or 2. Wash your hands in warm, soapy water after working with hot peppers.

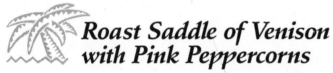

Roast Saddle of Venison with Pink Peppercorns

A visit to the dining room at the King Charles Restaurant in the Don Cesar Beach Resort in St. Petersburg, Florida, may put a slight dent in your wallet, but the experience will be memorable. So treat yourself to a midnight dinner in their elegant dining room overlooking the Gulf of Mexico. I highly recommend it. I also recommend this recipe, should you be fortunate enough to get some venison. Allow time for it to marinate overnight.

1 4-pound venison saddle
1 pound salt pork for larding*
2 cups port wine

*Larding is the process of adding fat in some form to prevent the meat from drying out during roasting. First, cut the salt pork into strips narrow enough to be threaded through the eye of a larding needle. Thread short lengths of the fat (2 or 3-inches long and about ¼-inch thick) at intervals through the venison, about ½-inch deep and on all sides. A thin knife may be used instead of the needle. If desired, rub each strip with garlic and other herbs before larding.

*See Cooking Terms.

2 cups port wine
1 small onion, roughly cut
2 stalks celery, roughly cut
2 carrots, roughly cut
1 tablespoon thyme
4 bay leaves
1 tablespoon peppercorns

4 tablespoons unsalted butter
4 tablespoons pink peppercorns (available at most gourmet shops)
3 tablespoons raspberry vinegar (available at most gourmet shops)
2 cups demiglace* (reduced veal stock)
2 pinches salt
Pinch of white pepper

Trim any skin or sinews from the venison saddle. Lard* the venison by threading short lengths of fat through the meat. Marinate overnight in the port wine with the vegetables and herbs. Turn it every 3–4 hours.

Preheat oven to 400°. Remove the meat from the marinade and pat dry. In 2 tablespoons of butter, saute the saddle until brown on all sides. Place in the oven for about 20–25 minutes until medium rare (135°–145° per meat thermometer). Remove from the oven and set aside. Drain grease from the saute pan. Add the pink peppercorns and vinegar. Reduce until almost dry. Add demiglace, stir and reduce by ⅓. Adjust seasoning and finish with remaining 2 tablespoons of butter.

Remove larding strips from the saddle. Slice venison very thin. Place sauce on the bottom of the serving dish. Arrange the venison over the sauce. Serve with vegetable purees such as celery, onion, and carrot.

Serves: 6

Jerk Pork

In Jamaica, the men who prepare this dish are known as "jerk men." "Jerking" is a very uniquely Jamaican cooking technique which is over 300 years old. It consists of blending a combination of herbs and spices into a marinade for meats or poultry, and slowly cooking the food over a pimento (allspice) wood fire. The meat is sold by the "jerk man" at the markets to vendors who then sell it to their customers. It lasts for several weeks after cooking and is simply delicious.

It was not easy to find a recipe for "jerking," since preparation generally consists of roasting a large pig or roast. The recipes I found varied tremendously, but the basic ingredients remained the same. The Sugar Reef restaurant in New York City had a delicious version, as good as many I tasted in the Caribbean.

Pig's blood is an important ingredient in many of the preparations, but since many are squeamish about using it, I have come up with a recipe of my own that is good and to which pig's blood may be added, if one deems necessary. This marinade is easy to prepare and contains ingredients that you should not have difficulty in locating.

Allow at least 1 hour for the meat to marinate and decrease or increase the amount of pepper according to your taste. Leave hot pepper seeds in if you want a scorcher!

1 pounds pork, trimmed and sliced into 4 × 1-inch thick strips
18 whole black peppercorns, ground
5 whole allspice seeds, ground
½ medium onion, finely minced
1 cup scallion, finely chopped
2 tablespoons freshly chopped thyme leaves
½Scotch Bonnet pepper, or other hot chili pepper, finely minced
2 teaspoons Worcestershire sauce
Salt to taste
2 tablespoons vegetable oil

Blend all ingredients, except pork, in the container of a food processor or mix by hand. Rub mixture well into the pork and allow to marinate, refrigerated, for 1–3 hours.

Broil or grill at medium temperature, basting with meat juices. If you are able to obtain the allspice wood, use it with the charcoal, or you may substitute other fragrant wood such as mesquite.

Try this blend on beef and poultry, too—it's excellent.

Serves 8:

Vegetables

Curried Ackee*

Ackee is the national fruit of Jamaica. It is also grown on many other Caribbean islands and can be found in a few areas of south Florida. Unless it is picked at exactly the right time, the fruit is poisonous. This puts it somewhat in the category of wild mushrooms—get some expert local advice before you indulge. The aril, the edible portion, looks like scrambled eggs after it is cooked, and has a delicate lovely flavor. It is quite enjoyable, although at first it may take getting used to. If you ever have the opportunity, I hope you will try this delicacy. For peace of mind (and convenience) you can use canned ackees from Jamaica, available in most Latin American and West Indian markets.

The fruit is often cooked with salt fish, or prepared with a nice curry powder as in this recipe. If you prefer your curry very hot, use the Hot Curry Powder recipe on page 251.

8–12 open ackee pods or 1 19-ounce can ackee
1 tablespoon butter or margarine
1 tablespoon curry powder
Salt to taste
⅓ cup milk

If you are using fresh ackee, remove the shiny, black seeds (three per fruit body) from the pods. Remove the arils. Clean the arils, being careful to remove all connecting tissue. Pour ½ cup water in a pan. Boil the arils until tender. Drain off water. Set aside. If using canned ackee, simply drain the can well and set aside.

In a small saucepan, blend together the butter, curry powder, and salt. Slowly add the milk and mix well. Drop ackee in the hot mixture. Warm and serve on toast points. Serve with salted codfish, sliced onions, tomatoes, and scallions.

Serves: 4–6

*See Tropical Glossary.

Garden Asparagus with Lemon Hollandaise Sauce

When preparing this recipe, be careful not to overcook the asparagus. After removing the skin of stalks with a vegetable peeler and trimming off the bottoms, I steam mine in an electric wok for just a few minutes.

1 pound fresh asparagus
4 tablespoons water
2 tablespoons white vinegar
1 teaspoon salt
1 teaspoon white pepper
5 egg yolks
1 cup melted clarified* butter
1 tablespoon lemon juice

Peel the asparagus. Steam for a few minutes.

Pour water and vinegar into the top part of a double boiler. Add salt and pepper, and reduce by about ½ over direct heat. Add the egg yolks and place pan over hot, but *not* boiling water that you have heated in the bottom of the double boiler. Whip very energetically with a wire whisk until the eggs are well mixed and slightly thickened.

Remove the pan from the heat. Adding a little at a time, beat in the clarified butter. Continue beating until the sauce reaches the degree of thickness desired. Correct seasoning with salt and fresh lemon juice.

Pour over freshly steamed asparagus.

Note: If your hollandaise sauce separates, beat in a tablespoon of hot water to smooth it again.

Yield: About ½ cup

*See Cooking Terms.

Picnic Beans

Although these beans must cook all day, you can easily prepare them in the morning, leave them in the oven on a low temperature all day, and arrive home to find them done. I've been preparing these beans for picnics in the tropics for many years. The liquid evaporates to leave an almost chewy texture.

4 16-ounce cans Campbell's Home-style Beans
1 cup ketchup
4 tablespoons brown sugar
½ cup chopped green pepper
4 tablespoons minced onions

1 cup molasses
2 teaspoons prepared mustard
1 teaspoon salt or salt substitute
½ cup chopped bacon or ground beef, drained
1 green pepper, sliced, for garnish

Preheat oven to 375°. Mix all ingredients well. Bake beans for 30 minutes at 375°. Then reduce oven to 225° and bake uncovered for about 7 hours. Garnish with slices of green pepper.

Serves: A crowd (10–16)

Winged Beans* with Bacon

I experienced a great love affair with the winged bean during a visit to Betty Mascoll's home in Sauteurs, Grenada. They were served as part of a buffet that included pepperpot stew, yam cakes, and several other island favorites.

This protein-filled bean is not easy to locate but can be found in some "very" gourmet shops around the United States. However, I'm sure that once word gets around it will become as popular as the once-little-known kiwifruit, which became the rage in a very short time.

The pods of the bean are larger but lighter in weight than a shell bean. They are crunchy (if not overcooked) and taste quite a bit like string beans. The bean makes such a refreshing presentation with its star-like appearance. Here's a variation of Betty's recipe.

1 pound winged beans, rinsed
4 slices bacon
2 scallions, thinly chopped
2 cloves garlic, pressed
Dash of hot pepper sauce
2 teaspoons sugar
1 teaspoon red wine vinegar

Cut beans on a slant into ½-inch pieces. Trim ends off and discard. Boil in a large saucepan of salted water. Cook for about 5 minutes or until tender. Drain and set aside. In a heavy frying pan, fry the bacon until very crisp. Remove from pan and cool. Break into small pieces and return to pan. Add the scallions and garlic to pan. Sauté for about 1 minute or until the garlic is just beginning to brown. Add a dash of hot pepper sauce.

Add the winged beans, sugar, and vinegar to saucepan mixture. Stir and simmer for a few minutes until well heated. Serve nice and hot.

Serves: 4

*See Tropical Glossary.

Hopping John

Mama Lo prepares this at her very popular eatery, Mama Lo's, in Gainesville, Florida. It's a classic, traditional Southern dish—with a little soul, of course. You need to soak the peas overnight.

        1 pound dry black-eyed peas
        3–4 thick slices salt pork
        6 cups water
        1 pound Uncle Ben's rice
        Salt and freshly ground pepper to taste
        1 tablespoon butter
        Pinch of sugar

Soak the black-eyed peas overnight in enough water to cover. Discard the soaking water. Mix black-eyed peas and salt pork in water. Boil gently for about 30 minutes. Add remaining ingredients and simmer for about 35–40 minutes longer. Add additional water as needed and stir often. It should have the consistency of stewed rice.

Serves: 6

Black-Eyed Peas

It is said you'll have good luck if you serve these on New Year's Day. Their taste is unique, if you haven't tried them before. They're not like the peas we Americans know, because these are really beans. Just like other beans, they need to soak overnight.

        1 pound dry black-eyed peas
        ¼ pound salt pork, thinly sliced with rind removed (may substitute a ham
            hock)
        1 teaspoon salt
        Freshly ground black pepper to taste
        2 cloves garlic, minced
        1 large onion, chopped

Place peas in a strainer. Rince twice with cold water and drain. Remove broken peas.

Place beans in a 6–8 quart kettle or stockpot and cover with water. Soak about 12 hours or overnight. Add the salt pork or ham hock and add more water to cover, if necessary. Bring peas to a boil. Reduce heat. Add the salt, pepper, garlic, and onion. Simmer for about 1½–2 hours or until peas ar quite tender. Do not stir as you may break the peas.

Serve with steamed rice, fresh tomatoes, onions, and cornbread or Carl's Cracklin' Corn Bread (page 119).

Serves: 4–6

Boniato (Tropical Sweet Potato)

When I first tasted this vegetable, I thought I was in heaven. By its outer appearance—reddish, fat, "potato-like"—one would never guess what a wonderfully smooth taste it will have once it's cooked. Cook with the skins on to retain the nutrients.

These potatoes can be purchased in very large sizes, but I find the smaller onces to be more tender and easier to work with. My Columbian friend, Miryam Ionita introduced me to this unique and special taste.

1 boniato (available at most Latin American markets)
Unsalted butter or margarine
Salt and freshly ground pepper to taste

Cut the boniato into quarters. Remove any brown spots with paring knife. Cover with water and bring to a boil. Then, simmer for about 20–25 minutes depeding on the size of the vegetable. It's done when you can poke it easily with a fork. The skin will become very loose during cooking. Remove it with a paring knife when cooked.
Serve topped with butter, salt, and pepper.

Serves: 2–4

Mess of Greens

Go out and buy a "mess of greens," but be sure they are select, young ones—they will be much more tender. Salt pork is a terrific seasoning for these tasty veggies.

2 pounds collard greens
4 cups water
¼ pound salt pork
½ cup chicken stock*
1 teaspoon salt or salt substitute
1 teaspoon sugar
Freshly ground black pepper (optional)
Bottled green pepper vinegar (optional)

Wash greens well several times in several changes of water to remove dirt, sand, and bugs. Remove stems and drain well. Discard yellow leaves and insect-bitten leaves. Chop greens well into small strips.

Add the water to a heavy, lidded pot. Then add the salt pork with the rind removed. Add the greens, chicken stock, salt, and sugar. Simmer for about 40 minutes. Test to see if they are tender—like spinach but not quite as soft. Season with pepper and vinegar, if desired.

Serves: 4–6

*See Cooking Terms.

Fried Corn

This recipe is from the Spring Creek restaurant in Spring Creek, Florida, a very old and tiny fishing village with about 100 residents. The restaurant is right near the fishermen's docks, so the catch is always fresh—but so are the accompaniments. This is a "fun" way to serve corn. If you're on a diet, this may not be the recipe for you.

6 ears fresh corn at room temperature
3 pounds all-purpose cooking fat, enough to cover corn
Melted butter (optional)

Pull husks and silk from the corn. Break ears in half. Heat the fat for deep-frying to 350° in a 3–4 quart kettle. Test for temperature with a thermometer. If you don't have one, dip a 1-inch bread cube into the fat. Be careful. If the cube browns in 60 seconds, the fat will be about the right temperature.

Carefully drop the corn into the fat. Cook until ears are brown and crunchy. Drain on paper towels.

Serve with melted butter, if desired.

Serves: 6

Malanga Chips

Malanga or yautia (the Cuban and Puerto Rican names, respectively) is a shaggy vegetable shaped much like a yam. Malanga makes some wonderful dishes including these chips which are light and delicous. Be careful though—it's a rather "slippery" fellow.

1 pound malanga*, scrubbed and peeled (available in most Latin American markets)
Vegetable oil for frying
Salt to taste

Peel the malanga and place in cold water—much like you would a potato until ready to fry. Preheat oil in a deep frying pan to about 350°.

Slice malanga very thin with a sharp knife or with the slicing blade of a food processor.

Place malanga slices in heated oil very carefully and fry for a few minutes on each side until golden brown. Drain on brown paper bags or paper towels. Serve while still hot, plain or with a zesty hot sauce. Serve with fried fish for a "Tropical Fish 'n' Chips" dish.

Serves: 4–6

*See Tropical Glossary.

Roasted Breadfruit

Breadfruit is avaiable in the United States primarily in the areas where there is a Caribbean population. It's a dietary staple in many of the Caribbean islands.

It was Captain Bligh of *Bounty* fame who first transported breadfruit seedlings from the South Pacific to the West Indies back in 1793. An earlier attempt to import seedlings had been thwarted by the mutiny. The English had planned to cultivate breadfruit as cheap provisions for the slaves they held there.

The mature fruit is roundish and can weigh anywhere from 2 to 10 pounds. Fully ripe, the pulp has a one-of-a-kind fruity squash-like flavor. Islanders love it roasted and are often seen preparing it in ground pits outside their homes.

It's also good baked or boiled—absolutely delicious!

1 ripe breadfruit (available in West Indian markets)
Butter
Salt and freshly ground pepper to taste

Remove the stem by pulling it out with your fingers. Place the breadfruit on a blazing charcoal fire. Cook it for about an hour, constantly turning it. When done, scrape off the black spots until the golden brown of the fruit appears. Cut into 4 pieces. Remove the threads inside. Serve with butter, salt and lots of pepper.

Serves: 1–2

Cassava Vegetable Chili

American cuisine has just recently discovered the mild-flavored cassava (yuca) vegetable. The cassava is a root vegetable with a woody exterior and a hard white flesh, much like a potato. It grows only in tropical climates. Although many of us are familiar with cassava in the form of tapioca, which is processed from the Brazilian cassava root, not too much experimenting has been done with this vegetable, which is naturally low in fat and contains no cholesterol.

Before cooking, it is very important to carefully remove the brittle outer bark and the pale pink undercovering with a sharp knife, thereby eliminating any harmful materials in the skin that could affect both taste and health. You'll like this for a nice change from the ordinary—it's delicious!

2 cups raw cassava* (available in most Latin American markets)
2 quarts water
¼ cup lime juice
¼ cup butter or margarine
6 fresh tomatoes, peeled and seeded

*See Tropical Glossary.

¼ cup chopped green chile peppers
½ cup chopped onion
3 cloves garlic, finely chopped
1 16-ounce can chick peas (garbanzo beans) with juice
¼ cup fresh chopped cilantro (coriander leaves)
¼ cup chopped scallions
1 cup grated Cheddar cheese

Peel the cassava carefully.

Cook in water with lime juice in a large open pot for 20 minutes or until tender. Drain and discard the cooking liquid.

In a separate pot, melt the butter and lightly sauté the tomatoes, green chile peppers, onion, and garlic. Stir in chick peas with juice and the cilantro. Next, add the already cooked cassava and heat thoroughly. Serve with chopped scallions and grated Cheddar cheese.

Serves: 4–6

Curried Mushrooms in Cheese

Curry was first introduced in the Caribbean by European sailors and later by laborers from India. The islanders place a high value on this spice, and use it in much of their cooking. My husband Richard, who also enjoys the taste of curry, created this simple side dish.

2 tablespoons butter or margarine
2 cloves garlic, finely chopped
1 medium onion, finely chopped
3 tablespoons finely chopped green pepper
1½ cups fresh thinly sliced mushrooms
2 tablespoons pimento
2 tablespoons cream cheese, softened
1½ teaspoons curry powder or more to taste
Freshly ground pepper
Salt or salt substitute
Toast points
Fresh parsley for garnish

In a heavy skillet, heat butter or margarine until sizzling. Add garlic, onion, green pepper, and mushrooms. Sauté for a few minutes until translucent. While stirring, add the cream cheese. Continue to stir until the cream cheese melts and combines with vegetables. Add curry, pepper, and salt to taste.

Serve on buttered toast points or in small sauce dish to accompany fish or fowl. Garnish with fresh sprigs of parsley.

Serves: 2

Hot and Cheesey Grits

Here's a touch of the South coupled with some flavors from "South of the Border" that will get your morning moving. Grits are actually coarsely ground white corn, and are to Southern cooking what pasta is to the Romans. True grits—not the sticky, cold, lumpy kind—are cooked slowly over low heat and stirred often.

   1½ cups grits
   6 cups boiling water
   1½ teaspoons salt or salt substitute
   ½ cup butter
   2½ cups shredded sharp New York State Cheddar cheese
   ¼ teaspoon ground cumin
   1 10-ounce can tomatoes and green chiles

Cook grits in the boiling water with salt for about 8–10 minutes until the water is absorbed. Add butter, 2 cups of the cheese, cumin, and tomatoes and green chiles. Mix well.

Spread in a greased 2-quart ovenproof dish. Sprinkle with remaining cheese. Broil until cheese is nicely browned.

Serves: 4–6

Okra and Tomatoes

The State Farmers' Market restaurant in Fort Myers, Florida, is a great choice for country-style cooking and plenty of local color. The restaurant is adjacent to the State Farmers' Market where produce is weighed and shipped to retail establishments throughout Florida. Produce truckers head straight over the restaurant after their work is done and proceed to order up the "Okeechobee Catfish Special," with a side dish of old-fashioned mashed potatoes (with "real" gravy) and an order of down-home Okra and Tomatoes.

   4 tablespoons margarine or butter
   1 pound fresh tomatoes, quartered
   2 pounds fresh okra, trimmed and sliced, if large
   1 onion, chopped
   1 tablespoon sugar
   Salt and freshly ground pepper to taste

Melt the margarine or butter in a pot. Add the tomatoes, okra, and onion. Bring to a boil. Cover and let simmer until the okra is tender. While the vegetables are cooking, mash the tomatoes from time to time. Season with sugar, and salt and pepper to taste.

Serves: 4–6

Mushrooms à la Crème George

Leonce Picot has often been referred to as the "King of Florida restaurateurs." His nearly fanatical attention to detail, along with that of his partner Al Kocab, has won them many of the prestigious awards in the food industry. Mushrooms à la Crème George is one of the most popular dishes at their Fort Lauderdale restaurant, the Down Under. I always receive rave reviews when I prepare this rich creation. Serve it as a side vegetable or as the main dish at lunch.

½ pound small fresh mushrooms and stems
1 tablespoon butter
1 tablespoon dry sherry
½ cup sour cream, at room temperature
¼ teaspoon monosodium glutamate (optional)
1 teaspoon Worcestershire sauce
Dash of Tabasco sauce
2 slices bread, cut into small triangles and toasted
¼ cup butter, melted
1 tablespoon fresh chopped parsley
Hungarian paprika for garnish

Sauté mushrooms in butter for 2 minutes. Add sherry and cook for another 2 minutes. Add sour cream, monosodium glutamate, Worcestershire, and Tabasco sauce. The consistency of the mixture should be that of a rich hollandaise sauce.

Toast points should be golden and very crisp. (Bake toast twice for maximum crispness.) Saturate them with the melted butter. Pour mushroom mixture onto toast points. Sprinkle parsley and paprika on top. Be sure to serve hot!

Serves: 2 as an appetizer, 1 as a main course

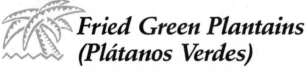

Fried Green Plantains (Plátanos Verdes)

The taste of the green plantain is quite different from that of the ripe fruit. It is fairly bland, and is very starchy. Plantains are served at most meals in the islands, just as potatoes or bread would be on the mainland. My friend, Miryam Ionita, a native of Columbia, South America, showed me her technique in frying these delicious fruits.

Consult the Can Do section of the book to find out how to easily peel a green plantain.

1 cup vegetable or olive oil
4 green plantains*
Salt to taste

Cut each plantain vertically in half, and immerse in hot water for about 5 minutes. Peel and dry. Cut into 1-inch thick slices. Heat oil in a skillet until it is about 350°. You need enough oil so that the plantains can be at least half-way submerged. Fry the pieces for about 7 minutes, turning frequently. Remove the pieces from the oil and place them between layers of paper towels. Press with the ball of your hand or use a block of wood to flatten the pieces. Carefully put the pieces back into the hot oil. Fry until light brown. Remove from the oil and drain on paper towels. Sprinkle with salt. Serve hot with pork, beef, or chicken.

Serves: 4

*See Tropical Glossary.

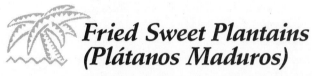

Fried Sweet Plantains (Plátanos Maduros)

On Cuban Independence Day in May, 1983, the regular menu at La Esquina de Tejas suddenly became famous. President Ronald Reagan came to town and stopped by for lunch. The visit had been carefully planned for months; however, the secret had been carefully hidden by co-owners Juan Vento and Wilfredo Chamizo.

When I am in Miami's Little Havana district, I often stop by there for lunch, too, and I always order the Fried Sweet Bananas, as they are called on the menu. Actually, they are not bananas at all, but ripe plantains, and they are a standard item in most Spanish and Cuban eateries.

For this dish, you must use very ripe plantains, which will look, on the outside, much like an overripe banana. The ripe plantains are much sweeter than the green ones, but even ripe plantains must be cooked before they are eaten.

1 cup vegetable or olive oil
4 very ripe plantains*, peeled and cut into 1-inch slices

Be sure plantains are very ripe. Heat the oil in a skillet until it is about 350°. You need enough oil so that the plantains will be at least halfway sub-merged. Fry the plantains for a few minutes until both sides are golden. Serve hot as a vegetable with Lali's Chicken and Yellow Rice (page 190).

Serves: 4

*See Tropical Glossary.

Coconut Fried Plantains

The plantain is often called the cooking banana, which is a very apt description. It looks just like a banana, but even at its very ripest, when the skin has turned totally black, it must still be cooked before you can eat it. Try this tropical delight made with the ripe fruit. Serve it as a side dish or as a dessert.

6 ripe plantains
½ pound butter or margarine
⅛ cup coconut oil
Juice of 2 lemons
Sugar for garnish

With a small, very sharp knife, peel the plantains. Slice the plantains diagonally into ½-inch pieces.

Heat the butter and coconut oil together in a heavy skillet until very hot. Place plantain pieces one at a time in the oil and fry for 2 minutes on each side, turning once. Drain on brown paper bags.

Sprinkle with juice and sugar. Serve hot.

Serves: 4–6

Banana Grumby

If you are tired of the same old "blah" vegetable casseroles, try this one. It's from the Delicious Landing restaurant in St. George's, Grenada, West Indies overlooking the harbor there. The nutmeg helps to orchestrate a rather unique blending of ingredients that excites one to declare, "Encore, please!"

Because fresh nutmeg has much more flavor than the ground variety sold in most supermarkets, you may wish to alter the amount used according to your taste. But whatever the case, you certainly won't grumble about this Grumby!

6 green plantains, peeled* and chopped
3 cauliflowers, trimmed of greens and chopped
4 carrots, peeled and chopped
¼ cup margarine or butter
½ cup evaporated milk
2½ cups freshly grated sharp Cheddar cheese
3 eggs, well beaten
1 teaspoon freshly grated nutmeg or to taste
6 medium stalks celery, peeled and chopped
2 large onions, grated

*See Can Do section.

1 tablespoon freshly ground white pepper
Sweet pepper rings for garnish
Salt to taste

Preheat oven to 325°. Boil or stem the plantains, cauliflower, and carrots.

In a large sauté pan, melt the margarine, or butter. Whisk in the milk, cheese, eggs, nutmeg, celery, onions, and pepper. Stir constantly until mixture is smooth. Stir in the prepared vegetable mixture. Gently mix. Place vegetable mixture in a baking pan laced with sweet pepper rings. Bake at 325° for about 20 minutes. Serve.

Serves: 10 as an appetizer or side dish, 6–8 as an entree

Baked Butternut Squash with Lime

Here's one of my favorite vegetables that is both economical *and* good for you. Be sure to use a fresh ripe squash. Ask your grocer to help you choose the best one.

You can use any Cheddar cheese, but it tastes especially good with a sharp one.

1 large butternut squash
2 tablespoons brown sugar
4 tablespoons butter or margarine
½ teaspoon freshly grated nutmeg
Salt and freshly ground pepper to taste
¾ cup sharp New York State Cheddar cheese, grated
Sprinkle of Hungarian paprika
4 fresh Persian lime or Key lime slices for garnish

Preheat oven to 350°. Quarter the squash. Scoop out and discard the seeds. Place the squash in a bowl of water and scrub the outer skin with a vegetable brush. Clean well.

Place flesh side down in a baking pan. Add water to cover the squash halfway. Bake for about 15 minutes.

Drain water. Turn squash cut side up. Add to each piece the following: a tablespoon of butter, ⅛ teaspoon of nutmeg, salt, and freshly ground pepper. Return the pan to the oven and bake about 30 minutes more or until flesh is quite soft. Test with a fork to see if it's done. Cooking time depends on squash size.

Sprinkle cheese and paprika over each piece. Broil until cheese is melted and golden brown. Garnish with a fresh slice of lime on each.

Serves: 4–6

Potatoes Bonaventure

At a "Great Chefs of Florida" weekend at the Bonaventure Hotel and Spa in the Fort Lauderdale area, I tasted this delicious potato dish prepared by Sous Chef Peter Pethybridge, a graduate of the Culinary Institute of America.

2 medium potatoes
4 tablespoons butter
Salt and white pepper to taste
1 tablespoon chopped fresh chives or parsley
2 tablespoons finely chopped onions
4 tablespoons chopped pastrami

Bake the potatoes. Cut them in half and scoop out the insides. Mix the pulp with all other ingredients. Press mixture into a shallow baking pan so that it is ½-inch thick. Cut into 4 sections and brown in butter on both sides.

Serves: 4

Swamp Cabbage with Tomatoes

Here's one of Flora and Ella's popular dishes from their famed restaurant in LaBelle, Florida. Besides the swamp cabbage favorites, other "pioneer-style" sustenance served up there includes black-eyed peas with rice and fresh onion, collard greens, catfish, cornbread, and mile-high pies. Seven generations have enjoyed the food served here. I know you'll enjoy this classic.

½ cup diced salt pork or slab bacon
½ cup diced onion
1 pound raw swamp cabbage*, soaked in strong salt water for 20 minutes
  and drained, or 1 14-ounce can hearts of palm
1 16-ounce can stewed tomatoes, sliced
Salt and pepper to taste

Place salt pork or slab bacon in a 2-quart saucepan and cook for a few minutes over low heat. Add the onion to the pan and sauté until the onion is slightly browned and transparent.

Slice the swamp cabbage or hearts of palm across the stalks into ½-inch slices. Add to the saucepan. Add the remaining ingredients and mix well. Cook 10–15 minutes or until the cabbage is done.

Serves: 4

*Also known as hearts of palm. Available canned at most supermarkets. Many counties in Florida regulate and protect the Sabal palm, the species from which the swamp cabbage comes. If you desire the raw cabbage, the local county government office will know the regulations regarding the palm.

Sweet Potato Pone

The word pone originated with the Algonquin Indians and it means something that is baked. In the South, corn pone means a corn bread often made without eggs or milk, and baked or fried.

Many of the vegetables indigenous to Jamaica are not readily available in the United States, but one of those we have in common is the delicious and versatile sweet potato. You'll enjoy this Sweet Potato Pone, as served at the Trelawny Beach Club in Jamaica.

1½–2 pounds raw sweet potatoes, peeled and grated
1 cup milk
1 cup cream of coconut*
1¼ cups brown sugar
1 teaspoon ground ginger
1 teaspoon cinnamon
1 teaspoon vanilla extract
½ teaspoon nutmeg or mace
½ cup raisins
1 7-ounce package of dried coconut flakes
2 cups hot water
2 tablespoons melted butter or margarine

Preheat oven to 375° and grease an ovenproof baking dish very well.
Combine the grated sweet potato with milk, cream, sugar, ginger, cinnamon, vanilla, and nutmeg or mace. Mix well. Add raisins, coconut, hot water, and melted butter. Mix briskly and taste for sweetness desired. Add more sugar if necessary. Pour into 2-quart glass baking dish and bake for about 1 hour.

Serves: 6

*See Tropical Glossary.

Cottage Fried Sweet Potatoes from Joe's

Without a doubt, one of the most enterprising persons in Miami Beach is the maitre d' of Joe's Stone Crab Restaurant. He is the individual with the supreme power to decide who will quickly be awarded a table and who may have to wait for upwards of two hours. But, even if you have to wait, it is a joy talking with JoAnn Sewitz, granddaughter of founder Joe Weiss, Sr. Joe arrived in Miami Beach from New York in 1913 and opened a tiny sandwich shop which just happened to turn into a world famous restaurant. Of course, the restaurant is well known for its stone crabs, but these sweet potatoes are pretty good, too.

4 sweet potatoes
1 quart vegetable oil for frying
Salt

Cut the sweet potatoes into slices and thin as potato chips. Soak them in ice water until they are ready for use. At the very last minute before serving, heat the oil in a fryer or an electric frying pan to 400°. Blot the sweet potato slices dry and fry them for about 2 minutes or until crisp and golden brown.

Remove the chips with a slotted spoon and drain on paper towels. Serve at once.

Serves: 4

Carl Allen's Sweet Potato Pie

When I begin having food fantasies, I've often thought of moving to Auburndale, a quiet serene community in central Florida, just so I could be closer to Carl Allen's Historical Cafe. The food there is simple but delicious and carefully prepared under the supervision of Carl Allen who is a native Floridian or "cracker." The Sertoma Club, a statewide service club, named him Florida's "#1 Cracker" and "Polk County's Favorite Son." His sweet potato pie is truly mouth-watering.

1½ cups cooked or canned sweet potatoes
½ cup sugar
1 teaspoon cinnamon
1 teaspoon allspice
½ teaspoon salt
2 fresh farm eggs, beaten
1 cup evaporated milk
2 tablespoons butter, softened
1 9½-inch unbaked pie shell

Preheat oven to 350°. If using the canned sweet potatoes, drain and mash the potatoes until free of all lumps. Add sugar, cinnamon, allspice, and salt to the sweet potatoes. Mix well. Add the eggs and mix again, very well. Blend in the milk and butter. Continue to mix until all ingredients are well blended.

Pour into an unbaked pie shell and bake for 45–60 minutes. Serve hot. If you like, add whipped cream topping for an extra special treat. Can also be served as a dessert.

Yield: 1 9½-inch pie

Festive Yams

Yams are one of the most important food crops in the world, and in many cultures are revered as religious and ceremonial objects. In Cuba, for example, yams are considered "festive food," to be saved for special occasions. Anytime is the right time to serve these yams, though. Try them with a leafy green vegetable and a large chunk of delicately spiced Southern ham.

4 large hearty yams
4 tablespoons butter, softened
¼ cup milk
2 tablespoons pure maple syrup (may substitute pancake syrup)
1 tablespoon freshly ground nutmeg*
1 tablespoon fresh orange juice
1 teaspoon freshly grated orange zest**
Salt and freshly ground pepper to taste
Topping (recipe follows)

Preheat oven to 425°. Bake yams for 40–50 minutes or until centers are soft (prick with a fork to test for doneness). When cooled, slice in half and scoop out the pulp into a bowl, reserving the shells. Mash all of the yam filling well. Add the next 7 ingredients and mix well. Spoon the filling back into the shells and smooth tops with a spatula.

Spoon topping over potatoes. Bake about 15 minutes. Garnish each shell with an orange slice, if desired.

Topping

½ cup chopped pecans
½ cup brown sugar
¼ cup butter, softened
¼ cup flour
Orange slice for garnish (optional)

Combine all ingredients.

Serves: 4

*Nutmeg grows and is harvested in great numbers in Grenada, West Indies. After my visit to Grenada, I hoarded great amounts of this spice which is wonderful freshly grated in many vegetable dishes and as a necessary garnish for rum drinks. Nutmeg will keep for up to 25 years, so my tour guide told me.
**See Cooking Terms.

Yams in Orange Cups

I always serve this at our home on Thanksgiving Day and Christmas. They add such a nice festive touch. My girls think they're "fun," too.

3 cups mashed canned yams
3 tablespoons butter or margarine
½ cup orange marmalade, preferably homemade
2 eggs
2 tablespoons pancake syrup
½ tablespoon salt or salt substitute
8 firm oranges
⅔ cup chopped nuts (pecans or almonds)
Butter for topping
Parsley for garnish

Preheat oven to 400°. Combine the yams, butter, marmalade, eggs, pancake syrup, and salt. Mix well. Be sure all lumps are mashed.

Slice off the top portion of the oranges. With a sharp knife, carefully cut out the pulp and section it, leaving a small portion of the stem in the bottom. Fill the cups with yam mixture. Top with chopped nuts and a dot of butter on each. Bake for about 20–25 minutes. Serve garnished with parsley sprigs and the sliced orange pulp sections on the side.

Serves: 8

Sweet Potato Souffle

Here's one of Ma Hopkins's "regular" recipes. If you're staying at her boarding house in Pensacola, Florida, you'll probably think about staying a few extra days after just one meal. If the potatoes seem a little dry to your taste, add up to ½ cup evaporated milk.

4 cups cooked mashed sweet potatoes
½ cup sugar
½ cup butter or margarine
½ cup grated coconut
⅓ cup raisins
1 teaspoon lemon extract or fresh orange peel
Miniature marshmallows, to cover

Preheat oven to 300°. While the potatoes are still hot, add all other ingredients except the marshmallows. Mix well. Place in a casserole dish and cover with marshmallows. Bake about 20–30 minutes or until the marshmallows are brown. Serve with ham and a Mess of Greens (page 219).

Serves: 6

Broiled Tomatoes with Mushroom Bits

In Florida, Ruskin tomatoes are considered among the very best. Use Ruskins, or other large ripe tomatoes, for this classic side vegetable.

2 large ripe red tomatoes
2 cloves garlic, pressed
2 tablespoons fresh bread crumbs
2 tablespoons freshly grated Parmesan or Romano cheese
1 tablespoon chopped fresh parsley
Salt and freshly ground pepper to taste
½ teaspoon sweet basil
3 large mushrooms, finely chopped
3 tablespoons extra virgin olive oil

Preheat oven to 375°. Slice tomatoes crosswise in halves. Make a mixture of the other ingredients. Mix well. Spread the mixture on top of each half with a spatula, being careful to cover entire pulp of tomatoes.

Bake for about 8–10 minutes, then broil for about 5 minutes or until browned.

Serves: 2–3

Fried Tomatoes

Tomatoes are great for weight watchers. A medium-sized tomato has only about 30 calories, and contains no cholesterol and just a small amount of sodium. At the same time, this same tomato will provide about half of the daily allowance of vitamin C. Of course, this dish would not exactly qualify for weight-watcher status since it is fried. Be sure to use tomatoes that are fully ripe.

2 large tomatoes
1 cup flour
1¼ teaspoons salt or salt substitute
½ teaspoon freshly ground pepper
¼ cup extra virgin olive oil

Cut a thin slice from the stem end of the tomatoes and discard. Cut each tomato into 8 slices. Combine flour, salt, and pepper. Coat each slice well with this flour mixture.

Heat the oil to about 325°. Fry the tomato slices for about 1 minute per side. Serve immediately.

Serves: 4

Fresh Zucchini Cakes

A tender and delicate member of the squash family, zucchini is as tasty cooked as it is raw. I particularly like them fried in olive oil. It enhances the flavor, and cuts down on the fat content in comparison to other oils.

4 cups very lightly salted, grated zucchini
¾ cup flour, sifted
1½ teaspoons baking powder
Salt and freshly ground pepper to taste
1 egg, well beaten
Olive oil for frying
Freshly grated Parmesan cheese (optional)

Combine the zucchini with flour, baking powder, salt, and pepper. Add egg and blend all ingredients well. Refrigerate mixture for about 10–15 minutes. Drop mixture by teaspoonfuls onto a smoking griddle or heavy frying pan. Cook until browned on both sides. Sprinkle with freshly grated Parmesan cheese, if desired, and serve with Fried Tomatoes (page 233).

Serves: 4–6

Buddy Freddy's Zucchini and Tomatoes

Buddy Freddy's is the kind of place where the locals go to eat good down-home cookin'. The menu includes a mix of Southern and Florida recipes, many passed down through generations of Johnson family members, owners of Buddy Freddy's Restaurant. Here's a family favorite from this Plant City, Florida, establishment.

6 small fresh zucchini
1 clove fresh garlic, peeled and pressed
1 8-ounce can tomatoes, drained and diced, or ½ pound fresh tomatoes, diced
1 small onion, diced
1 tablespoon vegetable oil
1 tablespoon sugar
1 tablespoon salt or salt substitute
½ teaspoon freshly ground black pepper
½ cup water
Freshly grated Parmesan cheese

Cut zucchini into bite-size pieces. Combine with the other ingredients, except the cheese. Simmer in a covered saucepan for about 15–20 minutes or until the zucchini is just tender. For added flavor, pass some freshly grated Parmesan cheese when you serve the zucchini.

Serves: 6

Ma's Fried Squash

Ma Hopkins is as much an institution in the town of Pensacola, Florida, as is her Hopkins's Boarding House. A visit here will guarantee that you'll eat more than you probably should. But, you'll never regret trying it all.

2 pounds yellow squash (may substitute zucchini)
Salt
Self-rising flour for dredging
Fat for deep frying

Wash and slice squash into 1-inch pieces. Sprinkle salt over the squash so that all the pieces are lightly salted. The salt will draw out any extra liquid. Let sit for about 1 hour. Pour off the liquid.

Dip each piece in self-rising flour so that they're completely covered. Fry in deep fat at 350° until brown and crisp. Drain on paper towels.

Serves: 4–6

Black Beans and Rice

During the 10 years I lived in the sleepy west coast town of St. Petersburg, Florida, I reviewed local restaurants for the popular *PM Magazine* television show. One of my favorite segments involved a visit to a quaint Tampa eatery, the Lincoln Restaurant, where the food is plentiful and served *"con gusto."*

Each year during the month of February, Tampa surrenders itself to pirates who re-invade the city in a fully-rigged pirate ship as they re-enact the invasion of Tampa by the 19th century Spanish buccaneer, Jose Gasper. I'm sure that the famous pirate would have surrendered willingly to the taste of Black Beans and Rice, served to thousands during "Gasparilla" time.

The black beans need to soak overnight.

12 ounces (1⅔ cups) dried black beans (*frijoles negroes*)
4½ cups cold water or more, if necessary
4 teaspoons salt
1 cup olive oil
3 medium onions, chopped
2 green peppers, chopped
5 cloves garlic, minced
2 bay leaves
1 teaspoon oregano
Freshly ground pepper to taste
6 cups cooked white rice
Chopped onions for garnish

Wash beans well. Put the beans in a covered pot, with enough water to cover, and 2 teaspoons of salt and soak overnight. The next day, simmer the beans in the same water. While beans are beginning to boil, pour oil into a frying pan. Sauté the onions and peppers until tender. Add the garlic, bay leaves, and oregano to the onion/pepper mixture. Cook for about 5 minutes. Add to black bean mixture.

Season with remaining salt and pepper. Cook the mixture until the beans are very tender, about 1½–2 hours. Add a little more water if necessary. Boil beans gently and stir very little to prevent breaking of skins.

Serve over the white rice topped with chopped raw onions.

Serves: 6–8

Flora and Ella's Peas and Rice

Flora and Ella's Restaurant is an institution in LaBelle, Florida, home of Florida's famous Swamp Cabbage Festival. But they also serve other good and hearty foods like this peas and rice dish. Serve with cornmeal muffins and a nice casserole. The "pot liquor" helps make it all worthwhile.

Be sure to soak the peas overnight if you use the dried variety.

Rice

1 cup long grain white rice
2 cups water
2 teaspoons salt
2 tablespoons butter

Rinse the rice in water. In heavy pot combine the rice, 2 cups of water, salt, and butter. Cover. Bring to boil, then simmer according to package directions. Do not stir.

Peas

2 cups water
1 pound fresh black-eyed peas (may substitute dried or frozen)
¼ pound salt pork, diced
1 small onion, finely chopped

Bring the water to a boil. Add the peas and salt pork. Cook 45 minutes–1 hour or until tender.

Serve the rice in an attractive bowl. Top with peas and "pot liquor" (juice from bottom). Sprinkle chopped onions over all. Enjoy.

Serves: 4

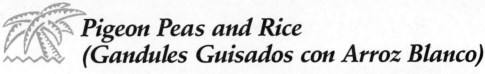

Pigeon Peas and Rice
(Gandules Guisados con Arroz Blanco)

I requested this recipe from a friend from Puerto Rico. She would not allow me to mention her name, but at least I can say—*"Thanks!"*

I have used several varieties of pigeon peas for this dish. Some varieties, as with most vegetables, are better than others. Choose a brand that is firm, not mushy.

- 1 clove garlic, pressed
- 2 tablespoons olive oil
- 1 small onion, chopped
- ½ green pepper, chopped
- ½ tomato, chopped
- 1 tablespoon tomato sauce
- 1 14-ounce package frozen pigeon peas or 2 cans, undrained, or regular garden peas
- ½ cup cooked pork pieces (optional)
- 4 cups cooked rice

Sauté the garlic in the olive oil for a few minutes. Add onion, green pepper, and tomato. Cook until onions are transparent. Add tomato sauce and pigeon peas. Bring to a boil. Reduce heat and simmer for 5–8 minutes. Serve over fluffy white rice.

This is great served alongside roasted pork, or add pieces of pork to the dish to make it into a main course.

Serves: 4–6

Caribbean-Style Rice and Peas

Rice and peas is a basic Creole dish, and is as common in the islands as mashed potatoes are in the United States. Serve this version with the Cinnamon Stir-Fry Chicken (page 182). This is how they do it at Delicous Landing restaurant in St. George's, Grenada, West Indies.

- 4 tablespoons margarine
- 4 tablespoons curry powder or to taste
- 2 cups chopped onions
- 2 cups cooked rice
- 4 cups cooked green peas (pigeon or regular)

In a sauté pan, melt the margarine. Sauté the curry powder and onions. Add the rice and peas and sauté until hot. Serve.

Serves: 4

Red Peas and Rice

Peas and rice is a traditional dish of the South. A variety of peas—which are actually beans to Americans—are used in these dishes including red kidney beans and black-eyed peas. In the Caribbean, the piegon pea, sometimes called the "gungo" pea is the mainstay bean. I've included a couple of recipes for each in this section, each of them prepared in a different way.

My friend, Elfreda Clarke, has to be one of the best Jamaican cooks in Miami. I've tasted mounds of "peas and rice," but this version alone makes one a true believer. You should see this lady whip it together—a true artist at work! Enjoy, but be sure to soak the beans (or peas) overnight.

2 cups dried red kidney beans, soaked overnight in enough water to cover
1 fresh coconut, cracked and meat removed from shell*
3½ cups water
½ pound smoked pork hocks
3 scallions, crushed and thinly sliced
2 cloves garlic, pressed
1 Scotch Bonnet pepper** (available in most West Indian markets)
1 tablespoon salt
4 cups white long grain rice, washed and drained

Crack the coconut and remove the meat. Discard the hard coconut shell. Dice the coconut into small pieces, leaving on the thin brown skin. Place the water in the container of a blender. Add coconut pieces slowly to the water. Blend until mixture is almost a purée. Now, strain the juice through a wire mesh strainer into a separate container. Discard the strained coconut.

Pour beans with the same water they soaked in into a large heavy pot. Add the smoked pork hocks. Pour in the fresh cream of coconut you just made. Mix gently. Cover and bring to a boil. Reduce heat. Allow to cook for 1 hour or until the peas get tender. (If you do not soak the beans, allow about 3 hours to cook.)

When the beans are tender, add the scallions, garlic, Scotch Bonnet, and salt. Simmer for a few minutes. Then, add the rice to the peas mixture and stir. Let cook on low heat for about 1 hour or until water is absorbed. You might need to add water.

Serves: 8–10

*See Can Do.
**Jamaicans like their food hot. Scotch Bonnet peppers are at least as hot as jalapeño peppers, so if you don't like your food too hot, don't use the whole pepper.

Sauces and Condiments

Old Sour

True "conchs"* rarely eat seafood without at least a few drops of their native Key lime juice. Here's a favorite lime concoction for use on conch and broiled, baked, or fried fish or meat. It has a potent flavor all it own, due to the Bird peppers. Bird peppers are also native to the keys, so it's not likely that you'll be able to find any in your locale, but any hot peppers will do.

1 cup Key lime juice (may substitute sour orange** or lemon juice)
1 tablespoon salt
2 whole Bird peppers or a few drops of hot sauce or cayenne to taste

Add the salt and peppers or hot sauce to the juice. Allow to stand at room temperature for 1 to 2 days.

Strain through cheesecloth until liquid is clear (about 3–4 times). Bottle tightly with a cork. Store at room temperature in an out-of-the-way place for 2–4 weeks to age.

Yield: 1 cup

*A conch (pronounced konk) is a person who was born and raised in the Florida keys or who has lived there for many years.
**See Tropical Glossary.

Sofrito (Spanish Sauce)

Cuba, with little doubt, is the most Hispanic of the Caribbean islands. Here's a great recipe for their popular multi-purpose sauce. It's available at most Latin American markets in a bottled version, but this is much better. It was given to me by Marina Polvay, a cookbook author who lives in Miami Shores, Florida.

Sofrito is the base of many typically Cuban dishes. The true secret is to let the mixture cook slowly to blend the wonderful flavors. There are many variations of this sauce. Use as a sauce over grilled meats and poultry or as directed in individual recipes.

1 cup diced salt pork
1 tablespoon annatto oil*
2 large onions, finely chopped
4 cloves garlic, minced
2 green peppers, finely chopped
2 cups diced cooked ham
3 large ripe tomatoes, peeled, seeded, and chopped
2 teaspoons minced fresh cilantro (coriander leaves)
½ teaspoon oregano
Salt to taste
½ teaspoon freshly ground pepper or to taste

Cook the salt pork in a large, heavy casserole over medium heat, stirring frequently until the pork cubes are brown and crisp. Remove the pork cubes with a slotted spoon and discard or reserve for another use. Add annatto oil to the drippings in the casserole. Heat the mixture until a haze appears. Add the onions, garlic, and peppers. Cook on medium heat, stirring frequently until the vegetables are just limp but not browned. Add ham, tomatoes, coriander, oregano, and salt and pepper to taste. Bring to a boil. Cover the casserole. Reduce heat and simmer for about 35–40 minutes, stirring frequently.

Pour sauce into jars with very tight lids. Cool completely and refrigerate until ready to use. The sauce will keep for 10–14 days in the refrigerator.

Yield: 3–3½ cups

*See Tropical Glossary.

Haitian Hot Sauce

Hot peppers of the Caribbean islands are extremely hot and often their flavors are one-of-a-kind. The seeds hold a great deal of the hotness, so remove the seeds for a milder taste. And be sure to carefully wash your hands with warm water after handling.

This sauce has a rich color and nice thickness. Use it on fish or fowl to enhance the flavor of the main course.

1 medium onion, finely chopped
3 cloves garlic, minced
2 scallions, mashed
¼ cup vegetable oil
2 stalks celery, peeled and chopped
4 Haitian peppers or other chili peppers, finely minced
2 carrots, finely grated
8 large ripe tomatoes, peeled, seeded, and chopped fine
1 teaspoon ground cloves
1 teaspoon freshly chopped thyme

Salt and freshly ground black pepper to taste
1 cup red wine

In a heavy saucepan, sauté the onion, garlic, and scallions in oil until the onion is translucent. Add the celery, peppers, and carrots. Cook over medium heat until vegetables are soft. Add tomatoes, cloves, thyme, and salt and pepper to taste. Cook over a medium heat, stirring occasionally for 40–45 minutes until thick. Add the red wine and cook for another 10 minutes. Cool and pour into sterilized jars. Seal tightly. Sauce will keep in refrigerator for a few weeks.

Yield: 2 ¼ cups

Key Lime Mustard Sauce

The Pier House Restaurant in Key West is famous for this mustard sauce—an excellent accompaniment to conch fritters, stone crabs, or your favorite seafood dish. Give it a try and you'll see how simple it is to make!
Key limes are not easy to find. Fresh Persian limes will do fine.

1 quart mayonnaise
1 cup Gulden's mustard
1 cup fresh or bottled Key lime juice (may substitute fresh lime juice)

Blend mayonnaise and mustard together well. Slowly add the lime juice, stirring well. Chill and serve on the side of fish or shellfish.

Yield: 6 cups

Joe's Stone Crab Restaurant Mustard Sauce

Here's a classic sauce that's a must for gourmets and gourmands to master in order to make their cooking repertoire complete! This sauce is the perfect one for stone crabs, but if you can't locate stone crabs, it's just as yummy on fish and meat.

3 ½ teaspoons dry English mustard
1 cup mayonnaise
2 teaspoons Worcestershire sauce
1 teaspoon A-1 sauce
⅛ cup light cream
⅛ teaspoon salt

Blend the English mustard and mayonnaise. Beat for about 1 minute. Add the remaining ingredients and beat until the mixture reaches a creamy consistency.

Yield: 1 cup

'Chovy Sauce

Since I'm a great lover of anchovies, this is one of my favorite sauces. Serve it drizzled over ice-cold shrimp and a bed of fresh vegetables. For true anchovy-lovers only.

1 cup mayonnaise
1 hard-boiled egg, chopped
1 teaspoon Coleman's dry mustard
2 cloves garlic, minced
1 teaspoon dried tarragon
2 cans flat anchovies, drained and chopped
1 teaspoon capers

Mix all ingredients well. Serve chilled.

Yield: 1 cup

Dill Sauce

The fresher the dill, the better the sauce. Try it on freshly poached salmon. It's superb.

1 cup sour cream
1 tablespoon minced parsley
1 tablespoon fresh lemon juice
1 teaspoon freshly chopped chives
1 teaspoon grated onion
2 tablespoons chopped fresh dill or to taste

Mix well by hand or for a few seconds in a food processor.

Yield: 1 cup

O'Steen's Shrimp Sauce

The lightness in color of this sauce will deceive you—it's quite tangy! O'Steen's Restaurant in St. Augustine, Florida, serves this with the freshest fried shrimp I've ever tasted!
Chill well before serving.

1 cup mayonnaise
¾ cup ketchup
3 tablespoons Worcestershire sauce
3 tablespoons horseradish
1½ tablespoons A.B. Hot Sauce or other hot sauce

Mix thoroughly and serve with hot fried shrimp.

Yield: About 2 cups

Zesty Shrimp Cocktail Sauce

This recipe calls for just 2 teaspoons of horseradish, but I add more for a hotter taste. My husband likes it *scorching*.

1 cup ketchup
2 teaspoons prepared horseradish, or more to taste
2 large dashes cayenne pepper
¾ teaspoon chili powder
2 cloves fresh garlic, pressed
Juice of ½ lemon or lime
Pinch of salt or salt substitute

Mix all ingredients together well.

Yield: 1½ cups sauce, enough for a pound of shrimp

Tropical Seafood Sauce

Spice up your hot seafood with this hot little sauce. It has just enough of that tropical lime juice to tickle your taste buds. You can also enjoy it as a shrimp cocktail sauce.

1 tablespoon lime juice
½ cup ketchup
1 tablespoon Worcestershire sauce
2 dashes Pickapeppa hot sauce or other hot sauce
Salt and coarsely ground pepper to taste
Lemon and fresh parsley for garnish

Combine all ingredients. Serve in a small glass dish next to a seafood entree along with a half lemon wrapped in cheesecloth and tied with a green ribbon, and sprigs of fresh parsley for garnish.

Yield: About ⅔ cup

Orange Hollandaise

Here's a refreshing change from your everyday hollandaise sauce. Serve it on asparagus and other green vegetables.

3 tablespoons orange marmalade
⅓ cup orange juice
⅓ cup water
1⅔ cup vegetable oil
1 egg yolk
2 whole eggs
2 tablespoons strawberry preserves

2 tablespoons minced fresh dill or ½ teaspoon dry
2 teaspoons minced fresh basil or ½ teaspoon dry
1 teaspoon minced fresh mint
1 tablespoon fresh cilantro (coriander leaves) or ½ teaspoon dry
Black pepper to taste
¼ cup white wine

In a medium-sized saucepan, mix together the orange marmalade, orange juice, and water. Cook at medium-high heat, stirring constantly until reduced by about ⅓.

In another small saucepan, heat the vegetable oil until warm. Place the egg yolk and whole eggs into the container of a blender. Whip for about 30 seconds. Add the strawberry preserves, dill, basil, mint, cilantro, and black pepper to taste. Blend until thick and pale yellow in color. Add the orange purée that you have already prepared and whip for 30 seconds. Pour vegetable oil slowly into blender with blender on low speed. Add white wine and whip for another 30 seconds.

Yield: About 2½ cups

Mango Spread

As a child, I grew up eating apple butter on Wonder bread, but now I like Mango Spread on hot muffins. It's also good on bread and rolls.

6 cups almost ripe or ripe mangoes, peeled and finely diced
2 tablespoons lime or Key lime juice
2 cups water
2½ cups sugar
¼ teaspoon freshly ground cloves
½ teaspoon cinnamon

Cook the prepared mangoes with water and lime juice for about 10–15 minutes or until soft. Add sugar and spices. Cook over medium heat. Stir frequently until the mixture is nice and thick. Pour into hot sterilized mason jars. Seal and process in boiling water for 10 minutes, according to manufacturer's canning instructions.

Yield: About 4 pints

Mango Butter

Mangoes are an important staple in most tropical countries. Consumption worldwide is believed to be second only to coconuts and bananas. The industry is a "mighty midget" and no wonder; the fruit is delicious and can be used in many different ways, like in this Mango Butter recipe. Use it on hot breads or biscuits.

½ pound butter
½ cup diced fresh mango
Fresh lime juice
2 teaspoons freshly chopped parsley
2 cloves garlic, minced
Dash of Worcestershire sauce
Salt and freshly ground pepper to taste

Combine all the ingredients in the container of a blender and blend well.

Yield: ¾ cup

Apricot Sauce

This sauce is particularly good for dunking fried shrimp and scallops. Make up a batch and store it in the refrigerator for when you need a quick seafood fix with a tasty dipping sauce.

1 10-ounce jar apricot jam
¼ cup sugar
¼ cup water
1 tablespoon rum or cognac

Combine the jam, sugar, and water in a small heavy saucepan. Stir over low heat until well blended and smooth. Strain the sauce by forcing it through a sieve with a small spoon or whisk. Let cool. Stir in the rum or cognac.

Yield: About 1½ cups

Lime Marmalade Sauce

Here's a flavorful sauce for dipping broiled or deep-fried shrimp or other seafood. If you'd prefer orange marmalade sauce, substitute orange marmalade for the lime marmalade.

1 cup lime marmalade
Juice of 1 lime
Pinch of freshly ground ginger
1 teaspoon prepared horseradish

Place the ingredients in the container of a blender or food processor. Blend for about 10 seconds on medium speed.

Yield: About 1 cup

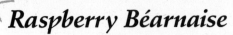

Raspberry Béarnaise

This béarnaise has a good shelf life; with refrigeration, it will keep for a week or more. It's delicious on duck and chicken. The recipe is from Patriccio's restaurant in Coral Gables, Florida.

1 6-ounce package frozen raspberries in heavy syrup
½ cup sugar
3 tablespoons Crème de Cassis
1⅔ cup vegetable oil
1 egg yolk
2 whole eggs
2 tablespoons strawberry vinegar*
1 teaspoon tarragon
¼ teaspoon finely ground black pepper

Purée the raspberries with syrup in a blender. Pour the purée into a saucepan. Add the sugar and Cassis. Simmer for about 30 minutes. Strain the purée into a bowl through a fine sieve and cool.

Warm the vegetable oil in a small saucepan. Meanwhile, place the egg yolks and whole eggs into the container of a blender. Blend for about 30 seconds. Add the strawberry vinegar, tarragon, and black pepper. Blend until thick and pale yellow. Blend in the raspberry purée. Turn blender to a low speed and slowly pour vegetable oil into mixture. Blend for additional 30 seconds.

Yield: 2 cups

*Make your own or purchase at a gourmet market. To make your own, place 6 quarts of hulled strawberries in a stainless steel bowl. Cover with 1 quart white wine vinegar or white champagne vinegar. Allow to stand in a cool place for about 20 hours. Strain, using a sieve and then cheesecloth, and pour the liquid into a glass or enameled pan. Bring to a boil and simmer 10 minutes. Cool, strain, and store in tightly lidded sterile jars.

Banana Chutney

This is a recipe from Gwen Tonge, an enthusiastic teacher who lives on the beautiful island of Antigua in the French West Indies. It is representative of their great local recipes that have been passed from generation to generation.

This is good with curry and also makes an excellent accompaniment to grilled fish.

2 cups diced ripe bananas
1 cup diced green papaya* (pawpaw)

*See Tropical Glossary.

3 tablespoons peeled and chopped fresh ginger
½ pound raisins
1 pound brown sugar or less
2 cloves, well mashed
¼ teaspoon chopped hot pepper
Salt to taste
1½ cup vinegar

Mix all ingredients in a heavy saucepan. Place on low heat and simmer until thick and the mixture leaves the side of the pan. Bottle in sterlilized jars and seal tightly. When sealed, be sure to store in a cool place.

Yield: About 2 pints

Mango Chutney

The mango was first cultivated in India more than 4,000 years ago. It is grown in tropical regions around the world. In the 1860s, the fruit was introduced in Florida and quickly became popular among local "crackers" (those born and raised in the state) and visitors alike.

Mango Chutney is a staple of tropical food lovers throughout the world. It's great served with curried meats, poultry, roasts, or as a relish. This recipe makes a huge batch, but then that's the only way to make sure you'll have a good supply. The "Dancin' Raisins" of the popular television commercial would surely jive to this one.

10 pounds green (unripe) mangoes*, cut up
1 large onion, chopped
½ pound seedless raisins
1 20-ounce can crushed pineapple
2 tablespoons chili powder
2 ounces fresh ginger root, peeled and diced
1½ teaspoons cinnamon
2 tablespoons dry mustard
1 tablespoon whole pickling spices
3 cups vinegar
3 pounds brown sugar or more to taste

Combine all ingredients. Boil slowly for 2–3 hours or until thick. Season to taste. Pour into clean sterilized jars and seal and process according to manufacturers canning instructions for 15 minutes in a boiling water bath. Store at room temperature.

Yield: About 3 quarts

*There are multitudinous varieties of mangoes and sizes. An average mango will weigh about ¾ pound. Be careful with the peel because it causes allergic reactions in some. See Tropical Glossary.

Mango Relish

I was demonstrating some Key lime recipes at the Epicure Row section of the Miami Book Fair International when I had the pleasure of meeting Ettabelle Mann. She came up to me, introduced herself, and handed me this absolutely delicious recipe. It's probably one of the juiciest relishes you will ever taste, and I'm very thankful that she wanted to share this family recipe.

You can make this with ripe or unripe mangoes—it's delicious both ways. Remember, there are many, many varieties of mangoes, so tastes will vary.

Use it on burgers or any meat—or just about anything!

2 quarts peeled ripe or unripe mangoes, seeds removed
4 large onions
6 medium green bell peppers, seeds removed
2 large hot peppers, seeds removed
3 small red bell peppers, seeds removed (may substitute pimento)
1 cup white vinegar
3½ cups sugar
1½ tablespoons mustard seeds
1½ tablespoons celery seeds
1 tablespoon salt

Coarsely chop the mangoes, onions, and peppers in the container of a food processor or by hand.

Combine the vinegar, sugar, mustard seed, celery seed, and salt in a large heavy Dutch oven. Add prepared vegetables and fruit. Mix well and bring to a boil. Reduce heat and simmer for about 10 minutes. Cover and let stand overnight.

The next day, cook until slightly thick, stirring now and then. Pack into hot sterilized jars, and process, according to manufacturer's instructions, for 15 minutes in a boiling water bath.

Yield: About 5–6 pints

Orangy Lime Relish

Here's a simple relish that makes a nice accompaniment to chicken or fish. Use sweet, juicy oranges, if you can.

2 very large oranges
3 seedless limes, thinly sliced
2 tablespoons wine vinegar
1–2 tablespoons sugar
1 tablespoon freshly minced onion

Peel the oranges over a bowl to catch any juice. Cut into medium thick slices. Be sure to remove any seeds. Thinly slice the limes. Add them to the oranges. Combine the remaining ingredients and pour over the fruit. Chill for several hours.

Yield: ½ cup

Mittie's Nine-Day Pickle Chips

My mother-in-law is one of the kindest, nicest people I know—besides being an excellent cook and gardener. Not only does she grow all of her vegetables from seed, she cans and freezes them for use year round. "Me-maw" gives us several gallons of these chips a year, but somehow there's never quite enough!

One can't be in a rush for these delicacies because they take nine days in the makin', but they're well worth the wait. They are the crispiest pickles I've ever eaten.

Do not refrigerate the cucumbers before pickling.

14 dill-size cucumbers
3 teaspoons alum
1 quart cider vinegar
8 cups sugar
1 tablespoon salt
1 tablespoon pickling spices
Green food coloring, several drops

Wash the cucumbers thoroughly and place in an enameled container. Cover with boiling water. Let stand for 24 hours. Pour off the water and cover again with fresh boiling water with a teaspoon of alum added to it. Again let the cucumbers stand for 24 hours. Repeat this step for 2 more days, using boiling water with 1 teaspoon of alum. On the 5th day, drain the cucumbers and cut into thin chips.

In a medium-sized saucepan combine the vinegar, sugar, salt, spices, and green food coloring. Boil for about 10–15 minutes, then pour over the chips. Let stand for another 24 hours. Drain off the liquid into a pot and bring the liquid to a boiling point. Then, pour it over the chips, again. Repeat this procedure for 4 days. On the 9th day, heat the liquid and chips together to the boiling point. Place chips into sterilized canning jars and seal according to manufacturer's canning instructions. Process for 15 minutes in a boiling water bath.

Yield: 6 20-ounce jars

Lake Suzanne Pepper Jelly

Carl and Vita Hinshaw of the Chalet Suzanne Restaurant and Inn in Lake Wales, Florida, took over the operation of this central Florida inn after it was begun by Carl's mom, Bertha. She was one of the best cooks ever. The Hinshaw's carry on her tradition and her reputation for great cuisine.

6½ cups granulated sugar
1½ cups cider vinegar
1½ cups coarsely ground green and red bell peppers (approximately 2 peppers)
¼ cup coarsely ground red, white, yellow, or green hot peppers (do not seed)
1 6-ounce bottle liquid pectin or 2 packages (3 ounces each) Certo

In a large saucepan, combine the sugar and vinegar until the sugar is dissolved. Stir in the peppers and bring to a rapid boil. Stirring to prevent sticking, boil for 3 minutes. Add the pectin and boil 1 minute. Remove from heat and let stand for 5 minutes. Ladle into hot sterilized jars, filling to ⅛-inch from top. Seal according to canning instructions, and let stand without disturbing for 24 hours.

Yield: 3 pints

Mango Jam

If you do not live in a climate where mangoes grow, you are probably puzzled as to the large number of recipes in this book that call for mangoes. The fact is, mangoes are as prolific as zucchini or tomatoes. In areas where they do grow well, when they are in season, folks may find themselves up to their ears in mangoes. In cases like this, it is good to know that mangoes freeze well. Peel them and purée the flesh in a food processor. Freeze them in small containers. They'll keep for months. It is best to put up this jam in small amounts that will be used up in a short time. Use fresh mangoes or frozen puréed mangoes. Either will do fine.

6 cups (about 3 pounds) half-ripe mangoes, peeled and sliced or puréed
½ cup water
3 cups sugar

Measure prepared fruit into a large heavy pan. Add water and cook about 15 minutes or until fruit is tender. Press fruit through a sieve or mash with a potato masher. Add sugar and simmer until mixture is thick. Remove from heat. Pour boiling mixture into clean, hot canning jars, leaving ½-inch headspace and proceed according to manufacturer's canning instructions. Wipe jar rims. Adjust lids and screwbands. Process for 10 minutes in boiling water-bath canner.

Yield: 3–4 pints

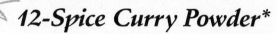

12-Spice Curry Powder*

Curry powder is really a blend of many spices. By varying the different spices and the proportions of the spices, you can make curries with a broad range of tastes. While it might seem more bother than it's worth to make your own curry powders, there are two good reasons for doing it. First, you can tailor the blend to your own tastes. Second, the most flavorful curries are those that are freshly ground. This is my own version, and it's fairly mild. In my last batch, I used cinnamon, cloves, turmeric, and ginger from the "Isle of Spice," Grenada, West Indies, where much of it is produced. Feel free to experiment.

¼ cup mustard seeds
½ teaspoon cardamon seeds, shelled
¼ cup black peppercorns
½ teaspoon cumin seeds
½ teaspoon coriander seeds
1 teaspoon fennel seeds
½ teaspoon ground cloves
½ teaspoon ground cinnamon
½ teaspoon ground turmeric
1½ teaspoons cayenne pepper
¼ teaspoon paprika
½ cup ground ginger
pinch of cornstarch

Grind all of the whole spices together in the container of a food processor, turning the processor on and off several times. Mix together the remaining ingredients and add to the freshly ground spices. Give it one brief pulse of the processor. Store in an air-tight container.

Yield: About 1½ cups

*The word "curry" derives from a Hindustani word, *turcarri*, shortened in India to *turri*. The British corrupted the word and pronounced in "curry." The color of most curry powders comes from the goldenrod yellow of turmeric.

Hot Curry Powder

Curry powders are the very best when spices are freshly ground or combined in a paste with onion, garlic, fruits, and vegetables as ordinary as carrots and celery and as unusual as pomegranate and breadfruit.

Here's one for those who enjoy a very hot curry.

½ cup coriander seeds
5 tablespoons black peppercorns
2 tablespoons cumin seeds
2 tablespoons cardamon seeds, shelled
1 tablespoon fennel seeds

½ cup ground turmeric
½ teaspoon cayenne pepper
1 tablespoon mace
1 tablespoon ground cinnamon
2 teaspoons ground ginger

Grind all whole spices together in the container of a food processor, turning the processor on and off several times. Mix together the powdered ingredients and add to the freshly ground spices. Store in an air-tight container.

Yield: 1¼ cups

Island Fish Seasoning Mixture

One of the treasured "secrets" in Caribbean cooking are the sauces in which the meats and fishes are marinated. The combinations of herbs and spices used in seasoning should be such that no single ingredient stands out and the blending is smooth and harmonious.

3 scallions, finely minced
1 medium onion, finely minced
1 tablespoon minced red bell pepper
½ teaspoon freshly ground cloves
½ teaspoon salt or to taste
2 sprigs whole thyme leaves, chopped
3 cloves garlic, finely minced
1 tablespoon fresh lime or lemon juice
Coarsely ground black pepper to taste
1 tablespoon chopped hot peppers (optional)

Chop all ingredients together with a very sharp knife. Wash fish well with lime juice and water and cut off gills. Score the fish deeply, about ½-inch. Place a little of the mixture into each pocket and rub all over the remainder of the fish. Marinate 1–5 hours or overnight in the refrigerator. This marinade is also good on pork. If desired, add ½ Scotch Bonnet pepper to make the fish hot and spicy.

Yield: Enough to coat a 4–6 pound fish

Meat Marinade, Island-Style

In Caribbean cooking, rarely is any meat, fish, or poultry cooked without being seasoned ahead of time. Of course, the larger the cut, the longer it will need to be marinated. Even a relatively cheap cut will taste good if it's marinated long enough. Here's a good beef marinade that will easily coat a 4–6 pound roast.

2 tablespoons apple cider vinegar
1 onion, thinly sliced
2 tablespoons rum or sherry
1 teaspoon Hungarian paprika
1 Scotch Bonnet pepper*, seeded and finely chopped or 1 teaspoon chili
   pepper
½ teaspoon celery salt
2 cloves garlic, finely chopped
½ teaspoon coarsely ground pepper

Combine all ingredients together well. Coat the meat with the marinade and marinate in the refrigerator for 2–4 hours or longer so the meat soaks up the flavors. Use the residue to make sauce for the meat.

Yield: Enough to coat a 4–6 pound roast

*See Tropical Glossary.

Chattaway's Quick Barbecue Sauce

If you were passing by the Chattaway Restaurant in St. Petersburg, you probably wouldn't stop in—unless, that is, you knew what good cookin' went on inside. The little wooden building was once a grocery, a gas station, and even a trolley stop. It is now an eatery frequented only by the locals "in the know." If you care to sit and enjoy St. Petersburg's famous sunshine (it used to be that you would get a free newspaper there when the sun didn't shine) you can take part in a casual feast *al fresco* at a picnic table under the graceful jacaranda tree.

You can use this sauce on beef, pork, chicken, or just about anything that requires a good barbecue sauce. The longer it sets, the better the flavor. But, keep it refrigerated in a tightly covered container.

½ medium onion, chopped
¼ green pepper, chopped
½ clove garlic, minced
2 tablespoons margarine or butter
1 quart ketchup
1 tablespoon chili powder
½ teaspoon Tabasco sauce or to taste
⅛ cup vinegar
¼ cup sugar
⅛ cup Worcestershire sauce
Dash of freshly ground pepper or to taste

Sauté the onion, green pepper, and garlic in the margarine or butter until soft. Add the ketchup and other ingredients. Mix well and simmer for about 15 minutes.

Yield: About 4 cups

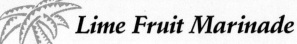

Lime Fruit Marinade

If you want to capture the essence of fresh lime, freeze the fresh juice in ice cube trays, then store in plastic bags in your freezer. When thawed, they'll provide fresh lime juice for all of your favorite recipes, any time of the year.

Here's an easy lime marinade for fresh fruits. Vary the fruits you use according to what is in season or what you have on hand at the time. The longer you marinate, the better the flavor becomes.

⅓ cup fresh lime juice
⅓ cup honey
½ cup sherry or other wine
1 quart cut-up fresh fruits (use strawberries, peaches, bananas, pineapples, papayas, grapes, or mangoes)

In a small bowl, blend the lime juice, honey and sherry. Let stand until the honey dissolves. Pour marinade over the fruits. Let stand for 2 hours or overnight, tossing occasionally.

Serves: 6–8

Desserts

Baked Apple Dessert

Did you ever wonder where cinnamon comes from? Well, the answer is not so astounding—from the bark of the cinnamon tree. "Spice," as the islanders call it, is one of the oldest aromatic seasonings known to man, and its uses are without number, but it's particularly triumphant in desserts. Here's a recipe I've prepared for years.

Filling

5 cups peeled and sliced tart apples
¾ cup sugar
2 tablespoons flour
1 teaspoon pure vanilla extract
½ teaspoon nutmeg
1 teaspoon cinnamon
¼ teaspoon salt
¼ cup water
1 tablespoon butter, softened

Batter

½ cup flour
½ cup sugar
½ teaspoon baking powder
¼ teaspoon salt
2 tablespoons butter, softened
1 egg, slightly beaten
Whipped cream for topping

Preheat oven to 375°. To prepare the filling, combine the apples, sugar, flour, vanilla, nutmeg, cinnamon, salt and ¼ cup water. Turn into a well greased 9 × 9 × 1¾ inch baking pan. Dot the apples with butter.

To prepare the batter, mix all the batter ingredients together well. Spoon the batter on to the apple mixture in about 9 portions—batter will spread. Bake for 30–40 minutes. Serve warm with whipped cream or Brazilian Snow from Bern's Steak House (see page 265).

Serves: 6

Boiled Plantains
(Plátanos Cocidos)

Yum, yum! There's no better description for the taste of this wonderfully sweet dessert. How could something so simple taste so great?!

4 very ripe soft plantains
⅛ teaspoon salt
Sugar to taste
Mozzarella cheese (optional)

Cut off ends of plantains. Slice in half and leave skins on. Place in boiling water.* Cover and cook for about 15 minutes. Remove, peel, and serve very hot. Top with salt and a little sugar. If desired, slice longitudinally and fill with mozzarella cheese.

These are very sweet. Serve as a side vegetable or dessert with a little cinnamon sprinkled on top.

Serves: 2–4

*When I prepare these, I usually boil them together with tropical sweet potatoes (boniato). This does not interfere with the taste and saves on the pot cleaning.

Cicely's Baked Bananas

I once stayed at the cozy hotel resort in Grenada, West Indies, called the Calabash Resort, where I had the good fortune to meet and speak with their excellent chef, Cicely Roberts. A pleasant and gentle woman, she was very helpful, taking time out of her busy day to demonstrate some of her favorite island dishes.

1 cup brown sugar
1 cup fresh orange juice
½ cup dark rum
½ teaspoon cinnamon
½ teaspoon nutmeg
1 teaspoon vanilla extract
4 ripe bananas, peeled and sliced lengthwise

Preheat oven to 350°. Grease well a 9-inch ovenproof pan. Put the brown sugar in a heavy saucepan. Heat carefully until it liquifies. Add the orange juice, rum, cinnamon, nutmeg, and vanilla. Boil for a few seconds. Then, pour over the bananas. Place in the oven and bake for about 30 minutes.

Serves: 2–4

Drunken Banana Fritters

I keep a nutmeg mill alongside the salt and pepper right on my dining room table. Freshly ground nutmeg . . . ummm, there's nothing quite like it! Along with the cinnamon and rum, it makes this banana dish an outrageous delight!

6–8 ripe bananas, sliced crosswide
½ cup rum
4 tablespoons sugar or sugar substitute
2 teaspoons cinnamon
2 pinches freshly grated nutmeg

Arrange the bananas in a glass serving bowl. Pour rum over each layer and sprinkle all of the bananas with sugar, cinnamon, and nutmeg. Allow the bananas to soak up the rum for about an hour. Serve as a dessert or an accompaniment to fresh seafood.

Serves: 6–8

Ambrosia Passion

Here's a light and easy dessert you'll have fun with. Add a touch of La Grande Passion Liqueur for a newly tropical feeling. Made with Armagnac, French brandy, passion fruit, and other natural flavors, La Grande Passion is delicious on fruits and ice creams.

3 grapefruit
3 oranges
1 cup fresh strawberries, hulled and sliced
3 tablespoons sugar or sugar substitute
La Grande Passion liqueur (may substitute other fruity liqueur)
¼ cup flaked coconut

Section the grapefruit and oranges. Combine the grapefruit, oranges, and strawberries. Sprinkle with sugar or sugar substitute. Add a touch of La Grande Passion Liqueur and sprinkle with coconut.

Serves: 8

Chocolate Curaçao Delight

"Chocoholics" will love this light, healthful dessert—except for the extra calories they will have to work off later. Be sure to chill the fruit well, and serve the sauce warm and freshly prepared. Use domestic or imported chocolates for an interesting variation on flavors.

    6 1.65-ounce bars of milk chocolate
    3 tablespoons heavy whipping cream
    2 tablespoons orange Curaçao liqueur
    ¼ teaspoon cinnamon
    Assorted chilled fruits: whole strawberries with stems; seedless orange
        and grapefruit sections; bananas cut into 1-inch chunks.

Break the chocolate into squares and dissolve in the top of a 2-quart double boiler. Stir until smooth. Then, add the cream and stir well. Add the Curaçao and cinnamon, and continue to stir until very smooth.

Remove from the heat and cool for a few seconds. Now, pour warm chocolate into tiny clear glass sauce dishes (these are available at most gourmet houseware stores or restaurant supply stores) and place each sauce dish in the middle of a chilled clear glass salad plate.

Arrange fruits around warm chocolate sauce. Serve with tiny forks or allow guests to dunk fruits into sauce with their fingers.

Serves: About 6

Strawberries Marguerite

Siple's Garden Seat is a lovely waterfront restaurant in Clearwater, Florida. It was converted from a private residence into a very fashionable tea room when Mary Boardman purchased it in 1920. Today, her grandson, Dick Siple, carries on many of her homey traditions. You can almost picture the fashionable young ladies sitting on the fragile white garden seats enjoying this dessert, one of my favorites. Make the Meringue Shells ahead of time.

    32–40 fresh whole strawberries
    1 cup brown sugar
    2 cups sour cream
    2 ounces Cointreau liqueur
    2 ounces orange Curaçao liqueur
    8 Meringue Shells (recipe follows—may be ordered from bakery)

Wash and remove stems from strawberries.

Combine the brown sugar, sour cream, and liqueurs. Blend thoroughly with a wire whisk. To serve, place 4–5 strawberries around the inside of each Meringue Shell and top with ⅓ cup of liqueur sauce.

Meringue Shells

1 cup sugar, sifted
3 large egg whites
½ teaspoon pure vanilla extract
Dash of salt

Preheat oven to 200°.

Heat the sugar and egg whites in a small saucepan until approximately 120°. Stir often to prevent burning. Using an egg beater or an electric mixer, begin mixing on high speed. Add the vanilla and salt. Beat until stiff. Place the meringue in a pastry bag with #3 star tube. Pipe out onto a cookie sheet that has been lined with either silicone or waxed paper. Make a 3-inch solid circle for the bottom. Then build up the sides approximately 1½–2 inches in height.

Put the cookie sheet on the rack at the highest point in the oven. Bake for 1 hour. Shut off heat. Leave shells in oven until thoroughly dry. Place in air-tight container until ready to use.

Serves: 8

Fresh Strawberry Pie

Some of the world's best strawberries are grown in Plant City, Florida. Their Strawberry Festival, held in February of each year, is one of the best, with tons of prize-winning strawberries served in huge mounds and topped with piles and piles of whipped cream.

One of the longest lines at the food booths is the one for the huge slices of Fresh Strawberry Pie. Local growers gave me this recipe about five years ago. I've used it ever since and have served it to a lot of friends who keep coming back for more. Use your favorite pie crust.

1 quart strawberries, hulled
1 cup water
1 cup sugar
4 tablespoons cornstarch
1 prebaked 9-inch pie shell
Whipped topping

Simmer 1 cup of strawberries and ⅔ cup water for 1 minute. Mix together the sugar, cornstarch, and ⅓ cup water. Add it to the berry mixture and bring to boil. Boil until thickened. Cool. Slice remaining strawberries and add to cooled mixture. Pile the strawberry mixture high into the pie. Top with whipped topping.

Serves: 8

Cherries Flambé

Here's a wonderful dessert recipe that my guests often request. Yours will love it, too! Use any flavor ice cream—homemade is preferred—that does well with cherries.

½ cup sugar
2 tablespoons grated orange rind
Grated rind of 1 lemon
1 teaspoon pure vanilla
½ cup 100-proof brandy
1 tablespoon cornstarch
1–2 tablespoons water
1 16-ounce can dark red sweet pitted cherries
4 sugar cubes soaked in overproof rum
4 huge scoops ice cream

In a heavy saucepan, mix together the sugar, orange rind, lemon rind, vanilla, and brandy. Bring to a boil. Stir the cornstarch and water together. Using a wire whisk, add it to the sugar mixture Add the cherries and cook for a few minutes on medium heat.

Soak the sugar cubes in rum. Pour the cherry mixture into a heated chafing dish to present tableside. Add rum cubes to the top of the mixture. Carefully ignite and let burn for a few seconds. When the flame has gone out, spoon the cherries over chilled dishes of vanilla ice cream.

Serves: 4

Key Lime Mousse

Key Biscayne, Florida, is the place for pampering yourself. Try this Key Lime Mousse at the Sonesta Beach Hotel there, or put a Jimmy Buffet record on the stereo and make it at home.

This recipe works just as well with regular Persian limes.

4 egg whites
14-ounce can condensed milk
4 egg yolks
1 cup fresh Key lime juice or Persian lime juice
6 dark chocolate cups, 1 inch high, 3 inches wide
6 slices candied lime (available at most candy stores)

In a small bowl, beat the egg whites to firm consistency. In another bowl, mix the condensed milk and egg yolks. Add Key lime juice. With your hands, fold the egg whites into the milk mixture, using a circular motion (from bottom to top). This will form the mousse.

Pour into chocolate cups and decorate with candied lime slices.

Serves: 6

Palm Breeze Lime Mousse

When shopping for limes I look for those with very smooth, shiny skins and deep green color—they seem to have the best flavor. I like seedless Florida limes so I don't have to worry about picking out the seeds. They'll stay fresh in your refrigerator for 6–8 weeks. Squeeze a little lime over chilled cantaloupe in the morning—it makes it even more delicious. Or try it in this breezy mousse.

    1 package unflavored gelatin
    ¼ cup cold water
    ¾ cup sugar
    ⅔ cup fresh Florida lime juice (about 6 limes)
    4 egg whites
    Dash of salt
    1 cup whipping cream, whipped
    Lime slices, grated lime peel, and grape clusters for garnish

In a saucepan, combine the gelatin and water to soften. Stir in ½ cup of the sugar. Warm over low heat to dissolve. Stir in the lime juice. Chill until syrupy.

Beat in the egg whites and salt until foamy. Gradually add the remaining ¼ cup sugar, beating to soft peaks. Fold in the chilled gelatin mixture, then the whipped cream. Pour into a 1½-quart mold. Chill for 4 hours.

Unmold. Garnish with lime slices, grated peel and grape clusters.

Serves: 8–12

Coconut Mango Mousse

Cooking in Jamaica is a most joyful and popular art. The native cuisine combines Jamaica's colonial influences—English, French, and Spanish—with the use of exotic indigenous foods, as in this Coconut Mango Mousse from the Hotel Inter-Continental in Ocho Rios, Jamaica.

    5 eggs, separated, whites whipped and chilled
    ¼ cup Rumona rum liqueur
    2 tablespoons fresh lime or lemon juice
    1½ cup sugar
    1 teaspoon vanilla
    Pinch of salt
    ½ cup milk
    ¼ cup cream of coconut* (available in most Latin American markets)
    2 tablespoons plain gelatin
    Pulp of 2 fresh mangoes of 1 12-ounce can mango nectar
    1 cup heavy cream, whipped
    1 7-ounce package dried coconut flakes

*See Tropical Glossary.

Separate the eggs. Reserve the whites. In the top of a double boiler, beat the yolks with the rum and lime or lemon juice until light and foamy. Now over hot water, whisk in the sugar, vanilla, and salt until slightly thickened.

Heat the milk and cream of coconut separately to dissolve the cream. Whisk the gelatin into the coconut mix and stir to dissolve evenly. Next pour the coconut mix into the egg yolk mixture. Stir and let cool for 20–30 minutes. With the electric mixer at low speed, fold in the mango, whipped cream, whipped egg whites, and ½ of the package of coconut flakes. Blend thoroughly and pour into soufflé dish lined with wax paper. Garnish the top of the mousse with the remaining coconut flakes. Chill until firm.

Serves: 6

Homemade Mango Ice Cream

Mangoes should be allowed to ripen at room temperature. When they're nice and ripe, why not make some tasty mango ice cream!

4 cups peeled mango slices, chopped fairly fine
1 cup sugar
4 14-ounce cans sweetened condensed milk, chilled
2 quarts half-and-half
6 eggs, well beaten
1 tablespoon vanilla extract
1 teaspoon almond extract

Combine the mango slices and sugar in a large saucepan. Heat until the sugar dissolves. Place in the refrigerator to chill.

In a churn, combine the sweetened condensed milk, half-and-half, eggs, and extracts. Add the chilled mango mixture. Follow manufacturer's directions for making ice cream.

Yield: 1 gallon

Pineapple-Orange Sherbet

Traditionally, pineapples have been associated with hospitality and friendship. This recipe will win friends for those persons willing to share!

5 10-ounce bottles chilled orange soda
2 14-ounce cans sweetened condensed milk
1 15¼-ounce can crushed pineapple in its own juice
Mint leaves for garnish
Fresh pineapple for garnish (optional)

Combine the first 3 ingredients. Blend well.

Pour into the container of a 1-gallon hand-operated or electric freezer. Freeze according to manufacturer's directions.

Serve in scooped-out pineapple halves with fresh pineapple and mint leaves for garnish.

Yield: 1 gallon

Mango Morada

A visit to Andre Mueller's Mile Marker 88 Restaurant will ensure your return to the Florida Keys, at least to Plantation Key. After a fine meal there you may not think there's room for more, but you'll change your mind when you see this! What the heck, you're on vacation!

4 scoops vanilla ice cream
2 large ripe mangoes, peeled and diced
½ cup Hershey's chocolate sauce
2 ounces Grand Marnier liqueur
½ cup sliced almonds, blanched and roasted
½ pint heavy cream, whipped

Place 1 scoop of ice cream in each of four dessert bowls. Top each scoop of ice cream with a portion of the peeled and diced mangoes. Add chocolate sauce, Grand Marnier, and almonds. Surround the creation with whipped cream.

Serves: 4

Pier House Key Lime Pie

I once participated, along with a number of other food writers and Florida chefs, in a program at the Waldorf Astoria Hotel in New York City. The purpose of the program was to illustrate the use of foods indigenous to Florida. The Pier House restaurant's demonstration on how to make this perfect Key lime pie was the hit of the evening. Incidentally, the Pier House is in Key West, "home of the perfect Key lime pie" as many "conchs" will tell you.

If you can't find Key lime juice, you can use regular lime juice, but then, technically, you couldn't call it Key Lime Pie.

4 eggs, separated
1 14-ounce can sweetened condensed milk
½ cup Key lime juice or Persian lime juice
½ teaspoon cream of tartar
1 9-inch graham cracker crust
4 egg whites
4 tablespoons sugar

Preheat oven to 325°. With an electric mixer, beat the egg yolks on high speed until thick and light in color. Turn off the mixer and add the sweetened condensed milk. Mix on slow speed. Still on low speed, add half the lime juice, cream of tartar, and then the remaining lime juice. Mix until blended.

Pour into a prepared 9-inch crust and bake for 10–15 minutes or until the center is firm and dry to the touch. Freeze for at least 3 hours before topping with meringue.

To make the meringue, heat the egg whites and sugar in the top of a double boiler. stirring frequently, to 110°. Beat on high speed until stiff peaks are formed. Top the frozen pie and return it to the freezer until ready to serve. It will keep for several days.

Serves: 8–10.

Mango Key Lime Pie

Chef Mark Militello of Cafe Max in Pompano, Florida, continues to gain kudos as one of Florida's best culinary artists. He has shown great promise in developing the new Florida Cuisine which is so rich with regional ethnic touches. His dishes are superb. This Mango Key Lime Pie is a fine example.

Key limes are difficult to purchase even in Florida, so you may have to opt for Mango Lime Pie which is also delicious.

½ pound graham cracker crumbs
1 tablespoon cake flour
2 tablespoons sugar
¼ pound butter, chopped up
1 medium mango, peeled and puréed
¾ cup fresh Key lime juice or Persian lime juice
2¼ 14-ounce cans sweetened condensed milk
6 egg yolks
4 egg whites
¾ cup sugar

Preheat oven to 350°. Place the graham cracker crumbs, flour, sugar, and butter in a bowl. Mix until blended. Press into a 9-or 10-inch pie pan.

Mix the mango purée and lime juice. Add the condensed milk and egg yolks. Mix until blended. Pour into the crust. Bake for about 7–10 minutes.

Place the egg whites and ¾ cup sugar in a stainless steel mixing bowl. Place the bowl in a pan of warm water and stir until the sugar is dissolved. Remove the bowl from the pan of water and beat the whites until stiff peaks form. Spread the meringue over the top of the pie and place under the broiler until golden brown.

Serves: 8–10

Coconut Cream Dessert

Put some Caribbean spice in your life! Try a little freshly grated nutmeg on this and that—whatever it is you're cooking—anything from your breakfast eggs to your evening dessert. Legend has it that nutmeg is an aphrodisiac. Try putting it on this dessert and you'll become a believer!

See the Can Do section for instructions on how to open a fresh coconut.

1 large coconut, drained (yields 2 cups of milk)
1 envelope unflavored gelatin
1 14-ounce can condensed milk
1 teaspoon freshly grated nutmeg
½ teaspoon salt or salt substitute
Fresh nutmeg for garnish

Drain the coconut milk from the coconut. In a medium-sized saucepan, soften 1 envelope of gelatin by stirring it with ¼ cup of the coconut milk. Now, add ½ cup more coconut milk. Heat on low temperature. Add the remaining coconut milk, condensed milk, and salt. Stir until dissolved. Strain mixture.

Pour into 6 individual containers. sprinkle with plenty of fresh nutmeg and place in the refrigerator to set until chilled.

Serves: 6

Brazilian Snow

What better way to cool off than with a little bit of "snow." Here's an easy little dish from Bern's Steak House in Tampa, Florida. Owner Bern Laxer, a dear friend of mine and fellow member of the Chaine des Rotisseurs, suggests using coffee 5–10 minutes after grinding—don't let the coffee sit for the aroma will not be as robust. If you like coffee, you'll love this.

4 ounces freshest coffee beans, roasted but unground
1 pint good quality vanilla ice cream
Freshly whipped cream
Ground coffee and maraschino cherries for garnish

To prepare this simple dessert, you will need a small grain grinder, like a Moulinex. Grind the coffee as finely as possible. Sprinkle a medium coating of the coffee onto the ice cream (save a little of the coffee for garnish). Mix the ice cream carefully with the coffee. Fold the coffee into the ice cream as many as 7–8 times to mix well. Top with a huge dollop of whipped cream. Garnish with a sprinkle of the ground coffee and a cherry.

Serves: 3–4.

Becky's Favorite Passion Fruit Sorbet

Becky Campbell is the wife of Dr. Carl Campbell, a well-known expert in tropical fruit production. This is a delightful palate cleanser. Serve it as a separate treat in between heavier dinner courses at your next fancy dinner or as a cooling tropical dessert.

    2 cups milk
    1 cup sugar
    ½ cup passion fruit juice, strained (available at most gourmet shops)
    ½ cup fresh lime juice

Combine the milk and sugar in a large saucepan over medium heat, stirring constantly until sugar dissolves. Cool the mixture to room temperature and then place it in the freezer. Freeze until crystals form. Remove and, with an electric mixer, beat in the passion fruit juice and lime juice. Return the mixture to the freezer. Check every 2 hours for formation of crystals and, as they form, beat the mixture with the electric mixer to keep a smooth texture. The sorbet is ready when it can be scooped into a ball and keep its shape.

Serves 6–8

Papaya Jam and Ice Cream

The flavor of the papaya is indescribably wonderful. It tastes like no other fruit on earth. The natives call it "paw-paw"—call it what you like, you'll want to prepare more right away.

You can gauge the ripeness of a papaya more by feel than by look. When fully ripe, it should have the same give as an avocado. A half-ripe papaya will have little give.

    1 large half-ripe papaya, peeled and cut into small strips
    1 cup water
    2 cups sugar
    1 teaspoon vanilla extract
    1 quart vanilla ice cream, divided into 4 servings
    Whipped cream for garnish

Place the papaya fruit in a heavy saucepan. Add the water, sugar, and vanilla extract. Cook over medium heat until the fruit is tender and nice light syrup develops. Serve warm over vanilla ice cream. Garnish with a twirl of whipped cream.

Serves: 4

Key Lime Baked Alaska

A trip to Florida would not be complete without a taste of the famous Key lime. Most Key lime pies have pretty standard ingredients. One of the most unusual I've enjoyed is this Key Lime Baked Alaska, a creation of Mile Marker 88 Restaurant's host/owner André Mueller. André began his culinary career in Switzerland as an apprentice to some of Europe's great chefs. But the locals are happy that he decided to settle down to the slower pace of the Florida Keys where his popular restaurant dishes up thousands of servings of his creation each year.

For this recipe, allow 24 hours for the pie to freeze, and since you probably won't be able to find Key lime juice, go ahead and use regular limes. They'll be just fine, although not as tart.

4 egg yolks
1 14-ounce can sweetened condensed milk
½ cup Key lime juice or Persian lime juice
½ gallon brick vanilla ice cream

Frosting

4 egg whites
½ teaspoon cream of tartar
½ cup sugar
Grated chocolate or toasted almonds

Beat the egg yolks. Blend in the sweetened condensed milk. Add the lime juice and stir.

Cut the ice cream into 1-inch slices. Arrange half of the slices on the bottom of the loaf pan. Pour the egg yolk mixture over this. Top with a layer of the remaining ice cream. Freeze overnight.

Unmold on brown paper and replace in the freezer for at least 15 minutes.*

Just before serving, preheat oven to 500°. Beat the egg whites with the cream of tarter, until very stiff. Gradually add sugar and beat until smooth. Frost the ice cream mold with the meringue (about ½-inch thick). Sprinkle with chocolate or almonds.

Place on a bread board so the heat won't melt the ice cream at the bottom. Bake for 5 minutes, watching carefully.

Serves: 12

*The mold may be kept in the freezer indefinitely before frosting. You can cut off just the amount needed and save the rest for another time. After frosting, it will keep in the freezer nicely for 2 days before baking.

Yearling's Lime Pie

Here's a no-fail recipe for a great lime pie. The local patrons of the famous Yearling Restaurant in Cross Creek, Florida, consume several carloads of this dessert each year. The restaurant is next to the former residence of Marjorie Kenner Rawlings, author of *The Yearling*, who lived and wrote about life in rural Florida.

1 9-inch graham cracker crust
3 egg yolks
1 14-ounce can sweetened condensed milk
6 drops green food coloring
2 tablespoons 151-proof rum
⅓ cup fresh lime juice

Topping

½ pint heavy cream
2 tablespoons confectioners' sugar
1 tablespoon 151-proof rum

Prepare the graham cracker crust or purchase one. Beat the egg yolks. Slowly stir in the condensed milk, food coloring, and 2 tablespoons of rum. Mix thoroughly. Add the lime juice. Pour into the graham cracker crust.

To prepare the topping, whip the cream, confectioners' sugar, and 1 table-spoon rum together until stiff. Spread on top of the pie, piling it nice and high. Chill before serving.

Serves: 8–10

Caribbean Lime Pie

In southern Florida there are two major species of limes produced commercially, the Mexican or true lime, known also as West Indian or Key lime; and the Persian lime, also known as the Tahiti, or Bearss, lime. The Persian is the lime most readily available.

Besides adding a lot of zip to your meals, limes are loaded with vitamin C. Their very special flavor helps bring out the flavor of foods just like salt would, but with barely a trace of sodium. They are also low in calories. When choosing limes, pick the ones that are firm and uniform in size with smooth shiny skins and a vivid green color.

1 9-inch graham cracker crust
6 eggs
2 cups sugar
Juice of 5–6 limes (about ⅔ cups)
¼ cup melted butter
Whipped cream
Lime slices

Preheat oven to 325°. In a mixing bowl, beat the eggs lightly. Add the sugar, lime juice, and butter. Beat well until blended. Pour into the prepared pie crust. Bake for 30–35 minutes or until the filling is set and the crust is golden. Cool. Refrigerate for several hours before serving.

Just before serving, garnish with freshly whipped cream and fresh lime slices.

Serves: 8–10

Blacksmith Pie

Chocolate lovers will rejoice when they taste this dark chocolate delight. It's served at the magnificent Forge restaurant in Miami Beach, Florida. Just a thin slice of this rich chocolate dessert goes a long way. To make it, you need to make some vanilla sugar. To make it, split 2 vanilla beans and put them, together with 3 cups of powdered or granulated sugar, into a jar with a tight lid. Wait 3 days and you'll have vanilla sugar.

Crust

1¼ cups graham crackers
1¼ cups Pepperidge Farm Chocolate Chip Cookies
½ cup melted butter

Vanilla Pudding

4 tablespoons cornstarch
3 tablespoons vanilla sugar
⅛ teaspoon salt
2 cups light cream
1 package unflavored gelatin
⅓ cup water
2 eggs
1 egg

Filling

12 ounces semi-sweet chocolate (1½ 8-ounce packages)
3¾ cups heavy whipping cream
1½ cups powdered sugar
2 egg whites
½ teaspoon vanilla extract or vanilla sugar
Chocolate curls and shavings for garnish

To prepare the crust, break up the crackers and cookies into crumbs with a rolling pin, mallet or food processor to make about 2 cups of crumbs. Mix with the butter and press into a deep 10-inch pie pan. Refrigerate for 1 hour.

To prepare the vanilla pudding, combine the cornstarch, vanilla sugar, and salt in a saucepan. Gradually add the cream, stirring until smooth. Cook over low heat, stirring constantly until thick.

In a small saucepan, combine the gelatin and water. Cook over low heat until melted and clear. Add to the hot pudding mixture. Beat the yolks and the whole egg together. Fold into the pudding mixture. Set aside to cool, then refrigerate.

To prepare the filling, melt the chocolate in a double boiler and stir in 1 cup of the chilled vanilla pudding. Whip the whipping cream with 1 cup of powdered sugar until stiff. Fold ⅔ of the whipped cream into the chocolate pudding mixture. Spread mixture over the crumb crust and refrigerate for at least 10 minutes.

Fold 1 cup of the whipped cream into the remaining vanilla pudding. Set aside. Beat the egg whites until foamy. Add the remaining ½ cup sugar and vanilla extract. Beat until stiff. Fold thoroughly into the remaining vanilla pudding mixture. Remove the pie base from the refrigerator and spread the vanilla pudding mixture on top. Refrigerate for 1 hour.

Frost the pie with the remaining whipped cream. Garnish with chocolate curls and shavings. Use a knife or vegetable peeler to shave the chocolate.

Serves: 10–12

Green Mango Pie

Marian Van Atta, a well-known expert on tropical fruits and vegetables who resides in Melbourne, Florida, is famous for her tropical dessert creations. Fans enjoy her mango pies made with ripened fruit, but also savor pies such as this one, made with unripened mangoes.

The green mangoes make this pie much like apple pie.

2 tablespoons flour
1 cup sugar
1 teaspoon cinnamon
½ teaspoon nutmeg
3½ cups peeled and sliced green mangoes
Juice of 1 lime
Pastry for a 2-crust pie

Preheat oven to 325°. In a medium-sized bowl, mix together the flour, sugar, and spices. Add the mangoes and mix well. Add the lime juice and mix lightly. Spoon into a pastry-lined pie pan. Cover with a lattice crust, and seal and flute edges. Bake 40–45 minutes or until crust is lightly browned and mangoes are cooked.

Serves: 8–10.

Fresh Mango Cheese Pie

Jeanne Cavallaro, a food writer in central Florida, has some of the best tropical fruit recipes. Here's a dessert recipe that she gave me several years ago. It tastes much like cheesecake, but it is very light and the combination with the fresh mango fruit is divine!

This pie needs to be refrigerated overnight and it's important to use a large rectangular baking pan.

2 cups lemon wafer crumbs or vanilla wafer crumbs
⅓ cup butter or margarine, melted
½ teaspoon grated lime zest*
½ teaspoon ground nutmeg
2 tablespoons cornstarch
2 tablespoons fresh lime juice
1½ tablespoons anisette
2 cups diced mango, cut in ¼-inch pieces
2 8-ounce packages softened cream cheese
1 cup sugar
½ teaspoon salt
3 large eggs, lightly beaten
1 teaspoon vanilla extract

Preheat oven to 325°. Process the wafers in the container of a blender. Add the melted butter and lime zest to the processed crumbs and mix well. Press on to the bottom of a 8 x 10 x 1½-inch deep rectangular baking pan. Set aside. In a bowl, blend the nutmeg and cornstarch, then add the lime juice and anisette and blend well. Stir in the mango pieces. Pour the mixture into a 2-quart saucepan and cook over low heat, stirring gently until the mixture is thickened and mango pieces are coated with cornstarch mixture, about 5 minutes. Cool to room temperature and then spoon the mixture into the prepared pie crust.

With a fork, work the cream cheese until light and fluffy. Add the sugar, salt and eggs. Whisk until very smooth and well blended. Blend in the vanilla. Pour this mixture over the mangoes, so that the entire pie is coated. Bake for 1–1¼ hours, until topping is a golden brown. Turn off the oven and leave the pie in the oven for another hour. Remove to a cooling rack. Refrigerate overnight before serving. Add whipped cream for garnish, if desired.

Serves: 10

*See Cooking Terms.

Mother's Orange Cheesecake

Here's a taste of Florida sunshine.

Crust

1⅔ cups finely rolled graham cracker crumbs
¼ cup sugar
¼ cup softened butter or margarine

Filling

3 eggs
2 8-ounce packages cream cheese
1 cup sugar
¼ teaspoon salt
2 teaspoons vanilla
3 cups sour cream
2 ounces frozen orange juice concentrate

Preheat oven to 375°. To prepare the crust, place the graham cracker crumbs in a bowl. Add ¼ cup sugar and the softened butter or margarine. Blend well using your well-washed fingers. Press this mixture into a 9-inch springform pan which is 2½-inches deep. Press the mixture evenly and smoothly over the bottom and sides of the pan.

To prepare the cheese mixture, beat the eggs well in a large bowl. Add the cream cheese and beat again. Add 1 cup sugar, salt, and vanilla. Beat until smooth. Add the sour cream and orange juice concentrate. Beat until smooth. Pour mixture into the prepared crust.

Bake for about 45 minutes. Turn off the oven and let stand in oven for 1 hour or a little longer. Remove and let cool.

Serves: 8–10

Lemon Cheesecake

Lemons range in size from a few inches to the size of a grapefruit. Varieties include the Meyer, an orange-lemon cross; the Bearss, a heavy fruit with tough skin; and the Ponderosa, a fruit that is very large but can be used as a lemon substitute.

Use any variety for the zest used in this luscious cheesecake.

Crust

¾ cup graham cracker crumbs
2 tablespoons butter, melted
2 tablespoons sugar
⅛ teaspoon cinnamon

Filling

2 8-ounce packages cream cheese, softened
½ cup sugar
3 eggs
3 teaspoons vanilla
1 teaspoon grated lemon zest*
2 cups sour cream
Thin slices of lemon peel for garnish

Preheat oven to 375°. In an 8-inch springform pan, mix the graham cracker crumbs, butter, 2 tablespoons of sugar, and cinnamon. Spread over the bottom of the pan and press down.

Whip the cream cheese until very smooth and fluffy. Beat in ½ cup of sugar and the eggs, one at a time. Beat in the vanilla and lemon zest, then the sour cream. Pour into the crust.

Bake for 40 minutes or until set near the sides, but slightly soft in center. Remove from the oven and cool. Chill several hours or overnight.

Garnish with thin slices of lemon peel and serve very cold.

Serves: 8–10.

*See Cooking Terms.

Hummingbird Cake with Cream Cheese Frosting

This cake—a moist, rich, fresh fruit cake—comes from an old Southern recipe. It was given to me by my very special friends, Phil Williams and Skip Mize, owners of a great restaurant in Dade City, Florida, Lunch on Limoges. This is very popular in their restaurant. I never asked them why it's called Hummingbird Cake, but I suspect it is because it makes you "hum" with joy with each taste!

3 cups all-purpose flour
2 cups sugar
1 teaspoon salt
1 teaspoon baking soda
½ teaspoon ground cinnamon
1½ cup vegetable oil
1½ teaspoons vanilla extract
1 8-ounce can crushed pineapple, drained
3 eggs, well beaten
1 cup chopped walnuts
2½ cups chopped bananas
1 cup chopped fresh strawberries or frozen whole strawberries, thawed
Cream Cheese Frosting (recipe follows)

Preheat oven to 350°. Grease and flour 3 9-inch round cake pans.

Combine the flour, sugar, salt, baking soda, and cinnamon. Stir in the oil, vanilla, pineapple, and eggs. Then, mix in the walnuts, bananas, and strawberries. Spoon the batter evenly into the 3 pans. Bake for 30–40 minutes. Cool completely before frosting.

Cream Cheese Frosting

2 8-ounce packages cream cheese, softened
1 cup butter or margarine, softened
2 16-ounce packages confectioners' sugar
2 teaspoons vanilla extract

Combine the cream cheese and butter. Cream until smooth. Add powdered sugar, beating until light and fluffy. Stir in the vanilla. Frost the completely cooled cake.

Serves: 12–16

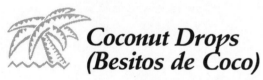

Coconut Drops
(Besitos de Coco)

Capture a few of the aromas of the Caribbean while these easy-to-prepare cookies are baking. This "light" cookie recipe was created by Executive Chef Willi Pirngruber of the Hyatt Dorado Beach Hotel in Puerto Rico and is just perfect after a lavish island buffet of Pumpkin Soup, Curried Goat, Rice and Peas, Pepperpot, and Roti. You can whip up the drops in just a few minutes.

2 3½-ounce cans Baker's Southern-style coconut
1 cup light brown sugar, firmly packed
8 tablespoons all-purpose flour
½ teaspoon salt
¼ cup butter
4 egg yolks
½ teaspoon vanilla extract
Grated rind of ½ lime

Preheat over to 350°. Grease a metal cookie sheet pan. Place all the ingredients in a mixing bowl and blend thoroughly. With your hands, form the mix into 1-inch thick coconut balls. Place about 2 inches apart on the sheet. Bake for about 20–30 minutes or until golden brown. Remove from sheet to cooling racks.

Yield: About 24 drops

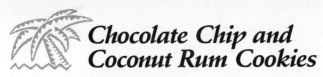

Chocolate Chip and
Coconut Rum Cookies

In September 1986, the Cerromar Beach Hotel in Puerto Rico opened the world's largest swimming pool. It is actually longer than New York's Empire State building is high! There is a river-like current in the pool that propels guests along on a float while allowing them to partake of tropical coolers. Ah, life in the tropics!

After your leisurely "float," you might get hungry from something oh-so-sweet, like these cookies created by Executive Chef Gerard Messerli.

1 cup plus 2 tablespoons all-purpose flour
¼ teaspoon salt
½ teaspoon baking soda
¾ stick unsalted butter, softened
½ cup firmly packed light brown sugar
¼ cup granulated sugar
1 large egg, lightly beaten
¾ teaspoon vanilla
¾ teaspoon light rum
½ cup grated coconut
½ cup semi-sweet chocolate chips

Preheat oven to 375°. Sift the flour, salt, and baking soda together in a bowl and set aside.

In another bowl, using an electric mixer, beat the butter, brown sugar, and granulated sugar until the mixture is light and fluffy. Add the eggs, vanilla, and rum. Beat the mixture well. Fold in the flour mixture, coconut, and chocolate chips. Form the cookies on a baking tray, using a small ice cream scoop. Bake for about 8–10 minutes.

Yield: 24–30 cookies

Flan
(Caramel Custard)

This dessert is a favorite of the locals at La Esquina de Tejas, a very popular Cuban restaurant in Miami's Little Havana. It can be served chilled, at room temperature, or slightly warm.

Many Cuban desserts require that the mold be caramel-lined. There are several different ways to line the molds, but the method described below is one of the easiest and works well.

1 cup white granulated sugar
1¼ cup water
1 ounce anisette liqueur

1 ounce cinnamon sticks
6 large egg yolks
¾ cup condensed milk
¾ cup evaporated milk
¾ cup whole milk
⅛ teaspoon salt
7 ounces freshly grated coconut

Preheat oven to 300°. Cook sugar and ¼ cup of water over high heat, stirring constantly until it browns and caramelizes. Be careful not to let it burn. Pour the resulting caramel into 6 metal molds and cool. As you pour, swirl the caramel around to that it coats the sides and bottom of the molds.

Boil together for 10 minutes 1 cup water, the anisette, and cinnamon sticks. Remove the cinnamon sticks and allow the mixture to cool slightly.

Stir in the remaining ingredients. Mix until smooth and creamy. Pour into molds that have been coated with caramel. Place molds in baking pan and fill with hot water that reaches halfway up the sides of the molds. Bake for 45 minutes or until a toothpick inserted into the middle of the flan comes out clean.

Serves: 6

Jamaican Custard

Some of the easiest to prepare desserts are the best, like this rich custard recipe which was given to me by my friend Elfreda Clarke. She is without a doubt one of the best cooks in southern Florida. This custard is great after a big bowl of Pepperpot Stew. It's very sweet, so serve in small squares.

6 eggs, well beaten
2 teaspoons vanilla
2 14–ounce cans sweetened condensed milk
1 cup brown sugar

Preheat over to 325°.

Add the eggs and vanilla to the milk and mix well. In a small saucepan, heat the brown sugar carefully until it liquifies. Put the brown sugar in a 9-inch square baking tin and coat the entire bottom of the pan very well. Pour the milk mixture into the tin and spread evenly.

Set the tin in a large pan of water and bake for about an hour or until a knife, when inserted, comes out dry.

Chill several hours or overnight. Turn the pan upside down to release the custard. Cut into squares. Top with whipped cream if desired.

Serves: 8–10

Cuban Banana Rum Custard Tart

Louie's Backyard restaurant in Key West, Florida, has one of the most dramatic settings for a memorable, romantic evening in the tropics. Dining outside and listening to the waves rolling in, near your feet, will assure very special memories indeed. This tart will be just the right touch for dessert.

Here's Louie's Executive Chef Norm Van Aken's delicious recipe.

Crust

5 ounces cashews, finely chopped
4 ounces butter, soft
2 tablespoons sugar
1½ cups flour
1 egg, lightly beaten
½ teaspoon vanilla extract

Custard

2 eggs
⅓ cup sugar
2 tablespoons flour
¾ cup heavy cream
4 tablespoons dark rum
2–4 bananas, sliced

Combine all the crust ingredients in a mixing bowl using either an electric mixer or a wooden spoon. This is not a typical crust in that you will probably find it difficult to roll out with a rolling pin. So press the dough into a 11-inch tart shell, using your fingertips, to even thickness. Chill the shell for at least 30 minutes. Preheat oven to 350°.

Line the tart shell with aluminum foil and fill with dried beans or rice. (This will prevent the dough from rising while baking.) Bake the tart shell for 15 minutes, then remove the foil and the beans. Bake 5 more minutes. Cool slightly while preparing the custard.

Beat the 2 eggs and sugar until light and frothy. Add in the flour and mix until smooth. Add the cream and rum. Pour into the partially baked crust and bake at 350° for approximately 20 minutes or until the custard is set.

Top the tart with sliced bananas. Start at the outside edge of the tart and work you way towards the center creating a neat pattern. Serve immediately.

Serves: 10–12

Jamaican Banana Bread Custard

Henry Towle, a young aspiring chef, is doing great things in Coral Gables, Florida. This dessert, one of his latest creations, has flavors one often dreams about!

5 tablespons butter
⅔ cup granulated sugar
12 slices dry bread with crust removed, broken into ¾-inch pieces
1 pound ripe bananas
2 tablespoons dark Jamaican Rum
3 tablespoons apricot preserve
3 ounces Eagle brand condensed milk
8 egg yolks
6 whole eggs
2½ cups milk
½ teaspoon cinnamon
¼ teaspoon nutmeg

Preheat oven to 350°. Butter the bottom of an 8-inch square baking pan with 1 tablespoon of butter and sprinkle with 2 tablespoons of sugar. Place the bread pieces in the bottom of the pan. Dot with the remaining butter and sprinkle with ¼ cup sugar. Slice the bananas lengthwise into halves. Place on top of the bread and sprinkle with rum. Spread the apricot preserves evenly over the bread and banana mixture. Ladle condensed milk over the bread.

In a medium-sized bowl, whisk together the egg yolks and whole eggs. Heat the milk and remaining sugar until the mixture begins to simmer. Pour the milk slowly into the eggs, stirring constantly until well blended. Pour over the bread and banana mixture. Sprinkle with cinnamon and nutmeg. Place a heavy platter or cutting board over the pan to weigh down the mixture. Allow to sit for 15 minutes. Bake in the preheated oven for 25–30 minutes or until an inserted knife comes out clean.

Serves: 6–8

Papaya Custard

Papaya is one fruit that has not yet been added to the dining repertoire of very many people; such a pity, as this is truly the food of the angels. My first experience with papaya came five years ago in Barranquilla, Colombia, where I was served huge papaya halves the size of half a basketball each day for breakfast. Just a squeeze of lime over the raw fruit enhances its lovely citrus flavor.

It's great cooked, too. This recipe was also given to me by Chef Henry Towle.

2 medium papayas, peeled, seeded, halved, and chopped
3 tablespoons butter
2 tablespoons dark brown sugar
2 tablespoons brandy
6 butter cookies
8 egg yolks
6 whole eggs
2½ cups milk
½ cup sugar

Preheat oven to 350°. In a skillet, melt the butter and add the chopped papaya. Sprinkle with brown sugar and brandy. Sauté until the papaya is very soft. Remove from heat and cool. Place in the container of a blender and puree. Crumble the butter cookies and stir into the papaya mixture. Spoon into the bottom of an 8-inch square baking pan.

In a medium-sized bowl, beat the egg yolks and whole eggs until slightly thickened. Heat the milk and sugar together and bring it to a boil. Remove from heat. Pour the milk slowly into the eggs, stirring constantly until well blended. Pour over papaya in the baking pan. Cover with foil. Bake in the preheated oven for 20–25 minutes or until an inserted knife comes out clean.

Serves: 6

Louie's Frozen Lime Soufflé

Executive Chef Norman Van Aken and Pastry Chef Susan Porter of Louie's Backyard restaurant in Key West, Florida, have done much to bring national recognition to Florida's regional cooking. When preparing this recipe, use Key limes if possible, but you may substitute Persian limes, the limes we use in most of our cooking.

Be sure to freeze the soufflé at least 4 hours before serving. You'll need six ramekins or individual soufflé dishes.

1 cup sugar
¾ cup water
2 teaspoons light corn syrup
6 egg yolks
Finely grated zest* of 1 Key lime or zest of ½ Persian lime
6 tablespoons freshly squeezed Key lime juice or Persian lime juice
¾ cup heavy cream

Prepare a strip of aluminum foil or parchment paper to form a collar for each ramekin that extends 1½ inches above the rim. Secure with tape.

Combine the sugar, water, and corn syrup and cook until the sugar dissolves. Keep over low heat.

*See Cooking Terms

To make the soufflé, combine in a mixer bowl the yolks and zest. Beat on high speed until very thick and pale. Slowly add the lime juice and continue beating on high speed for 3–4 minutes. Bring the corn syrup to a boil and add it to the mixture. Continue beating until cool. While this is mixing, beat the cream to stiff peaks, by hand, in a large bowl. Fold the lime mixture into the cream until thoroughly mixed. Pour the mixture into the prepared ramekins. Freeze at least 4 hours before serving. Serve with puréed fresh fruit.

Serves: 6

Persimmon Pudding

It is said that the Algonquin Indians used to collect the persimmon (an unusually sweet fruit when ripe), dry it, form it into bricks, and store it to eat in winter. Use ripe persimmons or the result will be very sour. To ripen persimmons, leave them in a plastic bag with a ripe apple for 2 to 4 days.

Try this classic recipe from Marian Van Atta, an author from Melbourne, Florida, who writes a popular cooking column called "Living Off The Land."

4 cups chopped persimmon*
3 cups milk
3 eggs
2 cups sugar
2 teaspoons baking soda
1 teaspoon baking powder
1 teaspoon cinnamon
1 teaspoon nutmeg
2 cups flour
3 tablespoons melted butter

Preheat oven to 325°. Wash the persimmons well, remove the stems, and chop. Combine with the milk. When well mixed, run through a colander to remove seeds. Beat the eggs and add to the milk-persimmon mixture.

Sift all the dry ingredients together and slowly add to the persimmon mixture. Add the melted shortening, slightly cooled. Mix well. Pour mixture into a greased 16 x 8 x 3-inch pan, or use 2 smaller pans.

Bake for 1 hour or until done. Cut into squares and serve plain or with fresh whipped cream or yogurt.

Serves: 8–10

*See Tropical Glossary.

Coconut Rice Pudding

Here's another rich and delicious dessert from Executive Chef Willi Pirngruber of the Hyatt Dorado Beach Hotel in Puerto Rico that is sure to please rice pudding lovers. Be sure to use short grain rice in this recipe because it cooks to a creamier consistency. Short grain rice is available as Arborio or Calrose rice.

6 cups milk
1⅛ cups canned cream of coconut
¾ cup short grain rice
1 cinnamon stick
½ teaspoon ground ginger
¼ teaspoon salt
2 tablespoons sugar
½ cup raisins
Ground cinnamon for garnish

In a large saucepan, bring the milk and cream of coconut to a boil over medium heat. Stir in the rice, cinnamon stick, ginger, and salt. Return to a boil. Reduce heat and simmer, uncovered, for about 30 minutes or until the rice is tender, stirring occasionally.

Stir in the sugar and simmer 5 minutes more. Add raisins and pour into a 1½-quart serving dish. Sprinkle generously with cinnamon. Chill at least 4 hours.

Serves: 8

Pudín Diplomático

I found this recipe in the *Miami Herald's* food column. Linda Cicero, the food editor, said the recipe was given to her by the late Rafael Casalins, who was the restaurant reviewer for *El Herald,* the *Miami Herald's* Spanish-language edition.

2 cups milk
1 teaspoon cinnamon
Grated rind of ½ orange
6 eggs
¾ cup sugar
1 teaspoon vanilla
⅛ teaspoon salt
¼ cup dark rum or fruit-flavored brandy
¼ cup sugar
2 teaspoons water
1 8-ounce can fruit cocktail, drained
1 pound cake (approximately 16 ounces), sliced ½-inch thick

Preheat oven to 350°. Combine the milk, cinnamon, and orange rind in a small saucepan and bring to a boil, then remove from heat and let cool to room temperature. Beat the eggs with ¾ cup sugar until light, then add vanilla, salt and liqueur. (If you do not like the alcohol's taste, you may substitute ¼ cup drained syrup from the fruit cocktail.) Beat in the milk mixture.

Caramelize the mold by placing ¼ cup sugar and a few teaspoons of water in a heavy saucepan over medium-high heat. Stir until the sugar is dissolved and turns a golden brown. Pour immediately into a 1-quart mold and swirl around to coat the bottom and sides. The caramel will harden very quickly.

Pour the egg mixture into the prepared mold, then spoon the fruit cocktail around the top. When the fruit is floating, carefully place the slices of pound cake on top, covering the surface as completely as possible. Place the mold in a pan that's at least 2 inches wider all around, and pour hot tap water in to reach halfway up the side of the mold. Bake for 1½ hours or until the custard is firm. Let cool completely and refrigerate for several hours before turning over to unmold. To unmold, dip briefly in warm water if necessary.

Serves: 8–10

 ## *Yum Rum Topping*

In the heat of the tropics, life can be made a lot simpler by preparing delicious but simple dessert recipes like this 1-2-3 rum topping.

½ cup Captain Morgan's Spiced Rum
1 cup water
1 cup sugar
Sponge cake or yellow cake

Combine water and sugar in a small heavy-bottomed saucepan. Bring to a boil over moderate heat. Cook about 1 minute without stirring. Remove from heat. Cool slightly and stir in the rum.

Serve over slices of sponge cake or yellow cake.

Serves: 4–6

Lime Cream Topping

After taking a bite of this simple-to-prepare dessert topping, you will agree that a lime is definitely not a lemon!

1 cup whipping cream
2 tablespoons freshly squeezed lime juice
¼ teaspoon vanilla extract
Pound cake
Chocolate shavings for garnish

Combine whipping cream, lime juice, and vanilla extract. Whip until soft peaks occur. Serve on bakery pound cake or your own homemade version. Garnish with chocolate shavings.

Yield: 1½ cups

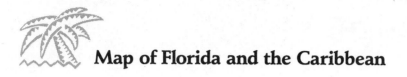

Map of Florida and the Caribbean

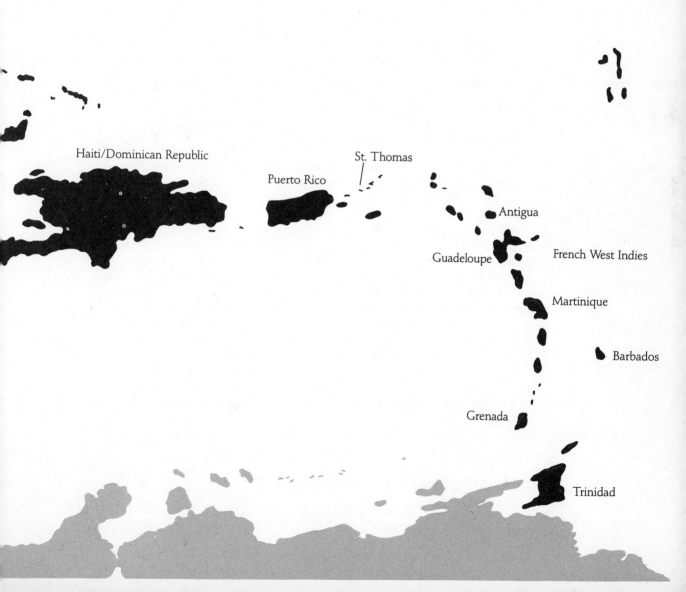

Haiti/Dominican Republic

Puerto Rico

St. Thomas

Antigua

Guadeloupe

French West Indies

Martinique

Barbados

Grenada

Trinidad

Can Do

This section covers the basic techniques for preparing some of the most commonly used tropical fruits—the ones you're going to encounter before you get very far into *Tropic Cooking*, but that you may never have handled before. You can read this whole section before you get started on your cooking adventure, or you can refer to it on an as-needed basis. When you get to the actual preparation, be sure you use a sturdy sharp knife. Anyone "can do" these preparations—it's simply a matter of a little know-how—and a good knife.

How to Slice a Pineapple

If you want to keep the rind intact to use as a serving boat, you need to cut the fruit away carefully, leaving enough of a shell for stability.

Place the pineapple atop a large cutting board with the stem facing you. Begin by placing the knife at the far end of the pineapple. Using a very firm, smooth stroke, gradually lower the knife and pull it toward you to cut the fruit in half. Using a similar stroke, cut each of the two pieces in half. Now, grasping the pineapple firmly with your left hand, cut off the base tip of each piece. Now, holding the fruit straight up, slice off the hard, fibrous center core with a firm stroke. Stand the pineapple upright again, hold the fruit firmly, and cut with a downward motion. If there are any "eyes" on the fruit, remove them with the sharp knife tip. Put the fruit back in place on the rind and cut it in half lengthwise. Make a series of crosswise cuts about 1 inch apart to create chunks. Divide in half if smaller wedges are desired.

If you are not concerned with keeping the rind intact, begin by cutting off the stem and the base of the whole pineapple. Stand the fruit on end and slice off the rind with eight or nine downward strokes. Use the sharp end of the knife to remove the eyes. Cut the fruit into fourths and cut out the fibrous core from each section. Lay each quarter on its side, and slice as desired.

How to Open a Fresh Coconut

First check to be sure the coconut is mature by shaking it. The mature coconut contains a large amount of "milk." Remove the outer husk, if there is one. Puncture the "eyes" of the brown hairy coconut by driving a nail or ice pick into these eyes. Drain the milk into a bowl for use later.

The coconut will be easier to crack if you bake it whole for 20 minutes in a 350° oven, or place it in the freezer—after removing the milk—for about an hour. Place the coconut on a very firm surface. Tap the shell lightly with a hammer in several locations until the shell cracks into several pieces. Separate the pieces of meat from the shell with a very sharp knife. Wipe the meat with a clean cloth. With a very sharp knife, trim off the outer brown layer. Slice into pieces or grab a hunk and enjoy.

How to Peel and Section a Grapefruit or an Orange

Place the fruit on its side. Cut off the top, slicing just deep enough to remove the rind and the white pith. Now, turn the fruit around. Cut off the bottom, slicing just deep enough to remove the rind and the white pith.

Set the fruit on the end now, so that you will be able to keep it stable while cutting. Make the first vertical cut, slicing only deeply enough to remove the rind and white pith and a small amount of fruit. Continue this procedure around the fruit, turning it slightly before each cut. By the time you are finished cutting, the fruit should be nearly free of any rind and pith. Easier done than said.

To cut the sections, hold the fruit firmly in the palm of your hand. Looking for the separations, gently free the sections with the tip of your knife. Hold the fruit over a bowl so that loose juice will flow into the bowl.

Another method is to peel by cutting the peel round and round spiral fashion, but I like the first method the best.

How to Peel a Green Plantain

Bananas are a cinch to peel, but green plantains can be somewhat difficult since the thick skin tends to cling tightly to its fruit.

For an easy method of peeling, slice off the end tips of the plantain, about ¾ of an inch, and discard. Cut the fruit in half vertically. Now make four evenly spaced slits lengthwise, cutting through the peel from the top to the bottom of the fruit. Beginning at the corner of each slit, lift the skin away, a strip at a time. Pull it off lengthwise rather than crosswise.

Slice the fruit diagonally or lengthwise for frying .

How to Slice a Mango

This fruit can be a slippery critter to slice, and some people show an allergic reaction to the skin, so be careful when handling one. In addition to being very slippery, the flesh clings to the large flat pit, so slicing a mango can be a tricky operation. The best way to accomplish this is to lay the mango on its side and cut a rather thick slice from the top (enough to clear the pit), and cut another slice from the bottom. Peel the skin from the center section and cut the juicy flesh off the seed, in slices or hunks, depending on your need. To dice the flesh from the top and bottom sections, cut the flesh almost to the skin, turn the skin inside-out and cut little squares away from the skin. To slice, gently carve the flesh out of the peel with a paring knife, trying to keep the piece intact. Then slice.

It is also possible (but don't count on it) to peel the whole mango first, then cut off the slices while holding the mango in one hand. Trying to get a mango to stay still on a cutting board is virtually impossible, so you'll have to hang onto it with one hand as you slice with the other. Give the seed to a passing child to suck on.

Both mangoes and papayas can cause allergic reactions in susceptible persons. The danger is not in the eating, but in getting the juices on the face or in the eyes. Allergic reactions include eruptions of the skin or swelling. Those who are allergic should wear rubber gloves when preparing either papayas or mangoes. As a precaution, everyone should wash hands thoroughly with warm soapy water after handling these fruits.

How to Handle Hot Peppers

The very volatile oil in hot chilies may burn your skin, make your eyes water, or cause other skin reactions. It is important to protect your hands by wearing rubber gloves when working with the hot chilies.

To prepare chilies for cooking, rinse the pods, and remove the stalks with your hands under cold running water. Break the pods in half and brush out the seeds with your fingers or a sharp knife. If the ribbings inside seem to be fleshy, cut them out. Use the chilies at once. After handling, wash hands thoroughly with warm soapy water.

If the chilies are not to be used right away, soak them in cold water. This may, however, take away some of the "hotness."

Tropical Glossary

Achiote
See Annatto.

Ackee (*Blighia sapida*)
(a-KI). Oblong-shaped red or yellow fruit of an evergreen tree that is very popular in Jamaica. The edible part looks like scrambled eggs. Flesh sections are generally cleaned, boiled, and sautéed with salted codfish, sliced onions, tomatoes, and scallions. Available canned in some West Indian shops. Also known as: channet and genip.

Allspice (*Pimenta officinalis*)
The dark brown berries of an evergreen tree grown in the West Indies. They look like large peppercorns and their aroma is that of a combination of cloves, nutmeg, and cinnamon. Allspice is often used in curries and marinades. Also known as: pimento and Jamaica pepper.

Annatto
A rusty-red dried seed used primarily to flavor and color cooking oil a bright orange yellow. Also known as: achiote.

Annatto Oil
Oil prepared from the annatto seed.

To prepare, heat 1 cup vegetable oil in a heavy saucepan. Add ½ cup of annatto seeds. Do not boil. Stir just until annatto turns oil orange. Strain out seeds. Oil will keep indefinitely if well sealed in the refrigerator.

Asopao
A Spanish word meaning "soup," used to describe a stew made with rice and fish, poultry, or meat. A Puerto Rican dish.

Avocado (*Persea americana*)
A pear-shaped, fleshy green fruit of a tropical American tree used often as an ingredient in salads and dips.

Bammie
(BA-mi). A round, flat bread made from the root of a grated cassava. This is delicious with fried fish steeped in a sauce of peppered vinegar.

Banana (*Musa acuminata*)
Crescent-shaped fruit which grows in tropical trees and has white, pulpy flesh and thick, yellow skin which is easily removed. Not to be confused with plantain.

Basil (*Ocimum basilicum*)
An herb. The chopped, green leaves of this plant are used in a variety of dishes.

Bellywash
A type of lemonade made in Jamaica.

Bijol
Ground annatto seed. It is often used to give rice a distinctive yellow color, much as saffron does, and a bit of fragrance. Usually found in Latin American markets.

Bird Pepper (*Capsicum frutescens*)
A fiery pepper whose tiny size disguises its bite. Bird peppers are used in pickles and condiments. Called bird peppers because birds love them!

Bitter Orange (*Citrus aurantium*)
Much more acidic than the sweet orange (*Citrus sinensis*). Used in juices and marmalades. To make your own, add an equal amount of lemon juice to regular orange juice. Also known as: sour orange.

Black-eyed Peas
Tropical white peas with little black "eyes" in the center of each. Actually, they're beans. Also known as: cowpeas.

Black pepper (*Piper nigrum*)
An all-purpose spice with a warm, pungent, and fiery taste. Also known as: pepper.

Blaff
Fresh fish poached and seasoned with spices and peppers. Popular in the French West Indies.

Bluggoe Figs
A species of banana, sometimes referred to as "bird figs." Reddish-purple and used as a vegetable.

Boniato (*Ipomoea batatas*)
A tuber that looks much like a common sweet potato, although the skin is usually mottled. It has white or yellow flesh. It is drier and fluffier than and less sweet than sweet potatoes—sort of a cross between a sweet potato and a baking potato. It is a staple in many countries of the world. Select rock-hard tubers. Also known as: batata, batata dulce, camote, Cuban sweet potato, and white sweet potato.

Breadfruit (*Artocarpus communis*)
A large green fruit with rough skin. The fruit is usually broiled or roasted. Roasted breadfruit resembles bread. When used as a bread substitute, it is sliced very thin. Also known as: fruit à Pain, pana de pepita, panapan.

Breadnut (*Brosimum alicastrum*)
The fruit of a tree grown in the West Indies, Mexico, and tropical areas of the United States. It is roasted and ground into a flour from which bread is made. Also known as: Maya breadnut.

Bulla
(BU-la). A round, flat cake made from flour and heavy dark sugar. Bulla with avocado is a traditional snack in Jamaica.

Bustamante Backbone
A tough sweet made from grated coconut, crude sugar, and molasses, named for Jamaica's first prime min-

ister, who was known for his firmness of character.

Calabaza (*Cucurbita moschata*) (kah-lah-BAH-sa). A round or slightly pear-shaped squash that grows to be very large (is rarely seen any smaller than a honeydew). Its fine-grained, orange flesh tastes similar to pumpkin but is sweeter and more moist. It is a staple in Central and South America and the Caribbean. Also known as: abóbora, ahuyama, crapaudback, Cuban squash, giraumon, toadback, West Indian pumpkin, zapallo.

Callaloo (*Xanthosma hastifolium*) [Also spelled calaloo, calalou, calalu, callilu.] (CA-la-lu) A vegetable closely resembling spinach in appearance as well as in flavor. The leaves are the size of elephant ears. Member of a diverse group of edible tubers that includes the dasheen or eddoe. It is grown in the West Indies. Also cultivated in Ceylon and India. One of the main ingredients of the popular Pepperpot Soup. Spinach or kale is a fair substitution. Also known as: bhaji.

Callaloo Greens
Term used for the young leaves of the dasheen or taro plant.

Capers (*Capparis spinosa*)
The unopened flower buds of the caper bush. Used as a seasoning in hot and cold sauces as well as in a variety of other dishes. Capers are usually packed in vinegar or salt.

Capsicium
See Peppers.

Carambola (*Averrhoa carambola*) (kah-rahm-BO-la). An oval-shaped, star-like fruit with a thin, shiny, yellow skin which has 4–6 longitudinal ribs. When sliced, carambola looks like a star and has translucent and juicy but crisp flesh. There are two varieties: sweet and sour. Also known as: five-angled fruit and star fruit.

Cassareep
Thick black seasoned syrup processed from the cassava root. Used for coloring, especially when cooking pepperpots. Can be purchased from West Indian markets or processed in your kitchen. Popular in Trinidad, Barbados, and other islands.

Cassava (*Manihot esculenta*)
A vegetable with long tuber-shaped roots (2 inches wide and 8 to 10 inches long) sometimes referred to as "sticks." The bark is dark, and is thick and tough . The flesh is white, and is hard and dense. Cooked cassava is gluey and somewhat sweet. There are two popular varieties: sweet and bitter. The sweet is generally boiled and used as a vegetable. The bitter variety is black, rough and with longer roots and is known to be poisonous until cooked. It is used commercially. Also known as: manioc, mandioca, tapioca, and yuca.

Cayenne (*Capsicum annum*)
A powder made from a combination of pods and seeds of pepper plants, hence, it is considered a pepper. Also known as: African pepper, chilies, hot pepper, red pepper, and zesty.

Chayote (*Sechium edule*)
(chy-O-tay). A green gnarled pear-shaped fruit which is used as a vegetable. Cooked, it tastes similar to a cucumber. A member of the squash family, the fruit is generally boiled and served hot with butter or grated cheese. Also known as: cho-cho, chocho, choko, christophene, christophine, chuchu, custard marrow, mirliton, pepinella, vegetable pear, sousous, and xuxu.

Chili Powder
A combination of chili peppers ground to a powder along with other herbs and spices.

Chive (*Allium schoenoprasum*)
The smallest member of the onion family with a delicate flavor. Often used as a garnish. It is a Caribbean herb; scallions seem to nearly approximate the flavor if one uses both the white and green of the stalk. Also known as: cebollino, ciboulette, cive, and simply "herb."

Chorizo
A very spicy sausage made with pork and pork liver, seasoned with cayenne pepper and juniper berries.

Christophene
See Chayote.

Cilantro
See Coriander.

Cinnamon
Made from the bark of the cinnamon tree, this spice has probably been around since the beginning of time and has a variety of uses.

Cloves
The unopened flower bud of a tropi-cal tree (*Eugenia aromatica*). It is brown and has a fragrant scent.

Coco
See Dasheen.

Coconut (*Cocos nucifera*)
Considered a fruit. A large seed of the coconut palm tree. A thick, hard shell encases an edible white flesh with a milky-fluid center.

Coconut Cream
See: Cream of coconut.

Coconut Juice
The liquid from a fresh coconut. Some call this coconut water.

Coconut Milk
To prepare, crack the coconut and remove the meat. Discard the hard coconut shell. Dice the coconut into small pieces, leaving on the thin brown skin. Place 3½ cups water in the container of a blender. Add coconut pieces slowly to the water. Blend until mixture is almost a purée. Now, strain the juice through a wire mesh strainer into a separate container. Discard the strained coconut.

Conch
(konk). A shellfish from the mollusk family that lives in a large spiral shaped shell. The meat is tough and must be tenderized before using through pounding and boiling the flesh. Widely used in many of the Caribbean islands and southern Florida. The word conch is also a slang term meaning a person who was born and raised in the Florida Keys, or has lived there many years. Also known as: concha, conque, and lambi (Carib name).

Coriander (*Coriandrum sativum*)
The leaves of this fragrant herb are widely used in Hispanic and Asian cuisines. The dried seeds of the plant are also used as a seasoning, notably in curries. Also known as: cilantro, culantro, culantrillo, Chinese parsley, and Mexican parsley.

Cream of Coconut
If coconut milk is allowed to stand, the coconut cream will rise to the top. For mixing tropical drinks, it is best to use the canned cream of coconut, which is slightly sweetened. Also known as: coconut cream.

Cumin (*Cominum cyminu*)
An herb commonly used in Italian and Hispanic cooking. Flavor is similar to caraway—hot and slightly bitter.

Curry
A combination of at least 10 spices usually ground at the same time. Can be used with fish, meat, poultry, and vegetables. It was first introduced to the Caribbean by European sailors and then by Indian laborers. The reason for its popularity is probably because hot and spicy foods allow the body to cool itself by perspiring. The yellow of turmeric generally gives curry its distinctive color.

Curried Goat
Spicy stew of goat (kid) meat cooked with curry, usually a feast food.

Dasheen (*Colocasia esculenta*)
A large, roundish tuber with a dark brown rough skin, white, cream or lilac-grey flesh, often with brown specks. It can be deep-fried or used in stews or soups. Hawaiians use it to make poi. Also known as: coco, eddo, eddoes, red-budded taro, sato imo, and taro. See also: Malanga.

Eggplant (*Solanum melongena*)
A smooth-skinned egg-shaped vegetable. The skin is dark purple, the flesh is cream flecked with brown. Also known as: aubergine, boulangere, and garden egg.

Empanada
A small pastry turnover filled with fish or meat.

Escallions
See Scallions.

Fennel (*Foeniculum vulgare*)
A crisp, fragrant vegetable whose leaves and seeds are used as a fresh sweet seasoning with fish, rice, and potatoes. The bulb looks much like celery, and is often used in place of celery. Also known as: anise, finocchio, Florence fennel, and sweet anise.

Fish Escovitch
(es-ko-VEECH). Freshly caught fish fried at a high temperature so that the skin is crunchy. It is highly seasoned with a mixture of red pepper, onions, and vinegar. Usually served cold.

Fish Tea
A broth made from boiling fish with green bananas and any available vegetable. The broth is highly seasoned with allspice, salt, and pepper.

Flan
A custard.

Garlic (*Allium sativum*)
A bulbous herb that has a distinct odor and taste. It is widely used in all types of cookery. It lends itself very well to a variety of Caribbean dishes.

Ginger Root (*Zingiber officinale*)
A pungent, aromatic rhizome widely used, especially in Asian and Hispanic cooking. Fresh ginger has a moist, juicy flesh with a brown, rather smooth skin, and a clean hot, spicy taste with sweet overtones. Ground ginger has a much less pungent flavoring; use fresh ginger if at all possible. Used often in curries, marinades, ginger ale, and liqueurs.

Ginger Tea
Made by boiling a small piece of ginger root in water. It is widely used as a home remedy for upset stomach.

Grapefruit (*Citrus paradisi*)
A large, round fruit that has a yellow rind and an edible juicy, acid pulp. A member of the citrus family, this fruit grows on trees.

Guanabana
See Soursop.

Guava (*Psidium guajava*)
(GWA-va). A round or pear-shaped fruit of an evergreen tree with small, hard seeds. About 3 to 4 inches in diameter with pale yellow skin and pink or white flesh. Eat fresh or make into jellies and jams. Very popular in the Hispanic Caribbean islands and Florida. Also known as: goyave and guayaba.

Hearts of Palm
See Swamp Cabbage.

Irish Moss (*Chondrus crispus*)
A variety of seaweed which when cleaned, dried and boiled yields a gelatinous cream-colored liquid. It is then sweetened with condensed milk and flavored with nutmeg and vanilla. A popular island drink with health food enthusiasts, Irish moss is believed to aid sexual prowess. Also known as: carrageen.

Jerk Pork
Barbecued pork that is highly seasoned with pepper, spices, and herbs and smoked over a fire made with pimento bark or guava wood.

Jira
The small, dry spicy seed from a sweet herb used to make the popular dish Roti and in other West Indian dishes.

Johnnycake
A popular bread substitute often served at breakfast. Made with flour, water, salt, and baking powder. The dough is usually shaped into medium-sized balls and fried in hot oil.

Kale (*Brassica napus*) and
Flowering Kale (*brassica oleracea* subspecies *acephala*)   There are two varieties of kale. Flowering kale is a leafy vegetable that looks like escarole but is heavier and a lighter shade of green. It is used for decorative purposes. Kale is a dark green, leafy vegetable with heart-shaped leaves. When steamed with butter and seasoning, it has a flavor similar to spinach. An important ingredient

in Pepperpot Soup. Flowering kale is also known as: flowering cabbage, flowering cole, ornamental kale, and salad savoy. Kale is also known as: bore cole, curly kale, and kail.

Key Lime
See Lime.

Kiwifruit (*Actinidia chinensis*)
An oval-shaped, brown-skinned, fuzzy fruit about the size of a large egg. The sweet-tart, emerald-green flesh tastes similar to a combination of citrus, strawberry, and melon. Also known as: kiwi and Chinese gooseberry.

Lambi
See Conch.

Lemon (*Citrus limon*)
A popular member of the citrus family, the yellow-rind fruit is the size and shape of a large egg. This tree-grown fruit has a yellow, acid, juicy pulp which is tart to the taste.

Lime
The most common variety of this citrus fruit is the Persian lime (*Citrus latifolia*), also known as the Tahiti or Bearss lime. The Key lime (*Citrus aurantifolia*), also known as the Mexican, West Indies, or true lime, is grown primarily in the Florida Keys. The Persian lime has the shape and size of a large egg. The skin can be anywhere from dark green to greenish-yellow. The Key lime is smaller, has a greenish-yellow skin, and is more tart.

Mace
The shell of the nutmeg seed that has a mild, fragrant odor and, when dried, a light orange color. Ground mace is used in cakes, cookies, chocolate desserts, pickles, and preserves.

Malanga (*Xanthosoma sagittifolium*)
A starchy tuber with a thin, shaggy brown skin. Similar to a sweet potato in shape, it can weigh from ½ to 2 pounds. The extremely crisp flesh may be beige, yellow, or red. Cooked malanga has a nuttier taste than potatoes. Also known as cocoyam, malanga amarilla, tannia, tannier, yautia amarilla, and yautia blanca.

Mango (*Mangifera indica*)
A fragrant, juicy fruit with a soft, moist, dense, sweet-tasting yellow-green flesh. It has a flat, large, and rather hairy seed. The skin is fairly thick, and ranges anywhere from green to yellow to red, depending on ripeness and/or the variety of mango. Ripe mangoes should be slightly soft and very aromatic. The skin may cause allergic reactions in some.

Mannish Water
A thick, highly seasoned soup made from goat offal, green bananas, and any available vegetable or tuber. Believed to be a tonic, it is an important dish at country weddings and other festive occasions.

Mauby
A sweet and slightly bitter drink, considered very healthy by many. It is made from the bark of a tree which grows in some Caribbean areas. The bark is dried and can be purchased in small pieces, boiled with spices and sugar, and served diluted with water to which ice is added.

Mustard
Seeds of the mustard plant, ground into a powder. Adds a spicy taste to dishes. Whole seeds are also used in salad dressings and pickling.

Nutmeg
The seed of the nutmeg tree. It is round and smaller than a walnut. It is processed in large quantities in Grenada. Freshly grated nutmeg results in a better aroma and taste than the commercially ground nutmeg.

Okra (*Hibiscus esculentus*)
Finger-length, bean-sized green pods, often used in soup and stews. Also known as: bamia, gombo, lady's fingers, ochro, okro, quiabo, and quingombo.

Orange, Sweet (*Citrus sinensis*)
The sweet orange is the most widely distributed variety of this most popular member of the citrus family. It is called sweet orange in the tropics in order to distinguish it from the sour or bitter orange. See also Bitter Orange.

Oregano (*Origanum vulgare*)
An herb made from the leaves of the oregano plant. Used in a variety of dishes.

Overproof Rum
Rum that is at least 81 proof. For best results, use 126–151 proof rum when overproof rum is called for in a recipe.

Papaya (*Carica papaya*)
There is an enormous variation in the size, shape, and skin color of this fruit. It can weigh from ½ to 20 pounds; it can be shaped like a banana, pear, or peach; it can be pink, orange, yellow or green. The flesh is yellow or orange when ripe, and there are numerous black seeds in the center. The fruit is a good source of vitamin A. Also known as: fruit bomba, lechosa, papaw, and pawpaw.

Paprika
A bright red powder ground from various sweet peppers. The best paprika is Hungarian paprika.

Passion Fruit (*Passiflora edulis*)
An egg-sized fruit that is oval and dusty purple-brown in color. It has a shell-like covering. The yellow pulp appears in liquidy teardrops. It tastes like lemons, pineapple, and guava, combined. Also known as: purple granadilla, maracudja, and maracuja.

Patty
A delicious crescent-shaped meat pie made with highly seasoned minced meat folded into a flaky pastry shell. Popular in the West Indies as a snack. Also known as: pastechi and pastelilos.

Pepper (*Capsicum annuum*)
This is a large family that includes the familiar red and green bell peppers.

Pepperpot
A highly seasoned stew made with poultry, game, or other meats and often thickened and flavored with cassareep in Trinidad. In Jamaica, it's very spicy and is made with meat, fowl, and vegetables.

Persian Lime
See Lime.

Persimmon

There are two basic varieties of persimmon available in the markets—the Oriental variety (*Diospyros kaki*) and the native American variety (*Diospyros virginiana*). Both have a shiny brilliant orange skin, and both tend to be quite "puckery," especially if they are not ripe. The native variety is smaller. The word persimmon is a corruption of the Algonquin Indian name for the fruit, *putchamin* or *pessemin*.

Picadillo

A highly seasoned Spanish dish made with minced raw beef or cooked beef. The Cuban picadillo is the most famous version.

Pickling Spice

A combination of herbs and spices that are used primarily for pickles and relishes.

Pigeon Peas (*Cajanus cajan*)

Round seeds the size of small garden peas, of African origin. They are very popular in West Indian cooking, dried and fresh. Also known as: arhar dahl, channa peas, gandules, goongoo, green peas congo, gungo peas, and tropical green peas.

Pimento

See Allspice.

Pineapple (*Ananas comosus*)

A fruit that grows in tropical areas, this sweet-tasting fruit has a juicy yellow pulp with a solid core. The skin is light brown and coarse and spiny.

Plantain ((*Musa paradisiaca*)

A member of the banana family. These fruits are not eaten raw. It is widely used in West Indian cooking green, ripe, and semiripe. Delicious fried as salted cocktail chips. Also known as: cooking banana, plátano, and plátano macho.

Pummelo (*Citrus grandis*)

A member of the citrus family that resembles a grapefruit but is usually larger, less juicy, and very thick skinned. The skin makes a nice preserve. Also known as: shaddock and Chinese grapefruit.

Pone

A word of Algonquin origin meaning baked.

Rum Punch

A sip of sunshine, made from potent rum, fruit syrup, lime juice and water. The traditional recipe for rum punch is: one of sour (one measurement of lime juice); two of sweet (two measurements of fruit or sugar syrup); three of strong (three measurements of rum) and four of weak (four measurements of water).

Run-Down

Jamaican name for salted mackerel, shad, or cod simmered in coconut milk, that has been boiled to a custard along with peppers, onion, and scallions.

Saffron

An expensive spice made from the dried stigmas of the saffron plant. In order to obtain a pound of the yellow powder, 75,000 blossoms must be hand picked. Used to impart a yellow-orange color to dishes as well as a delightful taste.

Salsa

Spanish word for sauce.

Sangria
A drink made with wine, fruits, and sweetener.

Sapodilla (*Manilkara zapota*)
(sap-o-DI-a). A russet-brown fruit about the size of a peach. It has a thin edible skin with a pale brown pulp that is sweet and delicately flavored. Also known as: naseberry.

Sapote, Black (*Diospyros digyna*)
Sapote, White (*Casimiroa edulis*)
(sah-PO-tay). This fruit is available in two varieties: black and white. the black sapote has leathery green skin. When fully ripe, the flesh resembles chocolate pudding in color and texture. The white sapote is a thin-skinned fruit. The pale cream flesh has a light texture and a sweet, mild flavor. This is the variety that is most commonly available. It resembles a Greengage plum in size and shape.

Scallions
The tender seedlings of the onion which have a delicate flavor. They are completely edible and have a multitude of uses. Also known as: cyves, escallions, eschalot, green onions, groundnut, peanut, and spring onions.

Scotch Bonnet
A strong-flavored hot pepper, so called because its shape is somewhat reminiscent of a Scotsman's bonnet. It is a very popular recipe ingredient in the tropics.

Shallots (*Alium ascalonicum*)
A member of the onion family, this small bulbous herb has a mild fragrance and taste.

Sky Juice
A popular drink in Jamaica. Syrup over shaved ice.

Sorrel (*Rumex scutatus*)
A tropical flower grown in hot climate areas. Has a faintly acid taste. Used in drinks, jams, jellies, and sauces. Also known as: flor de Jamaica, rosella, and roselle.

Sofrito
This term means lightly fried. It is also the name of a basic Spanish sauce used in island cooking, usually made with onions, garlic, tomatoes, peppers, herbs, spices, and ham. All are chopped and then cooked in oil.

Sour Orange
See Bitter Orange.

Soursop (*Annona muricata*)
A large green-skinned fruit with a spiky, rough-textured coat. The juicy white pulp has black seeds. The refreshing flavor of this is an interesting mix of sour and sweet. Delicious as a punch with sweetened milk or in ice cream. Also known as: guanabana.

Stamp and Go
A small fritter made with salty codfish. It's made with a heavy batter flavored with annatto, onions, and chilies.

Sugarcane (*Saccharum officinarum*)
Considered a tall grass. The juice from the thick, tough stems is used to make sugar.

Swamp Cabbage (*Sabal palmetto*)
The tender heart of the Sabal palm tree. Can be eaten raw or cooked

and is sold in cans as hearts of palm. Also known as: chou coco, chou glouglou, chou palmiste, hearts of palm, and palmito.

Sweet Pepper (*Capsicum annuum*)
See Pepper.

Sweet Potato
A tuber vegetable that is indigenous to the Americas. There are a variety of skin colors and flesh colors. In the United States, yellow and orange varieties are most popular. But boniato, a white fleshy sweet potato, is gaining immense popularity. See also: Boniato

Sweetsop (*Annona squamosa*)
Grown on tropical trees, the heart-shaped fruit is segmented and has a thick green scaly rind, a sweet, white creamy pulp, and shiny black seeds. Also known as: sugar apple.

Tamarind (*Tamarindus indica*)
(TAM-a-rind). An acid-tasting fruit with a brittle brown shell that is similar to a pod. Tamarind is about 3–4 inches long and grows in bunches on large trees. Inside, large flat seeds are covered by a tangy brown pulp. Tamarind may be eaten as a fresh fruit, rolled in granulated sugar to produce candy, or mixed with water and sugar to yield a delightful summer drink.

Tannia
See Malanga.

Taro
See Dasheen.

Tarragon (*Artemesia dracunculus*)
An aromatic herb made from the leaves of the tarragon plant with a variety of uses.

Thyme (*(Thymus vulgaris*)
The leaves of the plant provide a spicy flavor to many Caribbean dishes. Sprigs of thyme are often used in seasoning. Used in poultry dishes, sauces, soups, stews, and with vegetables.

Turmeric (*Curcuma longa*)
A member of the ginger family, the dried root of this tropical plant produces a spice which is brilliant yellow and provides the distinct color to curry powder.

Ugli Fruit (a cross between *citrus reticulata* and *citrus grandis*) (OO-gli). A Jamaican citrus fruit. The skin, which ranges in color from lime-green to orange, is easy to peel. The acid-sweet pulp is virtually free of seeds.

Vanilla (*Vanilla planifolia*)
The dried bean of an orchid. Vanilla can be found in the bean form or in extract form. Both provide the unique flavor associated with quality vanilla ice cream.

Vinegar
An integral part of the sauce for Escovitch Fish. Jamaican vinegar is made from sugar cane.

Wash
A beverage made from brown sugar, water, and lime or sour oranges.

Wet Sugar
A deep brown, moist granular sugar produced by boiling concentrated

cane juice until it crystallizes. Different from refined sugar in that it contains all the rich nutrients found in cane juice. It's supposed to be good for the nerves.

Winged Bean (*Psophocarpus tetragonolobus*)
A tropical legume. There are four ruffled wings that run the length of each pod. A cross-section cut reveals a cross-like shape. The lightweight pods are larger than string beans. Also known as: asparagus bean, four-angled bean, goa bean, manila bean, princess pea, and tropical legume.

Yam
A large tuber-like vegetable that can grow to be very large. The flesh may be white, yellow, or red and is often sweet.

Yampie
(YAM-pi). A small, delicate-flavored white tuber, often served boiled.

Yuca
(YOO-ka). See Cassava.

Zest
The experience you have when you taste a chilled mango on a hot day. Also the thin pigmented layer of citrus rind.

Tropical Substitutions

Although it is best to use the ingredients called for in the recipes, there may be times when that is impossible. Here's a list of substitutions that you may find useful.

Ingredient	Substitute
Bird pepper	Any hot pepper
Boniato	Irish white potato
Calabaza	Any large yellow squash (butternut, acorn, Hubbard)
Callaloo	Kale, spinach

Ingredient	Substitute
Coconut, fresh	Canned unsweetened coconut
Coconut milk	Cow's milk
Conch	Clams, whelks, squid
Ginger, fresh	Powdered ginger (1⅛ teaspoon for each tablespoon fresh ginger)
Goat meat	Mutton, gamey meats
Kale	Spinach, callaloo
Key limes	Persian limes (1 for every 3 Key limes)
Lemon, fresh	Bottled juice (2–3 tablespoons for each lemon)
Lime, fresh	Bottled juice (1½–2 tablespoons for each lime)
Mango, fresh	Peaches
Orange, fresh	Frozen, reconstituted (6–8 tablespoons for each orange)
Orange, sour	Equal parts of sweet orange juice and lemon juice
Pigeon peas, fresh	Garden peas, canned pigeon peas
Pigs' tails	Salt pork
Saffron	Bijol
Sapodilla, fresh	Peaches
Scotch Bonnet pepper	Any hot pepper
Soursop (guanabana), fresh	Canned soursop
Swamp cabbage, fresh	Canned hearts of palm
Tamarind, fresh	Canned tamarind
Tannia	Irish white potato
Wholewheat flour	White flour
Winged beans	French-cut green beans

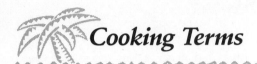

Cooking Terms

Blanch.
To parboil and, then, shock in cold water

Butterfly.
To cut against the grain or cut lengthwise, leaving meat attached on one side. This is done for appearance and to tenderize.

Chicken Stock.
Simmer together for 3 or 4 hours chicken bones and scraps, 1 carrot, 1 onion, 1 sprig of parsley, 2 cups of water, and thyme, white pepper, and salt to taste. Strain before using.

Chop.
Cut into ¼-inch cubes.

Clarifying Butter.
To remove all impurities from butter by heating and skimming off all whey or sediment as it rises to the top. Then, carefully strain.

Crème Frâiche.
To make your own, combine 1 cup of heavy cream with 1 tablespoon of buttermilk. Gently heat to not more

than 85°. Let stand at a temperature between 65° and 85° overnight, or until thickened. Refrigerate. Or use recipe on p. 128.

Deglaze.
To pour liquid (such as wine, water or stock) in a cooking pan, scraping sides and bottom to loosen residue used in sauce.

Demiglace.
Half-glaze. A reduced brown sauce. May purchase.

Dice.
Cut into ⅛-inch cubes.

Dredge.
To dip in flour.

Fillet.
Boneless meat or fish. To remove bones from fish.

Fish Stock.
Simmer together for 20 minutes the trimmings and scraps from a fish, 1 or 2 onions, chopped parsley stems, 1 carrot, 1 stalk of celery, 1 cup of

white wine, and 2 cups of water. Strain before using.

Flambé.
To cover food lightly with spirits and carefully ignite. It is to add flavor or spectacular beauty when serving.

Julienne.
Thin matchstick-like strips.

Purée.
To force food through a sieve or blend in a food processor until smooth.

Reduce.
To cook or simmer a liquid until there is a smaller amount in order to concentrate flavor.

Roux.
An equal amount of butter and flour cooked a few minutes until smooth. Used to thicken.

Sauté.
To cook in shallow pan in a small amount of butter or fat.

Score.
To make shallow cuts in surface of meat.

Zest.
The peel or thin outer pigmented skin of citrus fruits.

Zester.
A small utensil that easily lifts the peel off of the fruit. Available in most houseware stores.

Index

About the Author

Joyce LaFray Young is the coauthor of two popular Florida restaurant guide cookbooks, *Famous Florida!® Restaurants and Recipes* and *Famous Florida!® Underwater Gourmet.*

Mrs. Young studied at Loyola University in Rome, Italy where her fond interest in international cuisine was kindled. As a food critic, she was former host of *PM Magazine's "Florida Gourmet."* She now serves as consultant to Burdines popular Chef's Tour, and as advisor to many educational institutions throughout the state. As a guest of the Belgian Government in 1984, she interviewed award-winning chefs for a special project honoring the famed Salvador Dali museum.

Joyce is president of the Surfside Publishing Company. She also maintains a busy schedule of tennis, swimming, nutrition awareness, and recipe development along with her husband Richard and her two daughters Julie and Christy—her three best critics!